Finding Meaning in Life

Finding Meaning in Life

Logotherapy

Edited by

Joseph B. Fabry • Reuven P. Bulka • William S. Sahakian

With a foreword by

VIKTOR E. FRANKL

JASON ARONSON INC.

Northvale, New Jersey

London

THE MASTER WORK SERIES

First softcover edition 1995

The hardcover edition was titled *Logotherapy in Action*.

Library of Congress Cataloging-in-Publication Data

Finding meaning in life : Logotherapy / edited by Joseph B. Fabry,
Reuven P. Bulka, and William S. Sahakian.
p. cm.
Includes bibliographical references and index.
ISBN 1-56821-558-4 (softcover)
1. Logotherapy. I. Fabry, Joseph B. II. Bulka, Reuven P.
III. Sahakian, William S.
RC489.L6L64 1995
616.89'14—dc20 95-11818

Manufactured in the United States of America. Jason Aronson Inc. offers books and cassettes. For information and catalog write to Jason Aronson Inc., 230 Livingston Street, Northvale, New Jersey 07647.

Contents

VII
ADDICTION

VIII
COMMUNITY CONCERNS

Foreword

Since this book deals with logotherapy, it is natural that the founder of logotherapy has been requested to write a preface. I do so with pride and humility.

I feel pride because this book presents proof that logotherapy, as many people have asserted, speaks to the needs of the hour. This claim is not without justification. Western society, due to its technological progress, has the capacity—at least in principle—to satisfy all needs of humankind except one: the need for meaning. Under these circumstances it is not surprising to discover the appeal of a psychotherapy such as logotherapy which makes the will to meaning the focal point of its motivational theory and which goes so far as to define the human reality as a search for meaning.

Let us be frank: the Western world has solved the problem of survival. The struggle for survival is over. But the question of "survival for what?" is still open. That is exactly the question logotherapy has placed before us as the ultimate challenge. The answer? Who can claim to have final answers? True, some psychologies, such as behaviorism, are able to give exact answers—but only to questions of minor relevance. Other psychologies, such as psychodynamics, do raise important questions but unfortunately they cannot find the proper answers. The philosophy behind logotherapy attempts at least a first step in a direction which, judging from the response, seems to lead closer to the goal humankind is seeking for its survival to be worthy of the name "human."

I also feel a strong sense of humility as I survey the book while writing my preface. I see an expansion of my own ideas as I formulated them when creating logotherapy. Not every idea in the many chapters finds my full approval but the more the views of unorthodox logotherapists deviate from my own the more justified is its inclusion in this book. Logotherapy is no fixed set of dogmas. It is not a closed system. As I have stated on many occasions, it is open in two directions: open to the cooperation with other scientifically established psychotherapies, and open to its own evolution, to the full development of its own potential.

Ours is an age of pluralism, and we see pluralism also in the field of psychotherapy. Under the circumstances, the co-existence of a variety of schools is appropriate and a sound eclecticism is therefore mandatory. Why, then, shouldn't an "inner" eclecticism be justified—a variety of divergent views within logotherapy?

That is the reason why I grant any logotherapist the right to dissent from what I as the creator of logotherapy believe to be true. On the contrary, I have invited, encouraged, and welcomed criticism of my own teachings because I see in criticism, provided it is earnest and honest, the greatest chance still to learn.

I am indebted to my followers and students for giving me that chance. Many of them have provided me, in addition, with a discovery which I wish to share with the readers of this book: the discovery of the extent to which a practicing logotherapist can learn the application of logotherapy through his own efforts, without formal training, by a thorough study of my writings, even if his reading is limited to my five books available in English.[1] Among the best and most successful logotherapists—and their list extends from New Zealand to Newfoundland, from Japan to Argentina, from Sweden to South Africa—are some I have never met in person and some who have not even corresponded with me and whose existence I know only from their published work reporting their logotherapeutic practice and research. This may be an encouragement for those who up to now

1. Editors' note: In the meantime, a sixth book by Frankl has been published: *The Unheard Cry for Meaning: Psychotherapy and Humanism*. New York: Simon and Schuster, 1978.

have been looking in vain for the institutionalizing of logotherapy through institutes, societies, or journals.[2]

But back to the issue of divergent views within logotherapy: Many a school of thought has died out (as has many a tribe or race of people) because of incest. That's the reason why I—whom the *Journal of Existential Psychiatry*[3] in a special issue called "the father of logotherapy"—don't withhold a father's blessing, by way of a preface to this book, although it contains views to which I cannot fully subscribe. Is it conceivable that a father withholds his blessing from his children and grandchildren on the grounds that in them his blood has been blended with that from others? After all, that is precisely what enables his own blood to survive at all!

The divergence of views, as presented in this volume, sometimes goes so far, as the reader will notice, that some of the views seem to contradict each other. Logotherapy is such a many-faceted body of teaching that this is well understandable. If one thing is approached from opposite sides, it is necessarily depicted in contrasting views. But isn't it the very divergence between the pictures on the right and on the left retina that makes stereoscopic vision possible, thus gaining an entirely new dimension by opening up the perception of space?

To be sure, this state of affairs raises the question regarding what may legitimately be called logotherapy in the strict sense of its founder. But this merely academic question can easily be answered. Should the reader of this multi-dimensional book feel puzzled in this respect, he can resort to my own books and make his choices among "logotherapy pure," i.e., in the strictly Franklian sense, and logotherapy in the wider sense, be it Fabrian, Bulkanian, Sahakianian, or others. Each of the editors and each of the authors of chapters have made valuable contributions to logotherapy. I cannot but congratulate the editors on having such contributors, and congratulate the contributors on having such editors.

Viktor E. Frankl
Vienna
December 1978

2. Editors' note: An Institute of Logotherapy has now been established (1 Lawson Road, Berkeley, CA 94707) for the purpose of training and publishing. The institute publishes *The International Forum for Logotherapy* which reports continuing research on logotherapy

3. Vol. 1, no. 4 (Winter 1967).

REFERENCES TO VIKTOR FRANKL'S MAJOR WORKS quoted repeatedly in this book are indicated by the following symbols:

MS - *Man's Search for Meaning*
DS - *The Doctor and the Soul*
PE - *Psychotherapy and Existentialism*
WM - *The Will to Meaning*

References to other writings by Frankl are indicated by numerals referring to the listings at the end of each essay.

1

Prologue

Logotherapy—For Whom?

William S. Sahakian

For whom logotherapy? It is for you and for me; that is to say, everyone can benefit from it. People in all walks of life, those with or without problems, the mentally ill or well, all can avail themselves of the advantages offered by logotherapy. Moreover, it is not always necessary to see a therapist to profit from logotherapy, though for some that would be a desirable luxury and for others a virtual necessity.

This prologue indicates areas of action in which logotherapy has been successfully employed, either by the professional or by the layman. Subsequent essays will elaborate logotherapeutic tenets and techniques.

Happiness Is All That Counts

How many times have you heard someone say that happiness is all that counts? Such people assume that everyone knows what happiness is. The paradox of happiness is that if you make deliberate plans to pursue it consciously, it will elude you. Logotherapy indicates a way to capture happiness: happiness invariably accompanies a meaningful life. Consequently, by engaging in meaningful activity, a person enjoys happiness as a by-product.

The reason that happiness is so difficult to achieve is that most people confuse happiness with pleasure. When a person engages in pleasure, such as sexual pleasure, he expects to be happy. But sexual pleasure, as is typical of all physical pleasure, is momentary and devoid of any *lasting* feeling of satisfaction. The feeling subsides as quickly as it is aroused, leaving the person searching for some kind of happiness that will remain, if not permanently, at least for a reasonable period of time.

Most sexual episodes do not produce happiness because they lack sufficient meaning. Too often sexual activity merely relieves sexual tension, comparable to voiding oneself in the bathroom when the bodily relief is sensed as pleasurable. This pleasure does not last, because it is not meaningful. Thus, the secret of making sex a matter of lasting happiness is to make it the adjunct of meaning—to render it a meaningful experience, and not a matter of egoistic relief. The same holds true for any experience of life directly aimed at happiness.

The Hedonistic Trap

Hedonism is the philosophy of a person who makes his sole aim in life the pursuit of pleasure. Consequently, if life affords no pleasure, then for the hedonist it is no longer worth living. For him, the good life and the pleasurable life are synonymous.

As I shall discuss in a subsequent essay, hedonism can be a dangerous philosophy, because a person predisposed toward hedonism will turn to suicide once he is convinced that life has dealt him a low blow and that the future holds no promise of pleasure.

People in this predicament can be and have been helped through logotherapy. Viktor E. Frankl, the founder and principal developer of logotherapy, found that those who committed suicide in German concentration camps were not necessarily those who were treated worst but were those who had convinced themselves that life no longer held any pleasure for them.

Frankl, however, himself a prisoner in three concentration camps, asserted that the fundamental question of life is not "What can I expect from life?" but "What can life expect from me?" By responding to the demands of life we render it meaningful, and make it possible for us to endure the most dire circumstances.

True, we are not in concentration camps, but many of us are in predicaments or jobs that strike us as unbearable. A student was miserable because he was stuck with a job of washing dishes, which he detested. In a logotherapeutic session he came to the realization that his employment, a temporary thing, served to finance him through law school. Eager to become a lawyer and aware that were it not for that job his life's ambition would not be realized, he developed an appreciation for his job to the point of actually liking what he once detested. In becoming meaningful, the job was transformed from distasteful to quite acceptable.

A student and a relatively uneducated young man, both employed in a hospital, were assigned menial tasks. While the student despised his work, his co-worker had pride in what he was doing because he felt that he was contributing to the health of many patients. Once anything becomes meaningful, it becomes fulfilling and more than merely endurable.

Happiness in Misery

It is possible for a person to be happy even in miserable circumstances, just as another can be miserable living in the lap of luxury and blessed with good physical health. The secret, to be sure, is in deriving meaning from one's situation. The logotherapist claims that there is meaning to be found everywhere, even in suffering; and that the only unendurable suffering is the kind of misery that has no apparent meaning. If you cannot understand the reason behind your suffering, you will find it intolerable. Misery per se is not unendurable; it is meaninglessness that renders it so. Unavoidable suffering when transformed into a meaningful experience is not only endurable but challenging. If you have a meaning for living, there is nothing in life you will find insurmountable, no misery you couldn't cope with.

The logotherapist can supply many cases illustrating the tenet that there is meaning in everything, even and especially in unavoidable suffering. A simple example is that of a man whose intense dread of blood prevented him from giving blood. But when he was told that his son's life depended on receiving blood transfusions, he rushed to the blood bank. Frankl relates the case of the physician who suffered miserably when his beloved wife died. He was helped to realize that he could have been spared the misery if he had died before her. On becoming aware of this alternative, he realized that his wife was spared the misery of widowhood. Perceiving the situation in this new light, he felt that he was sacrificing for her, and what was once for him unbearable suffering became a challenge with which he was prepared to cope.

The Sunday Neurosis

Arthur Schopenhauer, the German philosopher, was perhaps the first to be aware that many people do not know what to do with themselves on Sundays. The rest of the week's activities are prescribed, each person doing the job expected of him. But with businesses closed on Sunday and with no job to occupy them, many people do not know what to do with their free time and become bored.

A Sunday neurosis is bad enough; but when a person feels that life in general, and on weekdays too is empty, depression may set in. A Sunday neurosis or an existential neurosis (termed by Frankl a "noögenic" neurosis) is dealt with effectively by engaging in meaningful activity. This was realized by a patient who was bored with everything in life: his employment, his home life, his leisure activity, and his relatives. He discovered that getting junior high school students excited about literature fascinated him. He derived satisfaction from opening their minds to the subject. For him teaching was more than a new way of earning a living; it was a new way of life. The enthusiasm for teaching and being taught carried over into the rest of his life; his existential neurosis was forgotten.

Some time ago a New York college had a special program for individuals in their thirties and forties who found themselves in unsuitable jobs. Employment, so often not tailored to an individual, can cause an existential neurosis. Employment must be meaningful. If a person cannot change his place or kind of employment, it becomes vital that he change his attitude toward it. The college applied an important tenet of logotherapy, relating to "attitudinal values'': if you cannot change conditions, then alter your attitude toward them.

Logodrama

Logodrama, a logotherapeutic adaptation of psychodrama, may help patients find a direction toward meaning. One woman in her twenties came to her logotherapist complaining that she was miserable and had started taking drugs. She confessed that she resorted to drugs to escape a humdrum life.

She was asked to visualize herself in her eighties on her deathbed, and to reflect on her life and the accomplishments and experiences that had made life worth living. With little effort she enumerated a number of priorities: a creative life as an artist, teaching others the technique of painting and the history of art, becoming a respected art critic, and having a family. With these as her self-chosen priorities, it was easy for the logotherapist to help her structure a course of life that would rescue her from being a victim of undesirable drugs.

Within a few months she was associated with an art critic who had great respect for her ability; she taught emotionally disturbed teenagers art and was thrilled with the salutary effect art had upon them; she later became a worthwhile mother and wife. She had transformed an existential neurosis into a meaningful life.

Paradoxical Intention

Have you ever had to face your employer or superior and discovered your heart pounding or your palms perspiring? Next time you find yourself in this state caused by nervousness or anxiety, utilize paradoxical intention—the logotherapeutic technique Frankl developed as early as 1929 (but published for the first time in 1939). Say to yourself: ''Let my palms sweat. Let my heart pound. Let me see if I can get it to pound louder than it did the last time. Who cares how hard it pounds?'' Instead of the situation deteriorating, it tends to evaporate because you have struck out at the source of tension by releasing it.

Many people fail at successfully exercising paradoxical intention when trying it alone, because they haltingly say to themselves: ''Let my hands sweat,'' fearfully thinking they will aggravate the situation. In so doing, they only intensify their tension.

I know of a speaker who was about to deliver an important address to a huge audience. As he walked toward the raised platform, he felt his heart beating loudly, in anxiety. Rather than being frightened by this discovery, he seized the opportunity of proving the effectiveness of paradoxical intention. He said to himself: ''Let's get this heart pounding loud and clear. Let's see if I can make it pound so loudly that everyone in this audience will hear it.'' Even he was surprised to find that the pounding dissipated.

Humor

In paradoxical intention, as well as in other ways, logotherapy makes use of our sense of humor. By stepping away from ourselves and looking at ourselves with a sense of humor we are able to see the ridiculousness of our behavior and fears. Frankl is fond of quoting Gordon Allport's observation: ''A patient who is able to laugh at himself is on the way to recovery.''

Dereflection

The excessive concern which makes a person trip over himself is familiar to everyone; logotherapy calls this *hyperintention.* A simple example is sleeplessness; the more you concentrate on having to fall asleep the more you will stay awake. Counting sheep is the most common form of dereflection. Sexual dysfunction is another example of hyperintention. The more a man thinks of his potency and the woman of her orgasm the more they will fail. Logotherapy has developed methods to dereflect from the performance itself to the partner.

While worry and anticipatory anxiety are caused by hyperreflection, dereflection counteracts them. To a person who is worrying, it is inadvisable to say, ''Stop worrying,'' for that merely reminds him to worry. To say to someone, ''Don't be nervous,'' merely calls his attention to his nervousness.

To prove this point, try the following experiment: for the next thirty seconds do not think of green snakes. Abolish all thought of green snakes from your mind. You may think of anything you choose but green snakes. Need I ask what is transpiring in your mind at this moment? Get involved in something that interests you—a book, a talk with a friend, a work project—and you will quickly forget about green snakes.

Hyperreflection is not normal. The normal thing is to permit nature to take its course. On a physical level, it is best not to become preoccupied with activities that function on an unconscious level, such as the heartbeat; otherwise, our preoccupation could be disruptive to the normal beat. The same can be said for mental activity. It is best not to be continually delving into our subconscious mind to look for hidden motives and the like, for this too can do more harm than good.

Other essays will provide the reader with detailed information about the nature, scope, and technique of logotherapy. This prologue, it is hoped, will arouse the reader's curiosity to discover in greater detail what logotherapy has to offer.

Logotherapy In Action: An Overview

Joseph B. Fabry

Logotherapy is a method to help persons whose life has become empty and meaningless to lead a fuller existence. Lack of meaning may be experienced as frustration, doubt, confusion, unhappiness, a sense of failure, of being trapped, of having been betrayed by life, of not living up to one's potential. Meaninglessness often is felt in transition periods when vital decisions have to be made about career, marriage, divorce, retirement, life style, or when a person is faced with tragedy.

Logotherapy, then, is therapy through meaning (logos). The logotherapist does not "prescribe" meanings; he cannot tell his clients what the meaning of their lives is but may well show them that meaning exists. He opens doors to possible meanings and leaves it to the individual to decide which doors he wishes to enter in his search. Logotherapy provides guidelines not only for trained therapists, counselors, social workers, and others in the helping professions but also for the individual who wishes to find meaning in his own life.

Logotherapy distinguishes two kinds of meanings: "ultimate meaning," and "the meaning of the moment." The existence of an ultimate meaning is an unprovable assumption, as are all philosophical concepts. Ultimate meaning may be defined as the assumption that order exists in the universe despite apparent chaos; that each person is part of that order; and that he can decide whether and how he wishes to participate in that order. Many names have been given to that order: God, nature, life force, evolution and, recently, the ecosystem. The name does not matter. What matters is that the person believes in ultimate meaning—the religious person by faith, the secular by way of a working hypothesis: he can experiment in the unrepeatable situations of his life, and live *as if* ultimate meaning existed and *as if* he were able to search for it, and see if this mode of living brings fulfillment. Ultimate meaning is like the horizon: it can be approached but never be reached. Important is not the attainment but the search.

The second kind of meaning—the meaning of the moment—is more accessible. Ultimate meaning, like ultimate truth and ultimate beauty, remains beyond reach; but a person in his search can encounter many beautiful, true, and meaningful experiences. Logotherapy presumes that every person, from birth to death, goes through a sequence of moments each of which, though often similar to other moments, is unique for the particular person in the particular situation; and each moment offers him a unique meaning. To recognize the meaning potentials of the moment and to respond to them present a pathway to a meaningful life.

The meanings of the moment range from the prosaic (to drive safely on the freeway) to the heroic (to risk one's life to save a drowning child). It is the central belief of logotherapy that each person has the capacity to discover the meaning inherent in the situation. He cannot arbitrarily "give" meaning to a moment; he can only find the meaning offered by the special circumstances of the situation. In continuously having to look for the meanings of each moment an individual is assisted by the meanings other people have found appropriate in similar situations. These "general" meanings, called "values" in logotherapy, help a person find meaning in standard situations—in the form of moral guidelines, religious commandments, laws, and customs. But reliance on values does not relieve a person from making individual decisions. Because values cover the meaning experiences of many people, they may offer contradictory advice. It is not even possible always to follow the Ten Commandments: a child who can save his parents only by stealing food, must in a crisis situation decide between the commandment not to steal and the one to honor his father and mother.

Unlike values, the meanings of the moment cannot contradict each other because they change from moment to moment and are strictly personal. Following the meaning of the moment may prompt a person to contradict an accepted value in extraordinary circumstances. Human beings, however, are not well equipped to recognize the meaning of the moment and to respond to its call. In this sense, logotherapy is "education to responsibility"in the literal sense: it helps an individual respond to the meaning of the moment, to make him response-able. According to logotherapy, the "organ" that directs a person toward finding the meaning of the moment is his conscience. Its voice is weak, its owner may not understand it properly and may never be sure whether it was "right"—still, he is obliged to try. As Gordon Allport said, "We can be at one and the same time half-sure and whole hearted."

The Principles of Logotherapy

Logotherapy was born in the Vienna of the late twenties. Its founder, Viktor E. Frankl, was a disciple of Alfred Adler, the originator of individual psychology, who in turn was a disciple of Sigmund Freud, the creator of psychoanalysis. It was a time of searching for scientific knowlege about the nature of man.[1] Freud's research centered on the sick, those unable to function properly; and psychoanalysis explored ways to bring them back to health. His disciples, even those who split from him and pursued their own methods, moved in similar directions. Frankl, however, found more people in despair caused by emptiness than by sickness. "At that point," he recalls, "I suspended what I had learned from my great teachers and began listening to what my patients were telling me—trying to learn from them."

He learned from them that their distress was often not physical or psychological. Instead, they suffered from a lack of purpose. The therapy consisted in redirecting them toward meaningful pursuits.

1. An attempt was made to avoid the exclusive masculine forms for human being. But words like *person* provide only temporary relief until the personal pronoun has to be used. He/she and him/her are obstacles to readability. And plural forms ("people," "they") are not always appropriate. We did the best we could.

The principles of logotherapy, as Frankl developed them over the next forty years, seem so simple that he has been accused of offering nothing new. But his drawing from the oldest sources of truth about human nature and man's place in the universe is perhaps logotherapy's greatest strength. Logotherapy offers a life view that confirms what man has always intuitively known about himself but which has often been denied by his physical, political, or spiritual rulers who had a vested interest in subduing him, either for his own good as they saw it, or for their own advantage. Logotherapy sees man primarily as a meaning-seeking animal, concerned not merely with needs but also with purpose, shaped not only by his past but also by his future, in terms of his goals. Logotherapy does not dwell on man's limitations, although they are realistically acknowledged, but directs him toward his potentials. Socrates demanded of man, "Know thyself;" Freud put the emphasis on "Know your unconscious;" and Frankl advises, "Know your potentials."

Logotherapy maintains that man can be understood in his fullness only if he is considered as a totality of body, psyche, and spirit (noös).[2] He is an individual in the literal sense—he is "individable." His mental health requires the well-being of all three dimensions, but with a difference: his body and psyche can become sick, but not his spirit. His noös is his healthy core, though it may be blocked by physical or psychological causes. The task of the logotherapist is to identify and help the client remove these blocks and gain access to his spiritual and uniquely human resources: his will to meaning, his goal orientation, his ideas and ideals, his awareness of past and future, his responsibility, his capacity to love, his creativity, his faith, his intuition, his sense of humor, his conscience. This noëtic dimension is the medicine chest which the logotherapist seeks to make accessible to the client by counseling, education, and therapy.

In emphasizing the human spirit, logotherapy goes beyond psychoanalysis. Man is seen not only driven by the forces of his psyche, but also pulled forward by the forces of his spirit of which his will to meaning is an essential part. Man's main motivation is his will to meaning, not his will to pleasure or power, however strong

2. *Spirit* is used in logotherapy to imply the essence of man. Every human being, regardless of his or her belief, has a spirit. To avoid the misconception that spirit is limited to the religious person, Frankl speaks of man's noös (spirit) and of the noëtic (spiritual) dimension.

these may be. No activity is satisfying unless it satisfies a spiritual hunger for meaning. If a person represses or ignores his will to meaning, he feels empty, experiencing what Frankl calls the "existential vacuum." Although he does not think this vacuum is a disease in itself, he has shown that it may result in a new type of neurosis which he has termed "noögenic."

Logotherapy's basic concepts—the will to meaning, the existential vacuum, and the noögenic neurosis—have been validated empirically.[3] Consistently, 20 percent of the neuroses were found to be noögenic, caused by existential frustration and differing from the conventional diagnostic syndromes.

Prevention and cure of the noögenic neurosis are among the medical tasks of the logotherapist. His mandate, however, goes beyond the medical. He has the responsibility of diagnosing the existential vacuum that many people feel as anxiety, alienation, loneliness, aimlessness, boredom, frustration, or the vague sense of unfulfillment that has invaded homes, schools, churches, communities, offices, workshops, and the political arena. The logotherapist has the further responsibility of helping persons fill their inner emptiness—not, as they are desperately trying to do, with alcohol, drugs, violence, sex, busyness, money, power, and "fun," but with meaning. Frankl diagnosed the existential vacuum as the common problem of man today, and prescribed meaning as a cure. How the logotherapist can help the alcoholic, drug addict, juvenile delinquent, worker, student, and the aimless searcher in general, is the subject of this book.

Logotherapy's view of man as a meaning seeker provides a structure of ideas that makes logotherapy a useful tool for professionals in many fields, as well as for the layman who wishes to find direction,

3. Crumbaugh, J. C. "Cross-Validation of Purpose-in-Life Test based on Frankl's Concepts." *Journal of Individual Psychology* 24 (74), 1968; Lukas, E. S. "Zur Validierung der Logotherapie," in Frankl, *Der Wille zum Sinn.* Bern-Stuttgart-Wien Hans Huber, 1972; Volhard, R., and D. Langen, "mehrdimensionale Psychotherapie," *Zeitschrift für Psychotherapie* 3:1, 1953; Prill, H. J. "Organneurose und Konstitution bei chronischfunktionellen Unterleibsbeschwerden der Frau," *Zeitschrift für Psychotherapie* 5: 125, 1955; Kocourek, K. *et al.* "Ergebnisse der klinischen Anwendung der Logotherapie," in Handbuch der *Neurosenlehre und Psychotherapie,* Munich-Berlin: Urban and Schwarzenberg, 1959; and Werner, T. A. Opening paper, Symposium on Logotherapy, International Congress of Psychotherapy, Vienna, 1961.

break unwanted patterns, and assume responsibility for who he is and wants to become.

Logotherapy proposes some concepts which can help the layman in these tasks:

1. Meaning can be found in activities, experiences, and attitudes taken in apparently meaningless, tragic situations.

2. Every person has the "defiant power of the human spirit" that enables him to take a stand in all situations, to focus on growth, and to search for the specific meanings of his life.

3. He has the capacity of "self-transcendence"—to reach beyond himself toward people to love and causes to serve.

4. He has the capacity of "self-detachment"—the ability to observe himself and his life patterns, and to make changes in the direction of his goals.

5. Each person is unique. Situations in which he feels irreplaceable are likely to elicit meaning.

6. The meaning of the moment is not always instantly recognizable. Sometimes it is necessary to be truly a "patient" and wait until meaning manifests itself.

7. Tension is part of human existence. To be healthy, a person need not achieve "adjustment" or equilibrium but must face the unavoidable tensions of life with daily exercises that will strengthen his spiritual muscles. The healthiest tension is that between what a person is and his vision of what he might become.

8. Finding meaning is not a gift but an achievement. The achievement may be greatest when meaning is obscure as in situations of unavoidable suffering. (This does not mean a person should look for suffering. Avoidable suffering is meaningless masochism.) Nobody knows his limits until life offers him the opportunity to test them.

9. Life does not owe man pleasures, rather it offers him meanings. Mental health does not come to those who demand happiness but to those who find meaning.

10. The greatest obstacle in man's search for meaning today is reductionism: the attempt to reduce the human being to "nothing but" an animal or a machine.

A Timely School of Thought

The concepts of logotherapy offer many reasons why they appeal to man today:

They open new doors to meaning and thereby offer hope to those who have become doubtful about the traditional sources of meaning.

They offer self-discovery, creativity, and human relationships as goals to stimulate affluent persons who no longer can find meaning in the struggle for food and shelter.

They rely on the inner authority of the conscience, a risk worth taking in an age when outer authorities have brought mankind to the brink of nuclear and ecological disaster.

They call attention to the human spirit, which appears wholesome in a society that feels the consequences of worshipping material things.

They stress personal choice and uniqueness, which is welcomed in an age when people feel replaceable by machines and helpless in the presence of supergovernments armed with superweapons.

They affirm responsibility, which is therapeutic for people who sense the emptiness of a pleasure-seeking life.

They emphasize that the personal pursuit of meaning provides hope for those who no longer can accept the guidelines of institutionalized religion yet have to face the realities religions have helped man to bear—how to make sense of life despite injustice, suffering, and death.

They confirm the human being in his fullness, counteracting the reductionism of science and contemporary education.

They see commitment to other people and causes no longer as a pious demand of morality but a prerequisite to human survival. Ecology demonstrates the consequences of selfishness. In the ecosystem "ultimate meaning" (defined as order in the universe of which the individual is a part) has become visible: the air the industrialist pollutes will choke his children; the destruction of the distant plankton in the ocean affects the chain of life and may lead to human starvation; the freedom today to breed at will, to produce goods unrestrictedly, and to use up resources may result in mass death tomorrow.

Logotherapy will not save the world from all ills, but it redirects man toward his human qualities and away from reductionism. It provides a life view that prevents man from becoming a psychological hypochondriac who keeps asking what's wrong with him, and instead stresses the healthy core of his noös which asserts what's right with him. A growing number of psychologists, sociologists, educators, economists, and statesmen point to man's potential capacity if he had wider visions. Such persons are not all logotherapists, but the purpose of this book is to suggest that logotherapy provides a sound philosophical basis for the needed positive forces.

Logotherapy deals realistically with "existential frustration" of the individual, but it has been criticized for not dealing with the social ills, for accepting society and its institutions as they are. The essays in the last section of this book indicate how logotherapy is being used to change institutions. But its emphasis remains with the individual who must decide whether the meaning of the moment—and of many moments in his life—is to commit himself to a social, economic, political, or ethical cause. In so doing he sets an example that may inspire others to do likewise. Logotherapy's way to change society is to encourage individuals to take a stand against outdated values and find new specific meanings which, if accepted by others, will develop into new general values. It is an evolutionary, not a revolutionary approach. And even if revolutions occasionally are necessary to tumble institutions and clear away the rubble, the commitment to such revolutions must come from the conscience of individuals.

If the principles of logotherapy are accepted by a significant number of individuals, the result will be a revolutionary change extending beyond logotherapy's original horizons. One aspect of this change results from logotherapy's stress on the humanness of man. If the doctor, the nurse, the teacher, the foreman will no longer hide behind their roles, masks, uniforms, degrees, positions, and titles but act as human beings among other human beings who happen to be patients, students, or workers, the entire structure of society will shift. Guidelines for meaning will no longer come from authority figures but from the consciences of individuals. Responsibility will not be ordered from above but be developed from within.

Another aspect of revolutionary change, if the principles of logotherapy are widely accepted, will result from the shift toward meaning as the central objective of man. If the nurse, teacher, and foreman see as their main task to help patients, students, and workers find meaning, the structure of nursing, teaching, and working will have to change; and some tasks which now occupy much of the time of these professionals will have to be carried out by paraprofessionals or trained laymen. These shifts in the structure of traditional institutions carry the risk of chaos, at least during the transitional period, but the present conditions of our institutions indicate that the shift and the resulting chaos are already underway. A clearer understanding of the shift from efficiency to meaning, from quantity to quality of life, may shorten the chaotic transitional period.

The Five Areas of Logotherapy

According to Frankl, logotherapy has contributions to make in five areas.

The first area provides a view of man. It might be called, though Frankl does not use the word *logophilosophy*. No application of logotherapy is possible without its underlying philosophy. Logophilosophy itself is therapeutic for those who follow the principles listed in this introduction and in the essays by Gill, Weisskopf-Joelson, Arnold and Gasson, Ghougassian, Sahakian, and Purvis.

The second area where logotherapy makes a contribution to mental health concerns the "collective" neuroses caused by (1) "day-to-day living," an attitude—sharpened by the threat of nuclear war and pollution—that considers a search for meaning not worthwhile because life ends anyway; (2) "fatalism," that considers a search for meaning hopeless because man's fate is determined by psychological drives, early environment, and other influences; (3) "conformism," that tempts a person who no longer trusts traditional guidelines to meaning and has not yet developed his own, to do what most other people find meaningful; and (4) "fanaticism," that accepts uncritically the meaning dictates of a leader or a movement.

Thoughtless day-by-day living, fatalism, conformism, and fanaticism are caused by the person's refusal to make responsible meaning choices. Here logotherapy becomes "education to responsibility" in the various forms discussed by Wirth, Bodenheimer, Briggs, Meshoulam, Sargent, and Phillips. This second area of assistance may be called "logoeducation."

The third area where logotherapy is pertinent deals with unavoidable suffering, as in a case of inoperable cancer. Here the logotherapist, not able to change the facts that have caused his client to suffer, refocuses the attention of the sufferer to meanings attainable by a change of attitude—away from what can not be avoided and toward the human possibilities still available under the circumstances. An example is Helen Keller: As long as she considered herself as deaf, dumb and blind, her life was meaningless. Only when she conceived of herself as a human being with many resources, but unable to hear, speak, and see, did meaning emerge, especially when she used her very shortcomings as her unique contribution to help others in similar circumstances. Here logotherapy operates as what one may call "logoministry." The essays by Brandon, Takashima, Tweedie, and Lunceford discuss this facet of logotherapy.

The fourth area of logotherapy treats and cures noögenic neuroses—those not caused by events in the past but by current conflicts of conscience or values or by frustration of the patient's will to meaning. Here logotherapy functions as medical therapy. The patient is directed to the resources of his noös and encouraged to mobilize them. This process is described by Hogan. But logotherapy can also be applied to persons who are not "sick" but simply bewildered as to the direction and content of their lives. Crumbaugh has called this application "logoanalysis," and similar modes of treatment are described for counseling situations by Fabry, Brandon, Tweedie, Leslie, and, on different levels, in the essays discussing the problems of youth, community concern, and addictions.

The fifth area, also a medical application, deals with neuroses and psychoses that have psychological or physical causes. Prominent among those are phobias, obsessions, and sexual disorders. To counteract such neuroses, Frankl developed the techniques of paradoxical intention and dereflection. They are described in the essays by Gerz and Kocourek. How these techniques are used to break unwanted behavior patterns in various other fields is discussed in essays by Takashima, Jepsen, Macaruso, Crumbaugh, and Brandon.

It is not unusual for a psychotherapy to have applications far beyond the medical field. Unlike other fields of medicine, psychotherapy cannot be judged entirely by the number of patients it has cured. Its impact on human health is measured by the extent to which it has contributed to the understanding of human nature and the relationship of the individual to his society. Psychoanalysis, for instance, revolutionized not only medicine but also education and child-rearing, politics, leisure activities, marriage relationships, writing and literary criticism, and sales techniques. This book is presented to indicate the impact logotherapy is beginning to have on medical and social aspects in the last third of the twentieth century, under conditions quite different from those of Freud's time. This book is the first presentation to demonstrate how widely logotherapy is being applied by its followers, and to inspire others who wish to apply it to their own field of interest.

Basically, this book seeks to help individual readers answer the central question about the meanings of the moments that make up their lives, but it also raises the wider question of what may be the meaning of the moment for psychologists, counselors, youth leaders, community leaders, and even of mankind as it approaches the end of our second millenium.

Conversation with Viktor Frankl

Derek L. T. Gill

Gill: Along with most laymen, I was introduced to your work through *Man's Search for Meaning.* How do you account for its extraordinary success?

Frankl: I see this success as a symptom of today's mass neurosis—of the fact that thousands are searching for the meaning of life. This search has been frustrated, and that is why people are turning to psychiatrists complaining of meaninglessness.

Gill: Can you give an example of this feeling of meaninglessness?

Frankl: I recently received in Vienna a letter from an American student. He wrote: "I am twenty-two years old with a university degree, a car, security, and the availability of more sex and power than I need. Now I have only to explain to myself what this all means." Here is an instance of a man experiencing a feeling of meaninglessness. Usually this feeling is associated with complaints of emptiness—the "existential vacuum."

Gill: How would you explain the occurrence of this existential vacuum?

Frankl: In contrast to animals, man is not told by drives and instincts what he *must* do. And in contrast to man in former times, he is no longer told by traditions and values what he *should* do. Now, neither knowing what he *must* do nor what he *should* do, he sometimes seems no longer to know what he basically *wishes* to do. Hence either he just wishes to do what other people are doing—this is conformism; or he does what other people want him to do—this is totalitarianism. But there is also a third effect of the existential vacuum: a new, unprecedented type of neurotic illness. Logotherapy terms it *noögenic neurosis* because it does not derive from complexes or traumas, but mainly from the frustration of man's search for meaning, from the fact that he can no longer see meaning in his life.

Gill: Is logotherapy a method to treat noögenic neuroses?

Frankl: Yes. The logotherapist aids his patients to overcome noögenic neuroses by helping them discover meanings in their lives.

Gill: Then this feeling of meaninglessness is a neurosis?

Frankl: No. This existential vacuum or existential frustration is not a neurosis but is existential despair—despair over apparent meaninglessness of one's life. This despair does not constitute an emotional disease or a mental illness. We must remember this fact when we offer "first aid" to a victim of an existential vacuum. Young people who are struggling with this inner crisis need not feel ashamed but may be proud because their acknowledgment of their vacuum shows their intellectual sincerity. Besides, it is the privilege of being human to dare to question whether life has meaning. No animal does this. Only man does, and it is a special prerogative of youth. But I have to add that this courage, notably on the part of young people, should be matched by patience. The questioner must be prepared to wait until sooner or later meaning will dawn upon him.

Gill: Is this feeling of meaninglessness more widespread in the United States than in your native Europe?

Frankl: Yes. Of my students at the University of Vienna Medical School, 40 percent confessed to a feeling of meaninglessness; of my American students, 80 percent.

Gill: How would you explain this alarmingly high percentage in America?

Frankl: The American student is more exposed to an indoctrination of a reductionist concept of man and a reductionist life view.

Gill: What do you mean by reductionism?

Frankl: Reductionism is a pseudoscientific procedure by which human phenomena are either reduced to or deduced from essentially subhuman phenomena.

Gill: That's too abstract for me.

Frankl: It is reductionism if you think of human life as nothing but a civil war between the clashing claims of the ego, id, and superego, or of man as nothing but the result of his environment or of economic forces.

Gill: Do you deny that animal mechanism operates in man?

Frankl: No, man is still an animal. He is even a computer. But he is an animal plus and a computer plus. The functioning of man's central nervous system may well be explained by using the computer as a model. But we have to open up the full dimension of the human phenomena and follow man, including the emotionally disturbed man, into this dimension of the distinctively human phenomena.

Gill: Why is it so important to include this dimension in psychiatry?

Frankl: Unless you enter the human dimension, or as long as you consider man as a mere animal or computer, you remain on the subhuman level and cannot understand the ailment of our age. How can you understand a man suffering from a meaningless life if you remain on the level of an ant or computer? Animals and computers don't suffer from meaninglessness. Only when you enter the human dimension can you understand the frustration of the search for meaning. Only when the therapist sees man as a human being can he help the patient mobilize his human resources.

Gill: How would a psychoanalyst, in contrast to a logotherapist, conceive of meaning and value?

Frankl: Two outstanding analytically oriented American psychiatrists came up with a definition of meaning and values as "nothing but reaction formations or defense mechanisms." I would not be willing to live for the sake of my reaction formations, even less to die for the sake of my defense mechanisms.

Gill: How widespread has the reductionist doctrine become?

Frankl: An indication is supplied in a book review in the *American Journal of Existential Psychiatry.* The book, two volumes, deals with Goethe, and now let me literally quote from the book review: "In the 1,538 pages the author portrays to us a genius with the earmarks of a manic-depressive, paranoid disorder, of homosexuality, incest, voyeurism, impotence, masochism, exhibitionism, fetishism, obsessive-compulsive neurosis, hysteria, megalomania, etc. The author seems to focus almost exclusively upon the dynamic forces that underlie the artistic product. We are led to believe that Goethe's work is nothing but the result of pregenital fixations. Goethe's struggle does not appear to aim for an ideal, for values, but for the overcoming of an embarrassing problem of premature ejaculation."

Gill: Are you serious? What is the impact of such indoctrination?

Frankl: The impact of such a reduction is the "nothing but-ness" approach. Man is nothing but . . . ; values are nothing but . . . . It is an approach that undermines and erodes the enthusiasm of young people. I predicted this erosion many years ago. Let me tell you of a young American, a Fulbright scholar who studied logotherapy in Vienna.

He told me about a young American couple that had served for two years in the Peace Corps in Africa. At the beginning of their training in America this young couple had to participate in a mandatory group session led by an American psychologist who played a game somewhat as follows: "Why did you join the Peace Corps?" "We wanted to help people who are underprivileged." "Then you must think that you are superior to them?" "Well, we of course have certain skills and knowledge which can help them." "So there must be in your unconscious mind a deep-down need to prove to people and to yourself that you are superior." "Well, doctor, we never thought of it that way. But you are a psychologist and must know better." That's the way it went. These young people are indoctrinated into interpreting their idealism and their altruism as nothing but personal hang-ups. Even worse, and now I am quoting my Fulbright student's report: "The group members were constantly on each other's backs, finally playing the 'what's your hidden motive' game among themselves."

Gill: Is this to say that you are against the unmasking of neurotic motivation?

Frankl: No, unmasking is legitimate, if there is something to unmask. But the unmasking psychologist has to stop at the point where he is confronted with what is genuine in man and therefore can not be unmasked. When he continues his "unmasking" beyond this point, he is really unmasking his own hidden motivation of debasing and belittling what is human in man.

Gill: What do you mean here by "human in man"?

Frankl: Essentially man's will to meaning. I do not see in man a being that is basically concerned with, say, gaining power, or with the pursuit of happiness. I see man's basic desire as seeking and fulfilling a meaning and purpose in his life.

Gill: You have been charged with presenting an idealistic philosophy. What is your reaction to this?

Frankl: Logotherapy is a practical philosophy, speaking to the needs of the day. Europeans are prone to see the typical American as mainly concerned with making money. The National Institute of Mental Health sponsored a statistical survey covering 8,000 American college students from 48 American colleges. There were indeed some young people who saw the making of money as their main concern. But this group accounted for only 16 percent while the highest-rated class of motivation, 78 percent of American youth, saw as their main concern "finding a meaning and purpose" in their lives.

Gill: But is it not dangerous to ascribe to each individual a will to meaning?

Frankl: You mean that by raising our demands too high, we might harm a person by exposing him to stress? My contention is that man needs a certain amount of tension, even though he may long for a tensionless state. When a man's basic concern is finding and fulfilling meaning rather than having prestige, pleasure and fun—this may look like idealism, but it is realism. I am a realist of that type of whom Goethe spoke when in rough translation he said, "If we take man as he is we make him worse. But if we take man as he ought to be, we promote him to become what he can be." Many idiots have become idiots simply because a psychiatrist misdiagnosed them as idiots and denied their capability to learn and advance. The same misdiagnosis is made by the mass media. As long as those responsible for the mass media regard the man in the street as half an idiot, they will make him a full idiot. Because the media fail to place intellectual demands or moral demands on the ordinary man, they underrate him and make him worse than he is. Here lies a great responsibility for those engaged in psychiatric diagnosis and also for those who run the mass media and who consistently underrate the intellectual and moral potential that is dormant in man.

Gill: As a veteran journalist, I regretfully agree with you. But on the other hand, isn't it true that man often seeks pleasure rather than meaning?

Frankl: Of course this is true. But I see in the will to pleasure—Sigmund Freud's pleasure principle—or Alfred Adler's will to power mere substitutes for the real thing. Only when the original motivational force in man—his will to meaning, his desire to see and fulfill a meaning in life—has been frustrated, the motivations called will to pleasure or will to power come to the fore.

Gill: What happens when man really sets out to make pleasure his goal?

Frankl: His efforts must fail. When you make pleasure or "happiness" a target, the aim is missed because man can become happy only by fulfilling a meaning or by loving another being. Meaning fulfillment and loving encounters give him a reason to be happy. If a man has such a reason, happiness ensues automatically. If we try to make happiness a goal, then we not only make it an objective for our intention but at the same time it is an object for our attention. The more we pay attention to happiness, the more we lose sight of any reason to become happy. Thus happiness itself fades away. In other words, "happiness" is something that must "happen," it cannot be pursued.

Gill: Today we seem to be obsessed with sex. Is the pursuit of sexual pleasure also doomed to failure?

Frankl: Of course it is. The more a man or a woman aims for sexual pleasure the less he or she is capable of obtaining it. Pursuit of sexual pleasure may cause impotence and frigidity. A male trying to demonstrate his sexual potency or a female trying to demonstrate for herself that she is fully capable of experiencing orgasm is likely to fail. The more a man or a woman give themselves, and the more they forget themselves, the more they will attain orgasm and potency.

Gill: Is selfless sex possible in an age characterized by pornography and the "sex for fun" ideology?

Frankl: We do live in a time of sexual inflation on a massive scale. But this is just an illustration of my contention of a vast existential vacuum.

Gill: How has this emphasis on sex affected sexual life?

Frankl: Any inflation, monetary or other, is accompanied by devaluation. Sexual life is devalued because it is being dehumanized. Human sex is always more than merely physical; it serves as an embodiment of human love.

Gill: What of the will to power? Is this also a substitute for a dissatisfied will to meaning?

Frankl: Yes. Not only libidinal but also aggressive drives and instincts enter the existential vacuum. In his book *History and Human Survival,* Robert J. Lifton says, "Men are most apt to kill or wish to kill when they feel overcome by meaninglessness." In the rehabilitation of juvenile delinquents distinctive success has been gained through logotherapy.

Gill: Is violence the only form of living out one's will to power, or are there also less brutal ways?

Frankl: There are. For instance, many people are dominated by a will to money rather than a will to power. These people cannot see any meaning in their lives and consequently focus on the means to the end rather than the end in itself: the will to money replaces a frustrated will to meaning.

Gill: How can a psychiatrist like yourself give meaning to his patient?

Frankl: He cannot. Meaning cannot be given. It has to be found. Meaning must be discovered by the individual.

Gill: I suppose many people must come to you and ask, "What is the meaning of life?" How do you answer them?

Frankl: Your question reminds me of a newspaper reporter asking a chess champion, "Maestro, could you tell me the best move in chess?" There is no best move in chess, but only a relatively good move when a player is confronted with a given situation in the game. Meaning is always unique. This uniqueness is related to the uniqueness of each individual and to the uniqueness of each life situation confronting him.

Gill: You put great emphasis on individual uniqueness.

Frankl: Yes, because awareness of this uniqueness results in a sense of responsibility. When we regard our life task—the meaning of our life—and, for that matter, the task of each single life situation as something unique, only then are we challenged to use our unique possibilities. In other words, our responsibleness derives from the awareness of the uniqueness of each situation confronting a person. An approximation of the statement by the Jewish sage of two thousand years ago, Hillel, illustrates these principles: "If I don't do it, who will do it? And if I don't do it right now, when shall I do it? But if I only do it for myself, what am I?" The first of these three admonitions refers to the fact that each person is unique and has his unique mission to carry out in life. The second refers to the uniqueness of each situation in which a person finds himself. If he lets these two unique possibilities pass, they will be lost forever. The third admonition seems to point to the fact that if I am purely selfish, then I am actually not a full human being. The humanness of the human being rests on his self-transcendence. What I see as self-transcendence is that being human always means being related to or pointing to something or someone other than oneself. To be truly human means to serve a cause or love a person.

Gill: I can see how meaning can come from our activities and our experience such as love. But are there no situations without meaning? Is life always meaningful? How about a situation where we have to face an unchangeable fate, say, an incurable disease like an inoperable cancer?

Frankl: It is then that we have the possibility to bear witness to the human potential at its best. This potential is the chance to turn a predicament or tragedy into an achievement or triumph on the human level. To bravely face an unchangeable fate offers the challenge to find the meanings of the moment in a life that "never promised you a rose garden," to quote the title of a well-known novel about just such a situation.

Gill: But does not life's transitory nature invalidate meaningfulness?

Frankl: I don't think so because once we have accomplished something, once we have experienced something or encountered someone, we have done so once and forever. In other words, the past is not lost. Rather, everything is safely stored there, and what we are doing is rescuing everything into our past—our deeds, loves, or honest sufferings. Usually man only sees the stubble field of transitoriness. But what he overlooks are the granaries of his past, those granaries in which he has harvested and stored everything. Nothing and no one can ever rob our granaries.

Gill: What about guilt? Guilt is spelled out in capital letters by so many psychologists. Can guilt, too, be turned into something meaningful?

Frankl: Let me quote from a letter I received from an American medical student: "All around me I see people desperately groping for a meaning for their existence. One of my best friends died as a result of his search. I know I could have prevented his suicide if I had taken the time to show my concern. I feel guilty, but I have learned my lesson. His death will always serve to pull me toward all people in distress. I think this is the most powerful motivation anyone can have. I have found a meaning despite my deep sorrow and guilt over my friend's life and death. If I can be strong enough to do my job and fulfill my responsibility, his death will not have been in vain. I want more than anything to prevent such a tragedy from happening to others." Doesn't this letter answer your question?

Gill: How can we get this crucial message across to the man in the street?

Frankl: By making conscious what he already knows intuitively: that every man retains his humanness up to the last moment of his life. We can get this message across because the man in the street knows in his heart that life has meaning under all circumstances and that he has the will to find meaning. I spoke to the prisoners at San Quentin, and they asked me to address a few words through a microphone to Aaron Mitchell who was awaiting execution on Death Row and was not allowed to attend lectures. What could I say? I felt I had to try. I said something like this: "You see, Mr. Mitchell, in a way I understand your situation because once I, too, had to live in the shadow of a gas chamber. But even then I did not give up my conviction that life has unconditional meaning. If life has meaning, then it must retain it even if life is short. If life has no meaning, then adding more years will not add meaning. Even in a life that seems to lack meaning, even in one that has been wasted, meaning can be found by the attitudes we adopt when confronted with an unalterable fate such as imprisonment and even death." I spoke to him in that vein, and a professor from Berkeley who was with me and later interviewed the prisoners found that they had gotten the message. And Mitchell, too, understood because before he was executed he was allowed to speak to the California press, and his statement was a moving document of humanness.

Gill: The message was, then, that life has meaning under all circumstances, and that everyone has a will to meaning.

Frankl: These are two of the three pillars on which logotherapy rests. The third is freedom of choice. Man is free to choose his own way of living, and if need be his own way of dying. Of course, his freedom is limited by many factors, biological, psychological, environmental. But even where his freedom is limited he always has the freedom of choice as to his attitudes. I know from my own experiences the incredible extent to which man is capable of braving the worst conceivable conditions.

Gill: How would you sum up the lesson you learned in the concentration camps?

Frankl: The lesson was that those who were most likely to survive such extreme conditions were oriented toward the future, toward a meaning to fulfill in the future. I learned that survival, all other conditions being equal, is dependent on the individual's awareness of meaning.

Gill: How does this lesson apply outside the barbed wire—to mankind as a whole?

Frankl: If humanity is to survive, people will have to become aware of some common denominator; they must find a common meaning. If people and peoples would see the meanings and values they have in common, they would be united by a common will to a common meaning.

Gill: Returning to the question of freedom: in America, many see freedom as the reason for and the motivation of this nation; do you see freedom in these ultimate terms?

Frankl: Freedom is only half of the story, half a truth. On its own, freedom is a negative concept that has to be complemented by its positive counterpart, responsibility, an awareness of being responsible. Freedom threatens to degenerate into arbitrariness or license if it is not lived in terms of responsibility. This is why I have been suggesting to my American friends that the Statue of Liberty on the East Coast be complemented by a Statue of Responsibility on the West Coast.

II

Logotherapy In Perspective

Logotherapy views man as the first creature in evolution that consciously seeks "logos," the presumed innate order of the universe. Plants and animals turn to it by chemistry and instinct; their search is carried out through their physical substance, and in case of animals through their instinctual drives. Man's conscious search for logos is made possible by the evolution of a third dimension, his spirit, the seat of awareness of potentials, goals, and meanings.

Logotherapy is not the only school of thought that seeks mental health through an understanding of man as a unity of body, psyche, and spirit. But it deserves credit for being the first school of psychology to see the human spirit as the core of mental well-being. It also deserves credit for presenting a consistent over-all picture of the mentally healthy person.

In contrast to the philosophy on which psychoanalysis rests, logophilosophy sees the mentally healthy person striving not for equilibrium but for the strengthening tension that comes with a reaching out for meaning. In contrast to the philosophy behind behaviorism, logophilosophy sees man not reduced to the level of animal or computer but challenged to live as close as possible to the uniqueness that resides in his *human* nature. And in contrast to religious and secular pollyannas, logophilosophy sees the mentally healthy person not escaping but facing the realities of the human predicament and living meaningfully within its limitations. The logotherapist helps his patient approach the goals of the currently popular prayer that asks for the strength to change what can be changed, for the courage to accept what cannot be changed, and for the wisdom to know the difference.

Logotherapy projects a humane philosophy into the psychological arena. Its view of man provides the basis for an art of healing, an art of learning, and an art of living that is accessible to everyone who familarizes himself with its principles.

Past and future, the roots and the orientation, form the first section of this book. Arnold and Gasson examine the place of logotherapy in the evolution of psychology. Sahakian explores its roots in philosophy. Ghougassian shows how logotherapy is the vehicle through which the return to true humanness in the clinical setting can be realized.

The guidelines for sane living suggested by logotherapy need to be tested in the laboratory of life. The essays in this first section provide the philosophical tools for such tests.

Logotherapy's Place in Psychology

Magda B. Arnold and J. A. Gasson

Every form of psychotherapy requires some notion of the normal personality and its organization. Only when we know something about the normal functioning person can we dare to diagnose any malfunctioning or devise techniques of correction. Hence, all types of psychotherapy had to work out a theory of the "normal" personality.

Freud, the first genuine psychotherapist—the first therapist who tried to analyze and change psychological functioning—found himself constrained to construct a coherent theory of psychosexual development which in turn forced him to develop a theory of personality. Every psychotherapist after him has been forced to do the same. It may be unfortunate that most early personality theories came from clinical psychiatrists and therefore were based on abnormal development or abnormal functioning. But the psychiatrists did generate a number of personality theories. Without them, academic psychologists might have preferred to research discrete little areas and leave personality theory in limbo.

Eventually some academic psychologists, too, turned to the clinic and the marketplace and developed a number of psychotherapeutic techniques rooted in academic psychology rather than psychiatry. These personality theories had the advantage of being based on normal development, because psychologists rarely deal with severe neurotics, let alone with psychotics.

Finally, the abundance of personality theories stemming from clinical efforts, whether in psychiatry or psychology, gave rise to a few theories that came from the scientific rather than the clinical side. Most of these theories paid scant attention to the abnormal personality, and still less to possible techniques of correcting such abnormality. For this reason, our effort to set logotherapy in its historical context starts by discussing its place among the psychotherapies and personality theories of Freud, Adler, and Jung before showing its relation to some of the more academically oriented theories.

Personality Theories by Psychiatrists

Sigmund Freud saw man's life essentially as one of conflict and difficulty—conflict even in his own house, between his reality-oriented ego, his power-generating id, and his internal controls embodied in his superego. The simile of a rider (ego) on an untamed horse (id) bedeviled by a monkey on the rider's back (superego) illustrates Everyman's troubles.

For Freud, the Oedipus complex is the divide between normal and abnormal development. If this complex is properly resolved, the personality will develop normally. If not, various types of abnormality are bound to develop. To correct these, the patient has to be brought back to the critical period in his childhood and so be enabled to make a correct turn this time. Freud's method of therapy was "free association," an attempt to enable the patient to abandon his usual way of looking at things, to inhibit the working of normal defense mechanisms, and so lead him back to childhood traumata. Analytic therapy rests on the notion that such free association, when interpreted according to psychoanalytic principles, will bring insight: once the patient achieves insight into his past emotional reactions and sees how his unconscious past has lived on in his present symptoms, the neurotic structure will begin to crumble. Lying on the analytic couch, with the therapist behind him, the patient can let his mind range freely—in theory. In practice, he might not say anything for days, either because he "can't think of anything" or because he falls asleep. And when such resistance is surmounted and the patient acquires some insight, he does not necessarily want to do anything about it. In the end, Freud postulated that the patient must identify with his therapist, the new father figure, and so be *motivated* to act like him, that is, be motivated to get well.

Therapy on these principles was a long process with uncertain outcome. Later analysts looked for ways to shorten the therapeutic process. This had to be done at the expense of the free-association method.

Alfred Adler was one of the first to forsake the method of free association. He saw man as a creature confronting hostile nature with insufficient equipment; man is biologically inferior to many animals who have stronger natural weapons; he is also inferior in relation to parents and older siblings who have to care for him; and finally, his organs and organ systems are developed unequally, so that one or the other of them is bound to be defective or at least inferior. Accordingly, the child strives to overcome feelings of inferiority and in so doing often overcompensates and tries to get the better of all his rivals. The striving for power is the psychological reaction to a feeling of inferiority and provides the motive for human development. Unless a "feeling of fellowship" *(Gemeinschaftsgefühl)* keeps the inferiority in check, it can also lead to aggression.

To correct such maldevelopment, Adler insists that the power conflict must first be fought out between patient and therapist. While in Freudian psychoanalysis the patient identifies with the therapist, in Adlerian therapy the patient sees the therapist at first as an antagonist whom he has to defeat; in the end, he has to make peace with the therapist as a friend. The weapon in this fight is a simple talking over of the patient's conflicts. There is no free association, nor can there be because the patient starts with the present situation rather than with his childhood.

Both Freud and Adler saw psychotherapy as an attempt to correct faulty emotional attitudes. For Freud, the failure of the little boy to identify with his father and so resolve the Oedipus complex will result in abnormal development, anxiety, and neurosis. The identification with the therapist (i.e., an emotional attachment) will motivate the patient to embark on the course of action his insights have shown him to be desirable. For Adler, on the other hand, the way in which a person handles his threefold inferiority is decisive for his further development; if he overcomes his inferiority feeling so that his will to power does not defeat his feeling of fellowship, he has a chance of becoming an effective personality and avoiding neurosis. If he needs therapy, he must come to terms with his desire to defeat the analyst and his antagonism toward him: again, it is a therapy of the emotions.

C. G. Jung's theory of personality and his technique of therapy do not fit into the patterns of Freud and Adler. For Jung, the goal of life is to resolve archetypal projections and attain to the larger self. The projections of the archetype upon father and mother, lover and political leader, contain the emotional power that can subjugate the individual; and his emotions make it difficult to resolve the projection and see parents, friends, and leaders in their true light. In therapy, the patient, through the use of his imagination, is able to objectify these figures and so normalize his attitudes toward them. The therapist is not a loved or hated father figure, but a fellow explorer who helps the patient find his way through the labyrinth of conscious and unconscious images.

Even the choice of goal is determined for a person by his emotions, according to various depth psychologies. For Freud, emotions account for many so-called "rational" decisions; the way a person resolves his Oedipus complex may determine his choice of vocation, his philosophy, and his religious faith. For Adler, such matters are determined not by psychosexual development and the accompanying emotional desires, but by a person's reaction to people and their views that seem to coerce or attack him. Jung again is in a category of his own: emotions make it difficult to attain to the larger self, but they do not determine the kind of selfhood a person will achieve. For Jung, the larger self is the destiny of every human being, and each individual has an unconscious drive toward it. But he can balk, let himself be dragged along, or go willingly.

Viktor Frankl contends that it is not enough to treat only emotions. Emotions are important, but there is more to human life; the human spirit has its own laws, which have little to do with emotions. Man must discover the meaning of his life and then try to fulfill it. A person with an inadequate philosophy of life will never discover that his life has meaning and will become frustrated in a much deeper sense than can be found in any emotional frustration. This emphasis on the meaning of life which every individual has to discover for himself distinguishes Frankl's personality theory from Jung's. For Jung, the individual psyche is only part of the collective psyche. What one man accomplishes is only the realization of the archetypal possibilities inherent in the species. Jung calls the progress toward the larger self "individuation," but in his system each individual is no more than a lone peak in a majestic mountain range. Frankl treats the human being as an individual who has to discover the unique meaning of his life and face his personal responsibility in living it—he is a free-standing mountain peak.

Both Jung and Frankl include in their system religious factors in addition to physiological, psychological, and social ones. But they differ considerably in their understanding of the religious side of human life. For Jung, religion is the symbolic expression of archetypal verities. Good and evil, gods and demons, are projections of the unconscious. As archetypes, they are real because all reality is psychic reality. In Jung's system, material reality itself is only an expression or, better, a condensation of psychic reality. It has developed from psychic reality in the same way as the individual psyche has developed from the collective psyche. Jung's philosophy is a panpsychism in which psychic reality is the only reality and has given birth to everything else, living and non-living. In "individuation," each person attains his larger self, a self of godlike stature. In this achievement, the collective psyche has reached its highest development and has become conscious of itself. Indeed, the larger self is the only god there is, the resolution of the last projection, the means by which a human being becomes what he previously had projected outside, the final power over his own life.

For Frankl, this solution represents mere psychologism, where all questions are answered on the dimension of psychology. Indeed, it may be asked: if every archetype has its counterpart in the real world (the mother, the father, the sage, the hero, the king), why not the god archetype? If every other archetype has to be resolved by taking back its projection without usurping its power and so inflating one's personality, why not the god archetype? To insist that the larger self is the only god means the same inflation of the personality by usurping an alien power, but this time on a cosmic scale.

For Frankl, the question why the divine has been worshipped everywhere all through time cannot be answered by resorting to a collective psyche that goes on producing the same god archetypes. Such an answer is an evasion, a refusal to face the possibility that there is a divine reality beyond all psychic reality, a divine reality that can be experienced by human beings. Indeed, Frankl would say that an individual's life has meaning only with reference to a god who is not bound by space or time, who is the ground and anchor for the human spirit.

At the same time, Frankl refuses to make all therapy a noötherapy in which all conflicts are seen as religious or philosophical difficulties. Among academic psychologists, O. H. Mowrer is close to such a solution. He insists that neurosis is sin, a transgression of moral laws. With this notion he brings back views held through centuries in which man was considered absolutely responsible for his actions, with no allowance for illness or other afflictions which may diminish his responsibility. Frankl admits that many neuroses do stem from emotional conflicts; and both psychoses and neuroses may be the result of organic causes. There are other neuroses that are produced by a relentless conflict of conscience, never acknowledged and thus inaccessible to resolution.

For Frankl, every life has a meaning. Life is a task that is given and has to be carried out. Its meaning is to be found in objective values. These values exist but have to be discovered anew by everyone. Every goal implies a value. Some values must be realized in deliberate action, as creative values that depend on the manner of acting rather than the significance of each action: man must act responsibly, his action must be a commitment. There are also experiential values (realized in the enjoyment of a painting or a symphony, the beauty of nature, the warmth of love). Even when it is impossible to realize either experiential or creative values, as, for instance, during periods of illness, deprivation, mental or physical suffering, or in the face of death, the human being can realize an objective value in the degree of courage and steadfastness with which he meets such catastrophes. It is God, as it were, who is the guarantor of these values, the silent witness when no one seems to know or care. It is God to whom man is responsible for his actions and his life.

Logotherapy is not a therapeutic technique in the usual sense. It considers any approach that becomes a mere technique as depreciating the human being and as reducing him to a "psychic apparatus." Nevertheless, logotherapy does use an approach, paradoxical intention, to put distance between the person and his emotions. As discussed elsewhere in this volume when emotions tend to overwhelm a patient, he can master them by challenging them to do their worst rather than by fighting them.

Psychological Theories and Therapies

So far, few of Frankl's views have been accepted by academic psychology. Nor have Adler and Jung been fully acknowledged. It seems that until the most recent past only Freud's views penetrated into this country.

Henry Murray, in a review of a book that he characterized as "another volume of Freudolatry," remarked that many deficiencies could be found in Freud's theory of personality, but, Murray said, his technique is the only one we have, so we have to use it—just like the gambler sitting in on a rigged-deck poker game, who said, "what can I do, it's the only game in town." Psychoanalytic notions have diffused through psychological thinking to the point where they almost monopolize it. This is especially true for psychotherapy which owes practically its entire form to Freud. And it was Freud who first advanced the notion that the affective side of life ("instinct and it affect charge") is the most important. He acknowleged that mankind has intelligence and reason, but neither of these lead to neurosis. Legend has it that he once remarked: "Mankind has always known it has a spirit; my task is to teach men that they have instincts, too."

Hence, in Freud's generation and the two following, psychotherapists took it for granted that therapy concerns itself only with the affective life, feelings and emotions. This was true even of those theorists and therapists who opposed Freud's theories and abandoned his technique. Psychoanalysis had shown itself to be a therapy requiring years rather than months or weeks. Thus many attempts were made to find shortcuts but none proved effective.

During this period also, there was a movement among analysts toward an ego psychology, away from id processes and explanations. Though in this movement the urge toward psychosexual development was still anchored in the libido, more autonomy and control was attributed to the ego. But in the end, insight into repressed emotional traumata was still the reason for change; the "cure," spontaneous upon insight, was derived from psychoanalytical interpretations and identification with the therapist. Too often, insight occurred but no change, or insight was long delayed by resistance; and the therapist found himself torn between his theoretical convictions that urged him to wait on the patient, and his conscience as a therapist that made him want to hasten insight or change. Many therapists eventually did decide to take a more active part in the treatment.

Therapists, including psychoanalysts, always claimed that the patient, not the therapist, worked the cure. But the patient was still *patiens* and patiently had to "undergo" treatment. Even if the analyst did not play an active role, he did give interpretations of free associations and dreams, and these could not help but shape the patient's insight.

Carl Rogers became dissatisfied with what was to be called "directive" therapy. Not a physician but a counselor, he did not have the attitude of the medical profession toward management of faulty functioning. More importantly, he came to see that advice and explanation were of little help in the troubles and difficulties people brought to him. Rather, what they needed was to take their feelings seriously, recognize them, acknowledge them, and have them taken seriously by the therapist. What troubled people need, he suggests, is to be accepted by the therapist and have his warm support. In an atmosphere of "unconditional positive regard" the client's (not patient's) confrontation with his problems will lead to their solution without active manipulation or explanation by the therapist.

Despite his break with the psychoanalytic tradition, Rogers also sees man's main task as coming to terms with his feelings and emotions. It is only Rogers' technique that differs from Freud's. Instead of using free association, the therapist acts as a mirror reflecting the client's feelings. But whether memory brings up traumatic situations and so confronts a person with his emotions, or whether he recognizes them in the counselor's factual reflections, it is still the client's feelings that are in the center of the counseling situation. By implication, if not by assertion, the client is led to believe that his feelings are the only things that matter, the only things that have to be changed. By concentrating on feelings alone, however, Rogers leaves out an important dimension. His clients may be more at home with themselves after nondirective therapy, but they never have a chance to face questions of deep human concern such as the meaning of life. A psychotherapist is not a spiritual counselor; but if such questions are of concern to the client, they deserve better than a bland reflection of his feelings about them. Curiously enough, it is Frankl, the medical man, who realizes the importance of the spiritual dimension, while Rogers, the former ministerial student, does not.

Nondirective therapy, as it came to be called, has had considerable success. As with most other therapies, there is no way to prove that it is the nondirective technique and not the skill of the therapist, or the client's willingness to change, that is at the root of such success. Despite the large following Rogers has gained, however, an unresolved doubt has remained. Does the therapist have the right to strict noninterference if the client decides on a course of action that is harmful to himself or somebody else? To warn or dissuade him, or otherwise prevent him from carrying out his intention may go counter to the principle of nondirective therapy. But not to keep him from harm would go counter to the over-all purpose of therapy—namely, restoration of health and happiness.

Rogers had his private doubts, too. He found it difficult to reconcile his life as a therapist with that of a scientist. What he found apt and effective as a therapist, he could not integrate with his explorations in science. When applied to his counseling procedure, his scientific method could not reach or measure the process of change (4).

Abraham Maslow faced the same problem in his psychological investigations. Although not a therapist, he was interested in personality, normal and disturbed, high-achieving and low-achieving, growing and stagnant. He urged other research workers to choose a significant problem and then devise methods of investigating and solving it, rather than choosing a method of inquiry and then looking around for a problem to which it could be applied (1). His own procedure followed his counsel. He turned away from the easy problems that had ready-made methods of approach and chose instead the significant human problems that could be approached only with less than scientific rigor. His concern with "self-actualization" and "human potential" gave rise to humanistic psychology, and gave theoretical support to the tremendous growth of training laboratories, encounter groups, and Esalen-type workshops. It also is sparking the beginning of a new look in psychotherapy.

Maslow's training in psychoanalytic theory biased him in the direction of instincts, or, as he put it, "needs." These needs he considered hierarchical: a higher need will not arise unless the more primitive needs are largely met. But given the ordered satisfaction of needs, the human being has the capacity for actualizing himself to the extent of his intelligence and his opportunities. What is distinctive in Maslow's approach is that he studied human qualities in normal people functioning at their best. For him, the norm of humanity is the healthy personality functioning harmoniously, smoothly, easily; the person who has growth (or being) needs—B-needs—as well as deficiency needs—D-needs—and who has "peak experiences" that give him ecstasy and illumination.

One problem in Maslow's personality theory is that it is essentially based on deficiency motivation. True, he claims that there is a switch from deficiency to growth motivation (self-actualization), once physiological, safety, love, and esteem needs are met. Actually, it could be said that there has been growth all along. The organism is growing, it has no "need" to grow. And because of this growth, the organism requires more food in childhood than when fully grown.

Psychologically speaking, the child reaches out lovingly, but he also has to have his love returned. This is not the filling of a deficiency; it is a mutual giving of love. If he cannot love or is not loved, his growth will be stunted. The child explores the world; but to do so, he needs a measure of safety and peace. The adult is active in his work and establishes a family, but he also needs the respect of others who let him keep what he has acquired. The self-actualizer is active on a higher level, but even he needs love. A need theory stresses the filling of a deficiency, instead of the human activity that leads to a goal transcending the individual.

Maslow calls the B-needs values and suggests that "these intrinsic values are instinctoid in nature; i.e., they are needed to avoid illness and to achieve fullest humanness or growth" (2, p. 316). If B-values are "instinctoid," Maslow is really saying that these needs are blind, as are all instincts. Even the self-actualizer, then, is merely obeying a blind urge, except that he has better conditions of growth and so manages to grow taller than others. Like the plant that has all the water and nourishment it needs, he can grow to the limit of his potentialities. But what really distinguishes the human being from other organic life is that he looks at the world around him, discovers things he values, and decides which of them he wants for his own. The search for goodness, truth, and beauty is not a search for what will fill a deficiency; that would restrict him to what is given in his environment. Man tries to improve his world; he makes things for his own purposes, he looks for truth or beauty where no one has found it before. The sculptor, the artist, the scientist, give more to the world than they take from it.

Maslow knew Frankl's work as he did that of other humanistic psychologists. He was an eclectic and took ideas and concepts where he found them. From Frankl, he took the spiritual dimension in man and noögenic disorders. But Maslow did not penetrate to the philosophical basis of these concepts, and he used them in a way they were not intended. Still, Maslow was aware of other views and was stimulated by them. The humanistic direction in psychology, inspired and carried by him, has developed practically into a new school of psychology, strictly apart from the mainstream of psychological thinking.

Behaviorism is the prevailing ideology of general academic psychology which has paid scant attention to either Frankl or the humanistic approach. Academic psychology considers behaviorism—its method, its facts, its inferences and conclusions—the only scientific psychology. That the hard-nosed behaviorist may have to lead a double life as scientist and human being is considered irrelevant. Even a psychologist like Carl Rogers, who is not a behaviorist, has found this a dilemma.

The core dogma of the behaviorist is that the animal, any animal, can be shaped to any behavior, no matter how complex, if the environmental stimuli are arranged so that the expected responses are given. Since contemporary learning theory holds that learning is the acquisition of new responses, it is not surprising that for most academic psychologists learning equals conditioning or, in the space age, programming.

It is easy to see how this concept can be reduced to practice. For E. J. Shoben, neurosis is a way of responding. If one neurotic pattern of responses is extinguished and another normal one established, the patient is "cured" of his neurosis. Whatever happens to the neurotic's thoughts, motives, desires, attitudes, or habits, if anything does, is presumed to follow behavior. His "mind" will be shaped as is his pattern of responses.

Behavior modification is the therapy of choice for many clinicians, even those who are in principle opposed to behavioristic notions of the human being and his goals. They may agree that behaviorist theory leaves out the humanity of man, but behavior therapy is convenient and easy to use. This technique makes thinking and decision-making, motives and purposes the froth that appears occasionally on a shaped response. And with small children, psychotics, and the retarded, for whom this method is more successful than with normal adults, such froth rarely appears.

In behavior modification, psychologists have gone back to the notion that the human being can and even must be managed, controlled, directed; but who controls the controllers? Learning theorists object to the "medical model" of psychotherapy and try to substitute the learning model. But they have taken over the most pernicious aspect of the medical model, namely the notion that it is the therapist who gives treatment and so brings about a cure. Now the patient is in truth "treated," controlled by cleverly arranged reinforcements. There is no appeal to a man's spirit, no acknowledgment of his autonomy. Whether a patient is aware of his problems or not, the therapist makes his diagnosis without even asking the patient.

But at least this much we ought to be grateful for: the therapist is at least trying to do something for patients who may not be helped by more humane methods. But as behavior therapists branch out from work with psychotics, children, retarded persons, and young people, to the more complex problems of adults, they will perhaps recognize that changes of outward behavior are not enough. At that time, some will perhaps go back to true humanists like Frankl for a more effective notion of the human being.

Frankl's place

This essay, by giving samples of personality theories and therapeutic techniques, attempted to show the place of Frankl in the emerging picture. There are many such theories, and more are being added constantly. Patterson (3), discussing theories of counseling and psychotherapy, lists fourteen of them, including Frankl's.

Psychotherapy seems to have started out as an attempt to help people solve emotional problems. Next, it became important to shorten the period of therapy. Emotional problems did not seem restricted to the upper classes, and salaried employees had neither the time nor the money, however much their inclination, to delve into their psyche for years. While shorter forms of therapy were successful enough, some therapists eventually felt that not only the monied and intelligent but also low-income and retarded people deserve help. So behavior modification came on the scene and had success where the older therapies had hardly been tried.

But in all these efforts to help human beings, only two major psychotherapists, Jung and Frankl, paid attention to the human spirit and human aspirations. Among academic theorists, Maslow is important because of the impetus he gave to humanistic psychology against the prevailing behaviorist ideology. Among humanists, Frankl was one of the first psychotherapists who took the human potential seriously, long before the advent of encounter groups and Esalen workshops. The questions he raised have to be answered in every human life. By insisting that every man has to find the meaning of his life and has the responsibility of carrying out his task, he has made the thoughtful, questing, creative personality the foundation of his personality theory, rather than extrapolating it from the neurotic caught in his emotions and preoccupied with his problems, or from the rat shaped in the Skinner box.

References

1. Maslow, A. J. (1946). Problem-centering versus means-centering in science. *Philosophy of Science* 13: 326–331.
2. ______. (1971). *The Farther Reaches of Human Nature.* New York: Viking.
3. Patterson, C. H. (1973). *Theories of Counseling and Psychotherapy.* 2nd ed. New York: Harper.
4. Rogers, C. R. (1961). *On Becoming a Person.* Boston: Houghton Mifflin.

Logotherapy's Place in Philosophy

William S. Sahakian

Logotherapy, based on the phenomenology of Max Scheler and the vitalism of Friedrich Nietzsche, is a philosophy applicable to everyday living. It is a *Lebensanschauung* (a conception of life) or *Lebensphilosophie* (a philosophy of life). As a philosophy, it agrees with existentialism. But unlike many forms of existentialism, logotherapy is marked by a buoyant optimism, an affirmation of life, acknowledging the reality of values and of a meaningful existence. Life is worth living because of the meanings and values it affords the individual. A meaningful life provides a perspective, a cause for which to live, and an anchor for psychological adjustment to the vicissitudes of life. It is as Nietzsche asserted, "If we possess our *why* of life we can put up with almost any *how*" (4, maxim 12).

The Hedonistic Paradox

Implicit in Freud's pleasure principle is the belief that man is a pleasure-seeking animal. Because of his natural constitution, man consciously or unconsciously pursues pleasure. The implication of this principle is that without happiness man is miserable. All hedonistic philosophies lead to despair, a fact known to the ancient Greek philosophers. The "death counselor," Hegesias, advocated suicide because he felt that life did not afford sufficient pleasure to make it worth living. If pleasure is held to be the only good of life, then Hegesias' *eudaemonistic pessimism* may have been valid thinking; since the frustration emanating from man's desires is a universal experience, a person ought to prefer death as a pain-free alternative.

Frankl learned firsthand that pleasure is an unreliable basis upon which to establish adjustments to life. Those inmates of Nazi concentration camps who were inclined to a hedonistic philosophy were the ones most susceptible to conscious or unconscious suicide. Barred from all pleasure and having no prospect of its return on the morrow, these persons concluded that they might as well give up since there was nothing else for which to live. But, Frankl contends, instead of asking what pleasure life has in store, the prisoners' survival chances would have been greater if they had been able to ask themselves, "What can life expect from me?" What makes a pleasure truly pleasurable is its significance or richness of meaning.

Since 1736, when Joseph Butler (1) uncovered the "hedonistic paradox," philosophers have been wary of advising the pursuit of happiness. According to the hedonistic paradox, no single or defined path to happiness exists; for example, a new home in the country may render one person happy but prove miserable, solitary, and confining to another. Although there is no direct path to happiness, happiness is attainable as a by-product of that which in itself is not identifiable as happiness, so that a harassed mother rearing her family or a man working hard to achieve his aspirations may well experience happiness. Still, the direct capture of happiness is impossible.

The hedonistic paradox (which is an important tenet of the philosophy of logotherapy) is not new with Frankl, but its use in conjunction with life's "meanings" for the successful attainment of happiness, is. The will to meaning provides a ground for happiness which in turn issues in happiness. "Both happiness and success are mere substitutes for fulfillment, and that is why [Freud's] pleasure principle as well as [Adler's] will to power are mere derivatives of the will to meaning" (WM, p. 36).

Stoical Character of Logotherapy

Logotherapy and stoicism share a number of ideas, for instance the existence of attitudinal values and the nonexistence of purposeless evil.

Stoics hold that an evil in itself—and not instrumental to an ultimate good—does not exist, hence all suffering is meaningful or for a purpose. Consequently, the stoic maintains that life's vicissitudes are to be viewed as God's wrestling with us as a sparring partner in order to strengthen our spiritual muscles. The stoic Epictetus admonished: "Difficulties are what show men's character. Therefore when a difficult crisis meets you, remember that you are as the raw youth with whom God, like a gymnastic trainer, is wrestling. For what end? That you may be an Olympic conqueror; and this cannot be without toil. No man, in my opinion, has a more profitable difficulty than you, provided you will but use it for exercise, as the athlete wrestles with his antagonist" (2, bk. 1, ch. 24). However, this exercise would be impossible if it were not for the fact that life is meaningful, especially with respect to its problems and sufferings.

Frankl's attitudinal value theory is unquestionably stoic in character. When a situation cannot be changed, a person still can alter his attitude toward his problem. This recommendation is paramount both in stoicism and logotherapy. "The essence of good and evil," wrote Epictetus, "lies in the attitude of the will" (2, bk. 1, ch. 29). "Where we can no longer control our fate and reshape it," advises Frankl, "we must be able to accept it" (PE, p. 128). The sting of life does not exist so much in the external world as it does within the personality as a state of mind, a condition of the soul. Consequently death and suffering have no more sting than an individual will allow them to have. Paralleling these stoic ideas of Epictetus, Frankl has written, "Whether any circumstances, be they inner or outer ones, have an influence on a given individual or not, and in which direction this influence takes its way—all that depends on the individual's free choice. *The conditions do not determine me but I determine whether I yield to them or brave them*" (3, p. 6).

Hence the role of the will in both stoicism and logotherapy becomes a prime consideration. The importance of will and its function is fundamental in stoicism and two of the three pillars on which logotherapy is constructed concern will (freedom of will, and will to meaning). Both philosophies view the will as unconquerable, that is, as lying within the power of the individual. Both philosophies hold that a person should transform his circumstances into more palatable ones if such transformation lies within his power, but that if it does not, an alteration of will or attitude is indicated. The stoics regard the will as inviolate, holding that it must remain invincible. That is to say, a person's will rests within his own power, consequently only he can yield it to another person or thing. However, Epictetus advised not to permit another to break your will. Even if a person has it within his power to put you to death, you must not allow your will to be broken. Anytus and Meletus, two politicians in Athens, worked it so that they brought about the conviction and execution of Socrates, hoping to break his spirit; but Socrates confounded his enemies with his attitude and invincible will by asserting, "Anytus and Meletus have power to put me to death, but hurt me they cannot" (2, bk. 1, ch. 29; 5, 30c). In logotherapy the exercise of will not only effects a change of attitude, it also is capable of producing self-detachment, resulting in paradoxical intention.

Personalistic Character of Logotherapy

As a philosophy, personalism views the person as of infinite intrinsic value, and regards the person as a *unitas multiplex* (multiple unity). As a psychology, personalism places the person in the center of concern. Distinguished personalists in philosophy include Borden Parker Bowne and Edgar Sheffield Brightman; in psychology two prominent ones were William Stern and Gordon W. Allport, but other psychologists who were personalistic in their outlook include William James, Mary W. Calkins, W. Dilthey, and E. Spranger. Current personalists in psychology are, in addition to Frankl, Carl R. Rogers, Henry A. Murray, and Erich Fromm.

Stern defined the person as "a living whole, individual, unique, striving toward goals, self-contained and yet open to the world around him; he is capable of having experience" (9, p. 70); then, Stern went on to assert that "the person is a totality, that is, a *unitas multiplex.*" Frankl likewise views "Man [as] a 'unitas multiplex.' Art has been defined as unity in diversity. I would define man as unity in spite of multiplicity" (WM, p. 22). A human being is unique in many ways; he is capable of humor, of evaluating, of willing, of grasping meaningful situations, of transcending himself, of pursuing goals, of intellectualizing, of acting as a free and responsible person, just to mention a few human or noëtic characteristics.

Logotherapy as a Form of Phenomenology

Phenomenology, as the philosophy of essence, is the descriptive analysis of subjective processes. It seeks to attain the ideal intelligible structure in phenomena. The phenomenology to which logotherapy is most closely related is that of Max Scheler. According to Scheler, a person possesses intellectual processes, but also emotional intuition and *a priori* apprehension of value; that is, genuine phenomenological experiences. "Phenomenological experience," asserts Scheler, "is at the same time *'immanent'* experience. . . . In phenomenological experience nothing is *meant* that is not *given,* and nothing is given that is not meant. It is precisely *in* this *coincidence* of the 'meant' and the 'given' that the *content* of phenomenological experience alone becomes manifest" (8, p. 51).

Not only does Frankl define "meaning" as "what is meant" (WM, p. 62), but he agrees with Scheler about the phenomenology of experience, especially that "meanings" are among the contents of phenomenological experiences. Thus meanings (in the plural) are genuine phenomenological entities existing out there in the real world along with music and other objective experiences that are peculiar solely to the human dimension. While meaningful experiences often are true for a specific individual, some are universally shared by all people and are called values. In this respect, logotherapy is a personalistic philosophy like Scheler's phenomenology.

Logotherapy as a Sophisticated Form of Existentialism

Unlike psychoanalysis, logotherapy conceives responsibility and guilt as human traits that should not be explained away. A person is a responsible being and as such should accept his obligations together with whatever guilt may result from such a nature. In contrast, psychoanalysis relieves a person from guilt no matter how responsible he is for it. The couch is a place to rid oneself of feelings of guilt and to shift responsibility to others or to an unhappy childhood situation. Anna Russell in her *Psychiatric Folksong* illustrates the psychoanalytic exculpation of a person's guilt:

At three I had a feeling of ambivalence toward my brothers.
And so it follows naturally I pursued all my lovers.
But now I'm happy; I have learned the lesson this has taught:
That everything I do that's wrong is someone else's fault.

Sartre's traditional existentialism does not permit excuses for demeaning behavior or taking recourse for such behavior by hiding behind passion or a deterministic philosophy that serves as an excuse for one's abominable actions. Sartre contended, "Those who hide their complete freedom from themselves out of a spirit of seriousness or by means of deterministic excuses, I shall call cowards; those who try to show that their existence was necessary, when it is the very contingency of man's appearance on earth, I shall call stinkers" (6, p. 55). Thus, for Sartre's existentialism, as for logotherapy, man is free; he is a "coward" who excuses his reprehensible behavior on grounds that he is a victim of his environment or his heredity. But responsibility, in logotherapy, goes beyond Sartre's view: Man is responsible for discovering the meanings of the moment that exist and must be responded to, and not simply for "inventing" meanings in an objectively meaningless existence, as Sartre recommends.

Logotherapy and French existentialism are equally humanistic, rather than reductionistic; both stress human in place of animalistic qualities. But logotherapy differs from traditional French existentialism in its optimism and panmeaningfulness. Whereas traditional existentialism is pessimistic and stresses the meaninglessness of life, optimistic logotherapy insists that the world is permeated with meaning. For existentialism "man is a useless passion" (7, p. 615); for logotherapy he is a being of intrinsic value, possessing dignity.

Logotherapy restores sanity by introducing meaningfulness in place of meaninglessness, optimism instead of pessimism with its attendant cynicism, and rationality as a replacement for irrationalism. In so doing, logotherapy plays an ascendant role over traditional existentialism.

Logotherapy is a youthful philosophy with an exuberance that conveys an atmosphere of hope. Being a young philosophy, it is undergoing an integration process from which is bound to emerge its ability to cohere with many more facts of human experience. It has the potential to develop into a maturity that could accord it a position among major philosophies. Currently, it offers one of the most adequate answers to the philosophical problems of natural evil such as the existence of human suffering. In this respect logotherapy is a philosophy of religion in addition to being a general philosophy of life.

References

1. Butler, J. (1726). Fifteen Sermons Preached at Rolls Chapel. London.
2. Epictetus. (1965). *Discourses.* In *The Works of Epictetus.* Boston Little, Brown.
3. Frankl, V. E. (1961). Dynamics, existence and values. *Journal of Existential Psychiatry* 2: 5–16.
4. Nietzsche, F. (1968). Maxim and arrows. In *The Twilight of the Idols.* Baltimore: Penguin.
5. Plato (1901). *Apology.* In B. Jowett, *The Dialogues of Plato.* 4 vols. New York: Scribner.
6. Sartre, J.-P. (1947). *Existentialism.* New York: Philosophical Library.
7. ______(1956). *Being and Nothingness.* New York: Philosophical Library.
8. Scheler, M. (1973). *Formalism in Ethics and the Non-Formal Ethics of Values.* Evanston, Illinois: Northwestern University Press.
9. Stern, W. (1938). *General Psychology: From the Personalistic Standpoint.* New York: Macmillan.

The "Rehumanization" of Psychotherapy

Joseph B. Ghougassian

Albert Camus, in *The Myth of Sisyphus,* raised a pertinent question which defies and challenges everybody who calls himself a true thinker, "There is but one truly serious philosophical problem, and that is suicide. Judging whether life is or is not worth living amounts to answering the fundamental question of philosophy."

Frankl is one of the few academic theoreticians and medical practitioners who has taken to heart Camus' challenge and answered positively that human existence is worth living even when life has become utterly unbearable because of incurable sickness or cruel suffering. He is the defender of the Renaissance "humanism," maintaining that values, meanings, freedom, responsibility, are intrinsic predicaments of the essence of man.

The Problematic of Man

Frankl has been influenced by Max Scheler who maintains that "at no time in his history has man been so much of a problem to himself as he is now" (6, p. 6). In our technological age, scientific control, understanding, and prediction have become the three most cherished intellectual ambitions. Accordingly, a reality defying these three tests of science will automatically be eliminated on the grounds that it is mysterious, disconcerting, or bothersome. Thus, the human being in the totality of his "humanness" is the very reality that science likes to becloud. Above all, the behavioral science of psychology and the science of psychoanalysis do not study man as a human being, but in the framework of some subhuman organism or in certain partial aspects of his humanness. This failure on the part of behavioral psychology and psychoanalysis to meet the challenge of man as man is the reason why Frankl is reviving the aims of humanism—to see man in all his dimensions of being.

Here lies the problem of man which gave birth to two opposite contemporary schools of thought: the *dehumanization* or reduction of the human being, and his *rehumanization.*

Dehumanization

Following Edmund Husserl, Frankl adopts the terminology of "scientism" and "psychologism" to criticize the internal contradictions of reductionism.

In the light of the philosophy carved on scientism, man is fashioned of the same material stuff as physical nature, and his behavior obeys the laws of physics and biology (7, p. 175). Only the physical is recognized as real; the ideal is refused any place in reality or is "naturalized" by being made a physical reality through the method of reductionism. Thus, scientism naturalizes consciousness and reduces it by comparing it with the "artificial consciousness" of machines; man's intelligence, so the argument goes, can be replicated in machines, and therefore "there is nothing essentially human" about any of the conditions "under which consciousness is attributed to human beings" (5, p. 12). The reducing of man to a "servomechanism" is a growing belief among eminent theoreticians: Dean E. Woolridge thinks that it is possible to construct cybernetic machines which are "completely indistinguishable from human beings produced in the usual manner" (10, p. 172); Marvin Minsky maintains that "there is no reason to suppose machines have any limitations not shared by man" (4, p. vii), an idea also held by the British mathematician A. Turing. Frankl terms scientism a "masked nothing-but-ness"—in the view of reductionism, man is "nothing but a complex biochemical mechanism powered by a combustion system which energizes computers with prodigious storage facilities for retaining encoded information." Man, however, is "infinitely more than a computer" (WM, p. 21).

The same nihilistic view of diminishing human nature is also advocated by both psychoanalysts and behaviorists, although their approaches differ from each other. Both fall prey to the fallacies of psychologism, which attempts to explain human phenomena such as consciousness, values, conscience, responsibility, love, and culture in purely psychological language. Psychologism reduces psychology to physiology, and physiology to physics and the laws of motion. The psychologism of both psychoanalysis and behaviorism is arrived at by the circuitous route of pure science. Psychoanalysis tends to reduce human motivations to the psychological dimension, while the behaviorists maintain that an equivalence of basic features exists between the animal kingdom and the human sphere—the latter simply being more complex but not of a different nature than animal species. Accordingly, in experimental psychology, many experiments are conducted on dogs (Pavlov), rats (Tolman), and pigeons (Skinner); and we are taught to believe that the results reached about the animal apply to human behavior.

These psychologists are avowed humanitarians. Skinner claims that his behavioral engineering science is "for the good of mankind." Watson expressed the same good intention of making "that God-given maze which is our world"—as his student Tolman once wrote—a place for "better ways of living and thinking." Our dispute with psychoanalysis and behaviorism is not so much a matter of "intentional" disagreement, as it is a critique of their methodology and philosophy which by their procedures and content depersonalize human nature. The more restrictive a theory is the more limited will be the results and, in our context, the more will human nature be dehumanized for lack of scope.

Rehumanization

If the growing movement of structuralism (under such philosophers as Michel Foucault), taking its vitalism from Marxism and Freudianism, has declared the "death of man" after the manner of the nineteenth-century deicide, and if Skinner has openly repudiated the "dignity of man," Frankl, inspired by the faith in monotheism, has professed his faith in "monanthropism" (unity of man). In this respect, logotherapy is a movement of "rehumanization"—it acknowledges the basic features of human existence and developed techniques of therapy through which the person can express and fulfill his humanity. The theory and method of logotherapy are scientific along the strict guidelines of Edmund Husserl, employing a "phenomenological analysis" which is empirical, observational, and includes a statistical polling of the experiences or behaviors of the man in the street (WM, p. 69). The purpose of the phenomenological method is to reveal through the study of behavior the essence of human nature. Although both psychoanalysis and behaviorist psychology are based on the same principle, the difference between them and logotherapy stems from their presupposed philosophical worldview. And here lies the difference between dehumanization and rehumanization. Both psychoanalysis and behaviorism restrict their explanations of behavior to a few human experiences, thus denying the reality of other facets of human behavior. Psychoanalysis, for instance, anticipates *a priori* only two dimensions of man—the organism and the mind. Behaviorism presupposes that there is only one dimension to human existence, the organism, and thus narrows its study of behavior to physiological processes. Logotherapy investigates all the original data and the reality the man of the street recounts, and the investigation reveals that human structure is an open system constituted by three interwoven dimensions: body, mind, and spirit. The dimensions are interrelated in their functions: one dimension *is* not the others. Although the characteristics of one are not inherent in the others, in actual functioning the dimensions interlace.

Logotherapy has rehumanized psychotherapy inasmuch as it makes the spirit the "highest" dimension that encompasses the more narrow dimensions of mind and body. The relationship of the spirit with mind and body could well be expressed by Gabriel Marcel's term "incarnate being." There is no action, regardless of how material or spiritual it is, that does not reflect the oneness of man. This genuine human reality is expressed in Paul Tillich's words, "Our whole being, every cell of our body, and every movement of our mind is both flesh and spirit" (8, p. 54).

The rehumanizing traits of the spiritual dimension predominantly include freedom of will and will to meaning.

Freedom of Will

The dispute among therapists as to whether man has enough power to determine his own destiny and to arrange a life of his own has become academic. Both the psychoanalysts and the behaviorists have answered in favor of strict determinism, but in practice neither school denies the patient a certain amount of self-determination in the process of the cure. However, Frankl, Carl Rogers, Rollo May and Karl Jaspers recognize the human phenomenon of freedom; and their practice is consistent with their philosophical speculation on the issue of free behavior. In his psychiatric credo, Frankl acknowledges a residue of freedom in the most deteriorated personality, "There is nothing conceivable that would so condition a man as to leave him without the slightest freedom. Therefore, a residue of freedom, however limited it may be, is left to man in neurotic and even psychotic cases" (MS, p. 211). Such a statement is corroborated by the fact that the patients themselves, assisted by their therapists, are capable of participating in their cure; they are not passive marionettes. In the words of Jaspers, the patient's free will is "an instrument of therapy."

One problem with the deterministic psychotherapies is their definition of freedom. Some define freedom as doing what one pleases (7, p. 29). The humanist psychotherapists, however, maintain that libertinism is no indication of free behavior; rather, capricious conducts are childish and most probably conditioned by internal physiological needs or by an unhealthy environmental upbringing. A free man is one who is ready to bear responsibly the consequences of his acts.

A second misconception about freedom is that whatever happens has a cause. Such a logic, which is exemplified by Skinner's behavior modification therapy, can be traced back to David Hume, whose influence on American psychology and philosophy is still felt. The confusion lies in the belief that causes and reasons, and causes and conditions, equal one another. A person acts because he has a reason or because he is motivated by certain conditions. A man empties a trash can because it is full; he has a reason to empty it. A teacher spends hours to prepare a lecture; lecturing intelligently is a condition for keeping his job. But we cannot say that the man emptying the trash can and the teacher have no other choices and therefore are determined in their actions. Man is a being-in-the-world; the world is made up of situations; and according to his circumstances, he has to act and adjust for survival.

A third misconception lies in a paradox: although there often is no freedom "from" conditions, there always is freedom "toward" and "in" conditions.

The determinists themselves implicitly acknowledge the paradox when they claim that human responses are conditioned reflexes due to stimuli but urge humanity to control the stimuli, choose the good from the bad conditionings, and reinforce the good ones in our children so a favorable world free from miseries can be built.

The freedom toward conditions, then, is a freedom of attitudes, whereas the freedom Skinner advocates is a type of reaction behavior meant to escape from the threat, pain, intentional control, aversion, to "avoid" them (7, pp. 24–40). His interpretation of freedom denotes a Freudian neurotic escape or defense mechanism.

The logotherapist advocates a more or less relative freedom for the individual. "Relative" because human actions are a blend of necessity and freedom, and also because man never will be able to dissipate completely the reality of necessity: no matter how much self-insight he gains about what determines him, there always will be some determinism that escapes his knowledge.

The question whether behavior is an expression of a person's self-assertion or a blind instinctual or habitual response has crucial therapeutic implications. The logotherapist contends that responsibility makes behavior self-determined. He helps the patient become "fully aware of his own responsibleness; [and] . . . leaves to him the option for what, to what or to whom he understands himself to be responsible" (MS, p. 173). To Frankl, freedom is a negative concept which requires a positive complement; and the positive element means responsibleness. Freedom without responsibleness is action in utter ignorance. Responsibleness adds a reflective knowledge about the what, why, and how of the action, and a sense of moral obligation about the consequences. Being responsible means listening actively to one's conscience. The more the person liberates himself from coercions the more he is responsible and the more he feels obligated toward someone or something. The person's conscience is experienced as an "ought," not as a "must." In contrast to the superego, which is the must-conscience of fear, punishment, and coercion, the ought conscience is a matter of private decision. Guilt, then, is not the result of the violation of tribal taboos but, to quote Allport, "a sense of violated value, a disgust at falling short of the ideal self-image."

Whereas the psychoanalyst aims primarily at strengthening the ego by making it more cognizant of the forces of the superego and of the id (the unconscious storehouse of the two major instincts: sex and aggression), and the behaviorist reinforces positively rewarding conditionings, the logotherapist strengthens the relationship between the individual's self-image and his values by making him aware of his responsibleness and tasks.

Logotherapy has rehumanized psychotherapy because it acknowledges the presence of the freedom of will and seeks to make the patients aware of their responsibleness. In contrast to psychoanalysis and behaviorism, it teaches that "man is by no means merely a product of heredity and environment. There is a third element: decision. Man ultimately decides for himself!" (DS, p. xvii).

The Will to Meaning

Psychoanalysis sees humans motivated by a will to impulses, a will to seek pleasure and avoid pain as far as possible. This "psychological hedonism" asserts that human behavior is a "push" from the internal desires of the id to find gratification for the two basic organic instincts, sex and death. Freud believed that the individual, in any life situation, will use all means to find pleasure; thus, for him sublimation operates by the reality principle, which is "a modified pleasure principle" (1, p. 120) or a "substitute" for the pleasure principle (2, p. 15). Moreover, Freud sees the foundations of personality fully established by the age of three (3, p. 13). In such a perspective what a man "becomes" is what he "is" and this essentially because of what he "was." Here lies Freud's determinism. Psychoanalysis reduces the variety of human experiences by drawing a chart of universal patterns of behavior, instead of enlarging the list of the causes of neuroses, and allowing, without prejudice, the manifoldness of human dimensions (freedom, conscience, responsibility, values) to unfold in the concrete existential moments of life.

Behavior therapy refuses man the "will to be free" (7, p. 39); denies the specificity of "human nature"; defines distinctive human phenomena (such as consciousness) in terms of "organic needs" which depend upon "the specific character in the environment" (9, p. 64); and minimizes the importance of "values" (pp. 96-120). Such an approach, though efficient in some pathological cases (deficiencies in organic needs and physiological processes), is ineffective in treating a noögenic neurosis of a patient suffering from existential despair, because behavior therapy rejects, on a prescientific speculative ground, the dimension of the spirit.

Frankl accepts the reality of a will to pleasure, a will to power, a will to biological homeostasis, but leaves room for a will to meaning and for further exploration of human behavior. Logotherapy is inclusive, open to new discoveries, and not "conclusive," shut to new insights; the subject matter of its studies, man, is himself an "open system."

The contribution of logotherapy is its persistent endeavor to recover human existence and the recognition that twentieth-century man suffers more than any of his ancestors from the anguish of meaninglessness, boredom-anguish-despair, and the existential vacuum. The man in the street is not so much afflicted by sex inhibitions nor, in affluent societies, by famine, though large parts of the world's population are still undernourished. The real challenge modern man encounters as a threat to his health and existence is Camus' question of whether life is worth living—a question which Frankl has incorporated in his system as a genuine psychophilosophical concern: "Our psychotherapy . . . is specifically designed to handle those suffering over the philosophical problems with which life confronts human beings" (DS, p. 23).

Like William James, Frankl sees freedom as a struggle for meaning as a dynamic motivational force. Behaviorism and S-R (stimulus-response) psychology stress the passive aspects of human conduct—the stimulus governs, directs, and determines the response. Logotherapy, on the contrary, maintains that the crucial determinant in behavior is not the stimulus but the values which the individual has formed for himself and which are decisive in his response. Actually, the best behavioristic formula applicable to logotherapy is the Allportian expression S-O-R. "O" stands for intentions, values, interests, responsibility, conscience, consciousness, love, morality—thus O determines the R (response) of the person. To the logotherapist, meanings are not absolute but relative; they account for the variability of the person's conduct. This is why man has the ability to change attitudes, value schemes, and intentions. This is dramatically illustrated in the story of Dr. J., the mass murderer who during the Nazi regime used euthanasia against the Jews, and completely changed his personality when he was imprisoned in the Lubianka cell, in Siberia (MS, p. 208).

If meaning-behavior is contrasted to the behaviorists' habit-behavior, we will see that meanings are flexible and allow for variability, while a habit is a specific response to a specific stimulus. In opposing situations the habit-behavior is destroyed while the meaning-behavior adapts easily, because equivalent meanings are perceived in different situations. Meanings do motivate the person to act in a repeated, consistent fashion, as for example, a student coming to class every Monday, Wednesday, Friday at eight, or a couple clearing the dishes after supper. To the questions why the student is prompt and the couple clears the dishes, the answers are: one sees the meaning "degree" as desirable, the other sees the meaning "neatness" as important. Their meaning of life and meaning in the equivalent situations sustain them in their long-range goals. This repeated behavior sustained by meanings should not be confused with the rigid habit response of the stimulus-response psychologists. Behaviors motivated by the will to meaning are free behaviors aimed at definite goals.

Logotherapy is rehumanizing psychotherapy because it helps the patient discover the situation where his responsibility, dignity, freedom, and conscience best can attest to the will to life-meaning.

References

1. Freud S. (1962). *An Outline of Psychoanalysis.* New York: Norton.
2. ______(1962). *The Ego and the Id.* New York: Norton.

3. Jones, E. (1957). *The Life and Work of Sigmund Freud.* New York: Basic Books.
4. Minsky, M. (1967). *Computations.* Englewood Cliffs, N.J.: Prentice-Hall.
5. Sayres, K. (1969). *Consciousness: A Philosophic Study of Minds and Machines.* New York: Random House.
6. Scheler, M. (1962). *Man's Place in Nature.* New York: Noonday.
7. Skinner, B. F. (1972). *Beyond Freedom and Dignity.* New York: Bantam Books.
8. Tillich, P. (1963). *The Eternal Now.* New York: Scribner.
9. Tolman, E. (1951). *Behavior and Psychological Man.* Berkeley: University of California Press.
10. Woolridge, D. (1968). *Mechanical Man.* New York: McGraw-Hill.

III

The Techniques of Logotherapy

Logotherapy's view of the human being would have remained restricted to philosophy had it not been developed by a physician. Frankl was determined to make the basic laws he had discovered, or rediscovered, therapeutically productive. Because logotherapy stresses the humanness of the person, it is cautious about applying techniques that would tend to manipulate the patient like a piece of machinery to be repaired. The logotherapist-patient relationship is an encounter between two caring human personalities.

Nevertheless, logotherapy has developed two important techniques—paradoxical intention and dereflection. Paradoxical intention was developed by Frankl in the thirties. Gerz shows how the patient, using his defiant power of the human spirit and the ability to laugh at himself, can use paradoxical intention to overcome some types of neuroses. Kocourek illustrates how the patient, by his ability to reach beyond himself toward meaning, can use another technique, called dereflection, to counter problems created by too much self-reflection. Lukas outlines the steps the logotherapist and logocounselor can take to help patients with noögenic neuroses for which logotherapy is most helpful and with non-noögenic neuroses for which it is supplementary therapy.

These techniques are not applied, only suggested, by the therapist. It is left to the patient to apply them to his specific predicament. They are not technical; they are founded on principles of humanness.

The practical applications of paradoxical intention have been adopted by some modern schools, including behavior therapy. Behaviorists help patients break unwanted patterns, such as phobias, by techniques referred to as "desensitisation," "implosion," and "flooding," which are similar to the previously developed paradoxical intention. Some behavior therapists, as A. Lazarus, Isaac M. Marks, and M. Jacobs, practice paradoxical intention and interpret their successes along the lines of behaviorism. While behaviorists and logotherapists use similar, and even identical, techniques, their underlying philosophies are worlds apart. Behaviorists "recondition" the patient whereas logotherapists enable him to take a stand against his unwanted pattern and assume the responsibility to break it through his own resources.

The techniques of logotherapy, as shown in later sections, are applicable beyond psychology to such fields as internal medicine, dentistry, addiction, juvenile delinquency, and labor-management relations. Properly understood, they can be applied by individuals who feel trapped in a behavior pattern they wish to change.

Paradoxical Intention

Hans O. Gerz

Paradoxical intention[1] is a technique based on logotherapy's concept of freedom, which is seen as freedom not *from* conditions but as the ability to take a stand *toward* conditions, even toward neuroses. This technique uses man's capacity of self-detachment, which enables him to rise above himself and his behavior patterns, and to look at himself from the outside, in an ironic way, making use of his sense of humor.

In clinical cases, paradoxical intention is applied on patients suffering from phobic or obsessive-compulsive neuroses. A phobia is a morbid fear, such as fear of blushing, open spaces, or heights. The obsessive-compulsive neurosis is characterized by disturbing anxiety-provoking thoughts and repetitive impulses to perform unwanted acts such as incessant hand washing or checking and rechecking. A clear differentiation between the phobic and the obsessive-compulsive neurotic is necessary because the behavior patterns to be broken are different. The phobic tries to *avoid* the fearful situation; the obsessive-compulsive runs *head-on* into his symptoms—he fights them and tries to get rid of them. Sometimes, however, that patient

1. For a fuller discussion of paradoxical intention see Frankl's *The Doctor and the Soul,* pp. 178 ff. and Gerz's "Experience with the Logotherapeutic Technique of Paradoxical Intention in the Treatment of Phobic and Obsessive-Compulsive Patients," *American Journal of Psychiatry* 123 (5), 1966.

suffers from a combination of both phobic and obsessive-compulsive symptoms, requiring a modification of treatment.

Why it works

A characteristic phenomenon of the phobic neurotic is anticipatory anxiety—a fear of the symptoms. It is precisely this anxiety that causes the phobic symptoms to become materialized. The more the patient fears his dreaded symptoms and the more he tries to avoid them, the more likely they are to happen. For instance, the patient who has a fear of blushing will actually do so when he is afraid that he might, when he tries hard "not to blush." What would happen, Frankl wrote in 1939, after he had developed paradoxical intention, if the patient instead of trying not to blush, tried to blush, instead of running away from his panic, made an effort to panic? The idea was to "encourage the patient to do, or wish to happen, the very things he fears. . . . Thereby the phobic patient stops fleeing from his fears, and the obsessive-compulsive patient stops fighting his obsessions and compulsions. At the same time, the feedback mechanism called anticipatory anxiety is broken up" (2).

The therapeutic effect of this technique may also be explained in a slightly different way. Our voluntary nervous system controls, by decision and will, the voluntary functions of our body, those muscles that make us act, move, or walk. We have no such control, however, over our involuntary nervous system which controls the functions of our inner organic systems such as respiration, heartbeat, digestive system, uro-genital system, but also our normal human emotions such as love, hate, sorrow, joy, anger, frustration, protective fear, and our pathological emotions such as phobias, obsessions, and compulsions. It is not possible, for instance, to decide on a heartbeat of 50 or 125. We cannot voluntarily command our kidneys to produce an ounce of urine or a gallon. Since emotional responses, both normal and pathological, are subject to the same autonomic nervous system, they too cannot be controlled by decision. By intentionally trying to produce his neurotic symptoms the patient is not only unable to do so but begins to change his attitude toward his neurosis. As he changes his attitude from being afraid of a symptom to producing or (paradoxically) liking it, he will find himself in a comical situation indeed. He will begin to feel humorous about his symptoms and laugh at them, and by so doing he will be able to place distance between himself and his neurotic symptoms. Humor is an indispensable ingredient in paradoxical intention.

One of my patients who had a fear of "getting the spell" spontaneously joked, "I try to get a spell and wind up feeling well." By this humorous attitude she "took the wind out of the sails of her neurosis." The technique can be used in severe cases as well in various small ways. For instance, a woman who frequently called me, complaining that she could not stop crying, was advised to cry as much as possible, "It is good for you and will release pent-up emotions"; and a patient who said, "I cannot breathe any more," was advised to stop breathing. Since in this treatment the patient is taught how to "treat his symptoms," the responsibility for getting (paradoxically) "worse" prevents him from becoming dependent upon his doctor; he becomes responsible and determines his own destiny by deciding on a certain stand toward his unwanted condition.

Paradoxical intention cannot be used with the severely depressed and suicidal patient. If he is told to "kill himself or jump out of a window, he will." Frankl stresses that paradoxical intention "is to be used only when suicide is the content of a true obsession, which is being *resisted* (and being reinforced by this resistance) by the patient. In a situation where the patient is prone to *identify* himself with the suicidal impulse (as may be the case in endogenous depression), paradoxical intention would serve to increase the danger and is, therefore, absolutely contraindicated. This should forcefully remind us that "there can be no differential therapy unless it is based on a thorough and solid differential diagnosis" (DS, p. 212).

In the differential diagnosis and treatment—to discover whether a phobic or obsessive neurosis is psychogenic or somatogenic—it is important to perform thyroid function tests because on rare occasions either neurotic syndrome can be caused by hyper- or hypothyroidism. Electroencephalography is required for diagnostic clarification. It is, however, important to exclude abnormalities in the electroencephalogram because what is called temporal misfirings or dysrhythmias (9, 10) can simulate any mental illness, including depressions, schizophrenic symptoms, and those of various neuroses.

Where such a possibility exists, a brain wave test should be performed before psychotherapy with paradoxical intention is started.

Procedures

The following pages present documented findings that enabled persons treated with paradoxical intention to reenter the main stream of life through work, pleasure, family relationships, and satisfying social and emotional experiences. These beneficial changes have been substantiated over a period of fourteen years of clinical practice.

Therapy, using paradoxical intention, begins with the therapist taking the case history. He then explains to the patient the neurophysiological mechanism that maintains his neurosis, and helps him understand how he is to apply paradoxical intention by discussing with him case histories of patients who have been cured from the same neurotic problem. When I started to use paradoxical intention in 1958, the patient and I discussed cases reported by Frankl (DS, 3, 5), Niebauer (12), Kocourek (11), and later my own. Initial discussion of paradoxical intention takes usually between 1½ to two hours. The patient learns to understand what we are trying to accomplish, and also gains confidence that this therapy is effective. It is helpful to have the new patient meet with one who has been cured by this treatment, either individually or in group therapy. Suggestion undoubtedly plays a part initially—but what physician can treat his patient without trust? The technique of paradoxical intention, however, is not suggestion alone. Quite the contrary: we do not tell the patient, as Coué did, "everything will get better and better," but instruct him to get "worse and worse." Benedikt (1) used tests to show that the success of paradoxical intention cannot be explained by suggestion.

Some Phobic Cases

A father of three children, 35, married, was treated successfully in 1959 and is still doing well. He had developed a fear that he would die from a heart attack, particularly after sexual intercourse. The referring family physician had performed a complete physical check-up including electrocardiogram, and had found the patient in good health. Yet, the patient was anxious, tense, fearful, depressed. He had always been a "worrier," he said, but "had never anything like this." That his sister died of rheumatic heart disease at 24, and his mother died of heart disease at 50 must be regarded as reasons for the development of his fear of a coronary. This latent anticipatory anxiety became activated one night when, after sexual intercourse, he went to the bathroom to wash. As he bent over the bathtub he suddenly felt "a sharp pain like something was pulling in my chest where my heart is." He returned to bed and broke out in a sweat. "I could not sleep. I figured this was the end."

From that time on he developed the phobia that he would die from a heart attack, particularly after intercourse, but also on other occasions "for no reason at all." He also developed a phobia of not being able to go to sleep, "It is a horror to go to bed." The anticipatory anxiety made him more fearful and caused heart palpitations via the autonomic nervous system and produced the need to frequently check his pulse. The patient was completely preoccupied with his fear of sudden death. Reassurances by his family physician that he was physically well provided him with temporary comfort, but he soon became tortured by his phobia again. He came to realize, in the course of the treatment, that on the evening his phobia had begun, he probably strained a muscle in the anterior chest wall as he was bending over the bathtub. This pain triggered off his anticipatory anxiety and brought on the vicious cycle of fear, causing sweating and heart palpitations, causing more anxiety. I told him to "make his heart beat fast and die of a heart attack on the spot." He replied laughingly, "Doc, I'm trying my best but I can't do it." At the end of the session I instructed him to try and have at least five heart attacks a day, and he said, "I feel better already." I saw the patient three times, and he reported four weeks later than he felt well and free of fears. He has had no recurrence.

Sometimes my attempt to get into the underlying psychodynamics is frustrated, as shown by the case of a 28-year-old married woman who for eight years had a severe fear of passing out in supermarkets and department stores. She became totally housebound, and her husband had to buy groceries; she herself ordered clothes and other merchandise through catalogues. When she applied for total disability, the examining psychiatrist refused to declare her disabled and referred her to me. In our first session I explained paradoxical intention to her and discussed other patients whom I had treated successfully with this therapy. During our second session, a few days later, I took her to three supermarkets and one department store, urging, commanding, and pleading with her to pass out "at least once." Each time she said, "I can't do it." Asked how she felt, she replied, "I feel perfectly comfortable." She cancelled the next appointment because, as she said, "a miracle happened, I am cured." Several days later her husband came to my office and angrily shouted, "My wife won't come here any more. Now she is on a continuous shopping spree." This remark indicated that a marital conflict might have brought on the phobia and maintained her symptoms. It is unfortunate that the therapy was interrupted. She may have to seek psychiatric help again if the marital conflict is not resolved.

During the first years, when I used paradoxical intention, I ignored psychodynamic factors. Working in a large mental hospital close to New York City, I saw numerous phobic and obsessive-compulsive neurotic patients who had been treated with psychoanalysis many years, who told me, "I know my psychodynamics exactly but my symptoms persist." Once the neurotic phobic defenses were removed by paradoxical intention, the patients, however, often began to talk spontaneously about "what really has been bothering me for a long time." It was at this point that we began practicing psychodynamically oriented psychotherapy, and in recent years we have more and more combined the logotherapeutic approach with the psychodynamic understanding of the symptom formation.

Frankl and I are aware that paradoxical intention does not cure all neurotic suffering *per se,* but must be regarded as a supplement to the entire psychotherapeutic program of the patient. Viewing phobias as displaced hostile impulses, the patient through paradoxical intention is permitted to act out symbolically the repressed hostile impulses. Oppenheim (13) as early as 1911 started "exercises . . . aiming to accustom" the patient to the phobic situation by the physician accompanying the patient in walking across a field or open places, and even Freud (6, pp. 392–402) stressed the necessity of exposing the phobic patient to the fearful situation, as he stated, "[A patient] can hardly ever master a phobia if he waits until the analysis influences him to give it up. He will never, in that case, bring for the analysis the material indispensable for a convincing solution of a phobia." Friedman (7) regards "psychoanalysis as the treatment of choice." He concludes his psychoanalytical chapter with a poem, which paradoxically praises, without intention, Frankl's paradoxical intention. The poem was composed by a phobic patient walking for the first time unaccompanied to her therapist's office:

Which Epitaph Shall Be Mine?

She couldn't try
For fear she'd die;
She never tried
And so she died.

or

She couldn't try
For fear she'd die;
But once she tried
Her fears—they died.

Obsessive-Compulsive Cases

The treatment of obsessive-compulsive neurotic patients is far more difficult and time consuming than those of phobic patients. Sandor Rado, who has a wealth of experience in treating obsessive-compulsive cases and is regarded as a renowned proponent of psychoanalytical therapy in this country, states, "Once the obsessive patient has reached the stage of chronic and severe tension, our attempts to reach him with psychotherapy are completely nil" (14).

Here is the case history of a 52-year-old man who had suffered from obsessive compulsions since childhood. At the age of ten he was tortured by the thought he would kill God. A priest, who obviously understood obsessions, told him to go ahead and try. Realizing the absurdity he forgot his obsessions. Three years later he became obsessed with the fear, which he was able to overcome by himself, that he would poison someone with farm chemicals. Still later he returned from the war with the obsessive thought that he had caught a venereal disease. It required several doctors to convince him that he was wrong.

He married and started in business, working 12 to 18 hours a day for years. During this time he developed several obsessions which, with the help of his wife, he managed to overcome: that he had cancer, that his wife was unfaithful with a priest, that he might become incestuously involved with his children. Eight years ago, at 44, he imagined he had fallen in love with a younger woman and suffered years of guilt some of which still remains.

Alcohol had not been a major problem until he approached 50. At that time he lost his best friend through a heart attack, and his fears and obsessions became unmanageable. He was almost totally confined to home and office, unable to drive on the highway for fear of killing people. He would turn around dozens of times, digging with his bare hands in briars until they bled, looking in ditches, culverts, and bushes for someone he might have killed. Panic-stricken, he kept looking in boxes, barrels, or anything that could hide a body. He was scared of little girls for fear of harming or raping them. When he read of a murder, he thought he had something do with it, even if it happened miles away.

"I often considered suicide," he recalled. "Words cannot describe the horrible thoughts and obsessions during these two years, and the depressions that have gone along with them. Eventually they even took their toll of my wife of 31 years, and she was under doctor's care.

"However, since Dr. Gerz first saw me in February of 1972, and treated me with paradoxical intention and medication, I am on the road back to good health. Though I have many bad days, I have many more good ones. Now (October 1972), I am able to function almost at a normal level. I can travel by myself, drive my car again, go to church for the first time in 42 years. I can walk alone or go into public rooms and rest rooms without fears and obsessions. I can stay at home or in my office alone, all of which I was unable to do six months ago. Some problems are still troublesome, but with the help of my doctor and paradoxical intention I am able to say 'to hell with most of my tortures and fears,' and I believe that in the near future I will be able to cope with all of my troublesome problems."

When I saw this patient for the first time I felt that, because of his profound depression, he would not have enough ego strength to use paradoxical intention. His depression was treated, with the concomitant application of antidepressant and tranquilizing medications. After about two months he was able to apply paradoxical intention. As he stated, after about nine months he can now function in his private and business life. Even though he still has the remnants of his major symptoms "in the back of my head," he can be expected, with further treatment, to recover almost completely. He probably will for the remainder of his life have, on and off, some obsessive thoughts or compulsive urges; but from my clinical experiences it can be projected that he will be able to disregard them, using paradoxical intention. A therapeutic side effect of our use of his particular antidepressant has been his complete elimination of alcohol because these two agents would clash and cause serious physical complications.

The basic theme to him was, "I don't give a shit about all this crazy stuff, let's rape them and kill them all. Yesterday I raped three little girls, tomorrow I will rape ten, and the day after that I will rape one hundred." It has been my experience when instructing people suffering from these kinds of neuroses, that to curse each time a neurotic symptom troubles them provides an immediate discharge of anger, which in turn makes the symptom formation pointless, and seems to diminish the overwhelming severity of the neurotic symptoms.

General Analysis and Critical Appraisal

Paradoxical intention is not always short-term therapy as reported in some of my cases. Usually the time required depends on the acuteness or length of the illness. In severe, long-standing phobic or obsessive-compulsive neurotic suffering, treatment up to two years sometimes has been necessary. The long range successes or failures of our treatment are difficult to assess because follow-up is sometimes impossible with patients treated in Europe or others in this country who moved frequently. Still, we estimate that 80 to 90 percent of all patients recovered or improved to the point of being able to function (8).

Once the phobic or obsessive-compulsive neurosis has existed for several years, the symptoms have become a vicious cycle and a separate autonomous entity. Such a neurotic reflex pattern, at least in the chronic cases no longer relates to the underlying cause of the symptom formation. Frankl as early as 1947 (4) pointed out that "psychoanalytically oriented psychotherapies are mainly concerned with uncovering the primary conditions of the conditioned reflex in which neurosis may well be understood; namely, the situation—outer and inner—in which a given neurotic symptom had emerged for the first time." He contended, however, that "the full-fledged neurosis is not only caused by the primary conditions but also by secondary conditioning. This reinforcement, in turn, is caused by the feedback mechanism called anticipatory anxiety. Therefore, if we wish to recondition a conditioned reflex, we must unhinge the vicious cycle formed by anticipatory anxiety, and this is the very job done by our paradoxical intention technique."

Concerning the efficacy of non-analytical therapy, Wolpe (15) reports that his first study of 249 patients whose neurotic symptoms improved markedly after psychotherapy other than psychoanalysis showed a relapse of only 1.6 percent. "This contradicts the psychoanalytical expectation of inferior durability of recoveries obtained without psychoanalysis and does away with the chief reason for regarding analysis as a treatment of choice for neurotic suffering."

In recent years I have increasingly modified paradoxical intention and interjected behavior therapy techniques that had been anticipated by paradoxical intention (5a), such as reconditioning and desensitization. The combination of Frankl's and Wolpe's approaches is helpful, but I have also learned that the application of paradoxical intention in some cases should not force the patient too quickly and too drastically into the phobic situation. Because most phobic symptoms are built up in a hierarchy, I advise the patient to attack the smallest fears and least anxiety-producing situations first and do not let him "jump into the most dreaded situation right away," as I practiced in earlier years. In fact, if the patient is forced into his most phobic situation too fast, he may panic even more and the anxiety will become more fixated. Wolpe stated (16) that "there is no question that this type of treatment is effective" but says, in essence, that paradoxical intention is more unpleasant than most other methods. Appreciating his experience in treating these conditions, I have in recent years modified paradoxical intention more to the individual capacity of the patient to employ it constructively. Recently developed behaviorist techniques such as implosion and flooding are even more painful and traumatic to patients than paradoxical intention.

References

1. Benedikt, Fritz (1966). Zur Therapie angst—und zwangsneurotischer Symptome mit Hilfe der 'Paradoxen Intention' und 'Dereflexion' nach V. E. Frankl, published dissertation, University of Munich Medical School.
2. Frankl, V. E. (1939). Zur medikamentösen Unterstützung der Psychotherapie bei Neurosen. *Schweizer Archiv für Neurologie und Psychiatrie* 43: 26–31.
3. ______(1959). Grundriss der Existenzanalyse und Logotherapie. In: *Handbuch der Neuorsenlehre und Psychotherapie* III. Frankl, V. E. von Gebsattel und J. H. Schultz, ed. München-Berlin: Urban & Schwarzenberg.
4. ______(1947, 1961). *Die Psychotherapie in der Praxis. Eine kasuistische Einführung für Aerzte.* Wien: Deuticke.
5. ______(1967). Paradoxical intention: a logotherapeutic technique in active psychotherapy. Harold Greenwald, ed. New York: Atherton Press.

5a. ______(1975). Paradoxical Intention and Dereflection. Psycho*therapy: Theory, Research and Practice* 12: 226–237.

6. Freud, S. (1959). Turning in the ways of psychoanalytic therapy. In *Collected Papers,* vol. 2. New York: Basic Books.
7. Friedman, P. (1959). The phobias. In *American Handbook of Psychiatry* vol. 1, Arieti, S., ed. New York: Basic Books.
8. Gerz, H. O. (1962). The treatment of the phobic and the obsessive-compulsive patient using paradoxical intention. *Journal of Neuropsychiatry* 3: 375–387.
9. ______(1972). Diphenyldantoin against 'painful touching' (dysthesia). *Physicians Drug Manual* 3: 11–12.
10. Jonas, A. D. (1965). *Ictal and subictal neurosis.* Springfield, Ill: Charles C Thomas.

11. Kocourek, K. (1959). Ergebnisse der klinischen Anwendung der Logotherapie. In: *Handbuch der Neurosenlehre und Psychotherapie,* III, Frankl, V. E. von Gebsattel, and J. H. Schultz, ed. München-Berlin: Urban & Schwarzenberg.
12. Niebauer, E. (1959). Ergebnisse der klinischen Anwendung der Logotherapie. In: *Handbuch der Neurosenlehre und Psychotherapie,* III, Frankl, V. E. von Gebsattel, and J. H. Schultz, ed. München-Berlin: Urban & Schwarzenberg.
13. Oppenheim, H. (1911). *Textbook of Nervous Diseases for Physicians and Students.* Edinburgh: Schulze, New York: Stechert.
14. Rado, S. (1959). Obsessive behavior. In: *American Handbook of Psychiatry,* vol. 1: Arieti, S., ed. New York: Basic Books.
15. Wolpe, T. (1961). The prognosis in unpsychoanalyzed recovery from neurosis. *American Journal of Psychiatry* 118: 35–39.
16. ______(1971). *Orientation on Behavior Therapy.* Nutley, N.J.: La Roche Co.

Dereflection

Kurt Kocourek

Dereflection is the therapeutic application of man's will to meaning and his capacity of self-transcendence. By making the will to meaning, rather than the will to pleasure, the central motivation of man, the logotherapist sees man not basically concerned with maintaining or restoring his inner equilibrium by gratifying his drives and instincts (1) but as directed toward something other than himself, reaching out toward other persons to meet and meaning to fulfill. The patient is "dereflected" from his disturbance to the task at hand or the partner involved. "Dereflection is intended to counteract [his] compulsive inclination to self-observation. Through paradoxical intention the patient tries to ridicule his symptoms, while he learns to 'ignore' them through dereflection" (DS, pp. 255–256).

Hyperreflection

A measure of self-observation or self-reflection is normal but under some conditions excessive or "hyper"reflection, and "hyper"intention (WM, pp. 33, 100) can cause disorders in the organism. The most widespread disorder caused by hyperreflection is sexual neurosis—impotence or frigidity. The sexual neurotic, unlike the obsessive-compulsive, does not fight *against* his obsessions and compulsions, but *for* his or her sexual pleasure (WM, p. 104).

Logotherapy maintains that the direct intent to find pleasure prevents the person from finding it. The more a man will think about his potency during intercourse and the woman about her orgasm, the more likely they are to fail.

Sexual failure often is intensified by anticipatory anxiety. The first failure may occur accidentally, through alcohol or drugs, or by the "demand quality" of the situation (2, p. 129). The demand may originate from the partner (a "liberated" woman), a situation (a motel room), or the patient who wants to show his or her sexuality (1, p. 128–30). Whatever the reason for the first failure, the person will approach the second attempt with added anticipatory anxiety. If he or she fails again, the vicious circle of failure-fear-new failure has started.

In such cases dereflection is indicated. However, mere preaching ('forget your potency, think of your partner") will succeed only rarely. It may have the opposite effect. The patient may react like the man who was given an alchemist's recipe to make gold from copper, with the admonition that it would work only if he would not think of a chameleon. He was not able to keep his thoughts off that rare animal although he had never before thought of a chameleon.

Improvisations

The therapist must improvise to reflect the patient's attention away from his or her sexual failure. To a woman who cannot reach a climax, the doctor may prescribe a harmless medicine, telling her that while taking the medicine she will not be able to experience orgasm. With her attention thus dereflected, she is likely to achieve it.

Many improvisations go back to a "trick" developed by Frankl. "We advise the patient to inform his partner that he consulted the doctor about his difficulty and was told his case was not serious, and that the prognosis is favorable. Most important, however, is that he tells his partner that the doctor has absolutely forbidden coitus. His partner now expects no sexual activity and the patient is 'released.' Through his release from the demands of his partner it is possible for his sexuality to be expressed again, undisturbed and unblocked by the feeling that something is demanded . . . of him. Often, in fact, his partner is not only surprised when the potency of the man becomes apparent, but she goes so far as to reject him because of the doctor's order. When the patient has no other goal before him than a purely fragmentary, mutual sexual play of tenderness, then, and only then, in the process of such play is the complete sexual act accomplished and he is faced, as it were, with the *fait accompli*. The vicious circle is broken'' (2). Sahakian and Sahakian (5) see this idea corroborated by Masters and Johnson in their research on human sexual inadequacy.

Sometimes a direct approach is possible—the patient's attention is diverted from sex toward his partner and the love that exists between them. Kaczanowski reports a case of impotence in a newly married bridegroom, ''He was downhearted and ashamed; the wife believed that it was her fault. They loved each other very much and their life together was most satisfactory, except in the sexual sphere. The husband's examination by two urologists had not revealed any organic abnormality. The husband stated that since he had been the lucky one to get the most glamorous girl of his acquaintance as his wife, he wanted to give her the greatest possible sexual pleasure which she deserved and certainly expected. The therapist let the patient ventilate his feelings and ideas about love and marriage. After a few sessions, the patient became aware of his desperate striving for sexual perfection and of his obsessive preoccupation with his failures. Guided by pointed questioning, he began to suspect that his hyperreflection upon the sexual situation and his hyperintention of virility could be the reason for his impotence. He accepted the explanation that the sexual act was an automatic function and could easily be disturbed by higher emotional processes, like worries and anxieties. The therapist helped him see that real love had many aspects worthy of cultivation. The patient learned that if he loved his wife he could give her himself, instead of trying to give her a sexual climax. Then her pleasure would be the consequence of his attitude, not an aim in itself (4). Here too, however, Kaczanowski supplemented the direct approach by Frankl's trick. He banned intercourse for a while. The patient, restricted to giving his wife sexual pleasure in other ways, broke the doctor's order; the wife tried to remind him but, fortunately, he disregarded that, too. Since that time their sexual relationships have been normal.

Similarly, Darrell Burnett, in an unpublished paper presented in 1971 to the Logotherapy Seminar in San Diego, reported a case of a woman "suffering from frigidity, who kept observing what was going on in her body during intercourse, trying to do everything according to the manuals. She was told to switch her attention to her husband. A week later she experienced orgasm."

Not all sexual failures will respond to dereflection, certainly not those based on physical or psychological causes. However, according to Frankl's experience and that of others, 90 percent of sexual neuroses are caused by hyperreflection on sexual activity or hyperintention of sexual pleasure; these are strictly human conditions. Only a human being, as far as we know, reflects on, worries about, and experiences doubt in sexual performance. A diagnosis by a psychiatrist must precede application of dereflection in every instance. But even where sexual failure is based on physical or psychological reasons, dereflection may be useful after the original cause of the neurosis has been removed because the vicious circle of anticipatory anxiety may continue.

Hyperreflection may be caused by a number of reasons, even by a "joke." A patient I treated for anxiety neurosis developed an eye disease and showed me a bottle of medicine his eye doctor had prescribed. He asked me if this medicine might have any side effect. I told him that it contained vitamins E and A, and added that the only possible side effect was that it might make him more potent. The patient left, laughing, but next time came back depressed. Since he had taken the eye medicine, he related, he was impotent. I remembered my "joke," and my questions established the fact that my patient kept observing himself "how and when the tablets will increase my potency." I explained to him how this enforced self-reflection led to his failure and advised him again to pay more attention to his partner than to his own performance. The patient left me with the remark, "Why didn't you warn me not to watch myself when you pulled the gag about sex on me?" A few days later he phoned me, saying, "All's well, doc."

Nonsexual Neuroses

Dereflection is not limited to sexual neurosis. A patient had become afraid her food would go down the wrong pipe, and she would choke. Anticipatory anxiety and compulsive self-observation disturbed her eating to the extent that she became underweight. She was encouraged to trust her organism and its automatically regulated functioning. The patient was therapeutically dereflected by the formula, "I don't need to watch my swallowing because I don't really need to swallow, for actually I don't swallow, but rather *it* does." And thus she was able to leave to the *it,* the unconscious and unintentional act of swallowing (DS, p. 206).

Another case: A nineteen-year-old youth suffered from a speech disturbance since a bolt of lightning had struck near him when he was six. For a week he had been unable to speak. He was given psychoanalytic treatment for five months and took speech and breathing exercises for another four months. The logotherapist applied dereflection by telling the patient that he would have to give up any ambition of becoming a great orator; however, to the degree to which he became resigned to being a poor speaker he would, as a matter of fact, improve his speech. For then he would pay less attention to the "how" and more to the "what" in his speech (DS, p. 207).

Dereflection is a difficult art because it requires the creative improvisation of the therapist. Kaczanowski considers it a logotherapeutic technique that is less specific and more difficult than paradoxical intention.

Although dereflection has been developed as a technique for the logotherapist, its principles have been applied since time immemorial. The best known example is counting sheep by persons who want to fall asleep. The more they reflect on falling asleep the less likely they are to succeed. Counting sheep is as good a method of dereflection as any. The method is used even unconsciously. An example is the woman who cannot become pregnant although she has tried for years, then finally gives up, adopts a baby, and soon afterwards becomes pregnant. It seems as if her body, freed from hyperreflection, is finally able to function.

The method of "natural" childbirth by which the mother foregoes anesthetics, also contains elements of dereflection. Instead of concentrating on her pains, her thinking is directed toward giving birth to a new human being, often in the presence of her husband. Her reaching out to her husband and child enables her to transcend her physical discomfort.

Dereflection is used by people without the help of a doctor or counselor, often even by coincidence. A middle-aged man took up jogging on a track, starting with one mile a day. He concentrated on his task, thinking, "Now I still have three laps to go, now still two, now one." He was out of breath after a quarter mile and had to walk a while before starting to jog again. One day he was worried about his daughter, and during his jogging was preoccupied with thoughts on how he might help her. To his amazement he had finished his mile before he realized it, without ever slowing down to a walk. Since then he keeps thinking of other things, and is now running three miles a day without difficulties.

Dereflection can work even with people who are ignorant about their situation as illustrated by a sexually inexperienced couple who married in their mid-twenties. During intercourse the wife could not experience orgasm except by masturbation because this had been her premarital pattern. The husband told her a misconception he picked up during his bachelor days: that masturbation—alone or mutual—was the only form of orgasm a woman could experience. A week later, to the amazement of both, the wife achieved orgasm in intercourse.

The physician may make use of these latent opportunities for dereflection, as I did with nine-year-old Katharina. For three weeks the child could not fall asleep at night; and medication, such as valium, had made her drowsy in the morning, interfering with her work in school. She was described as obedient, ambitious, a bit pedantic, and a better-than-average student.

It turned out that three weeks back, a family celebration had kept the girl up beyond her bedtime, and the next day she had failed in a memory test. The teacher, learning the circumstances, took the opportunity to lecture to the class about the consequences of going to bed late. My patient took the reprimand to heart and decided to go to bed early. "I do all I can to fall asleep early, but I can't," she complained. Her parents reported that Katharina went to bed at 7:30 P.M. but hardly ever could fall asleep before eleven.

I explained to the girl that the teacher had been right about children not staying up too late but that the main thing was rest, not necessarily sleep. I advised her to lie in bed quietly and think of something pleasant, so the night would not be too long for her. I persuaded her parents to leave the television on in the next room, so she could listen. Ten days later the mother reported that Katharina was falling asleep as she had done before the disturbance. At first she had dropped off while the television was on, usually within fifteen minutes. By now she did not need the TV any more.

Messages from the Unconscious

The effect of dereflection seems to support Frankl's contention that therapy needs to do more than make conscious what has been repressed. "No longer is one allowed today to believe that the goal of psychotherapy consists in making something conscious at any price. Becoming conscious is no more than just a transitory stage of the psychotherapeutic process. It has to make conscious the unconscious—including the spiritual unconscious—only in order to allow it finally to recede back to unconsciousness. . . . It is the task of the therapist, in the final analysis, to reinstate the spontaneity and naiveté of an unreflected existential act" (3).

In this context, he speaks of a violinist patient who made a great effort to perform as consciously as possible, from putting his violin in place on his shoulder to the most trifling technical details. This resulted in a complete artistic breakdown. The treatment of dereflection was aimed at eliminating his hyperreflection and at restoring the patient's trust in his unconscious, by making him realize how much more musical his unconscious was than his conscious. "This treatment oriented toward the patient's self-reliance on his unconscious did bring about the release of the artistic creative powers of his unconscious. Dereflection liberated the creative process from the inhibiting effects of any unnecessary reflection" (3).

The logotherapist helps the patient regain his trust in the wisdom of his noëtic unconscious—of what often is referred to as "the wisdom of the heart" which also is captured by the wisdom of the language (1, p. 732). We speak of "falling" asleep and "falling" in love. Sleep and love cannot be consciously willed, they escape us if we hyperreflect on them or concentrate our intention on them. Only by using the resources of the noëtic unconscious, primarily the will to meaning, can we transcend ourselves and reach the objects of our intention, which escape direct assault. Dereflection is a method to achieve this goal.

References

1. Frankl, V. E. (1959). Grundriss der Existenzanalyse und Logotherapie. In: *Handbuch der Neurosenlehre und Psychotherapie,* München: Urban & Schwarzenberg.
2. ______(1952). The pleasure principle and sexual neurosis. *International Journal of Sexology* 5.
3. ______(1975). *The Unconscious God: Psychotherapy and Theology.* New York: Simon and Schuster.
4. Kaczanowski, Godfryd (1967). Logotherapy—a new psychotherapeutic tool. *Psychosomatics* 8.
5. Sahakian, W. S., and B. J. Sahakian (1972). Logotherapy as a personality theory. *Israel Annals of Psychiatry and Related Disciplines* 10.

The Four Steps of Logotherapy

Elisabeth Lukas

My research (1, pp. 233 ff.) has confirmed findings in Europe, North and South America, and Japan that about 20 percent of today's neuroses are noögenic. Symptoms include depressions, fears, obsessions, and any number of psychosomatic illnesses. For really noögenic neuroses logotherapy is specifically indicated, while in non-noögenic cases of neuroses other psychotherapeutic techniques—along with logotherapy—may be applicable.

In logotherapy, the patient's uniquely human resources—or, as one might say, his "spiritual" resources—are tapped: his will to meaning, his goal orientation, his ideas and ideals, the awareness of what kind of person he is and what kind of person he has the vision of becoming, his awareness of conscience, his sense of responsibility, and his sense of humor.

The self-image patients gain in therapy affects their understanding of themselves and produces a continuing feedback. If they see themselves as "nothing but" machines that can be manipulated, their attention is focused on their biology. If they see themselves as "nothing but" animals that can be trained, their attention is focused on their psychological needs. Logotherapy insists that, although man has features like a computer and an animal, he is much more. He must be considered in his totality, including his noëtic dimension where he is concerned with meanings, values, goals, and tasks, leading him to accept an inner-directed responsibleness. Logotherapy is always education, but it must remain a self-generated education; that is, the patient learns to educate himself according to his own values. The value system of the therapist does not enter. Much of logotherapy is discussion but its subject is limited to arguments which help the patient in his search for meaning within his own frame of reference. The discussion never includes arguments which support the world view of the therapist.

In my practice, logotherapy proceeds in four major steps: (1) gaining distance from the symptoms; (2) modification of attitudes; (3) reduction of symptoms; and (4) orientation toward meaning.

Distance from Symptoms

From Frankl's writings we may distill certain guiding principles for the logotherapeutic treatment of neuroses—in addition to the two techniques discussed in the two previous essays, namely paradoxical intention and dereflection.

The first task of the logotherapist is to help his patients realize that they are not identical with their symptoms. The resources of the spirit are tapped, its defiant power is awakened so the patient sees that fears, obsessions, depressions, feelings of inferiority, and emotional outbursts are not an integral part of what he *is* but qualities he *has* and which he can modify, and possibly overcome. He learns that he is not the helpless victim of his biological shortcomings, his psychological drives, and his environmental influences, that he is not fated to remain the way he has been, and that there is no situation in which he cannot change unwanted patterns, either in fact or, where this is not possible, in the attitude he takes toward an unchangeable circumstance like the death of a friend or the loss of a limb.

The logotherapist helps his patients overcome their feeling of helpless dependence on circumstances "beyond their control" which they sometimes use only to explain their symptoms and their personalities to themselves, and which, in turn, result in a negative feedback that further reinforces their symptoms.

The logotherapist makes his patients conscious of what they unconsciously know: that they are, first and foremost, human beings with the capacity to find meanings; only secondarily are they individuals who have certain shortcomings which can be overcome and unwanted patterns which can be broken.

To break unwanted patterns, the patients have to be led to see themselves from outside, as observers, and not from inside their traps, as victims. How the therapist manages to bring distance between a patient and his symptoms is not decisive. It may require some techniques and much improvisation and patience. Mere persuasion, however, will not work. The more the therapist tries to persuade his patients that they are not really sick, that their symptoms are mere illusions, the more he will fortify their inner resistance against moving away from their symptoms. In my practice I rely on four methods developed by Frankl: paradoxical intention, dereflection, the Socratic dialogue, and what he once called "the appealing technique." These four approaches help patients to separate themselves from their symptoms. Paradoxical intention teaches them to laugh at their symptoms; dereflection helps them to stop concentrating on their symptoms; the Socratic dialogue elicits in the patients new insights into their symptoms and thus helps them become less dependent on these symptoms; and the appealing technique strengthens the will of the patients so they can use the defiant power of their spirit.

Modification of Attitudes

The second step in logotherapy is to help patients gain new perspectives of themselves and their life situation, and thus modify their attitudes. The therapist does not "give" perspectives but merely serves as midwife to bring out what already exists in the patient. The "birth," however, may require labor pains. The therapist educates his patients in the literal sense of the Latin word *e-ducere*—he draws out what is in the patient. The only considerations of the therapist are the patient's well-being and his truthfulness to himself.

The principal method to draw from patients their unconscious perspectives of themselves is the Socratic dialogue, in which the therapist challenges the patient with questions that touch on his spiritual resources, in order to clarify personal goals and commitments. At the same time, therapist and patient go on a common search to discover how the patient feels about himself and wants to feel about himself. That's why this method also may be called the "self-discovery discourse." The main aim of this quest is to find a perspective that can serve the patient in facing his particular life situation, strengthen him in his fight for existence, and help him overcome his sense of dependency.

Again: the uniqueness of the individual is respected. It is important that the new attitudes originate in the patient and grow out of his personality; they must not be tinged by the views of the therapist, but they must be meaning-oriented and psychohygienically positive. Exceptions to this rule are cases where immediate help is required, such as in urgent cases of the "tragic triad"—unavoidable suffering, guilt, and death. In such cases it may happen that the therapist does not have the time to explore and improvise. He may have to use shortcuts to pull the patient away from his close involvement with the tragic situation: the therapist has to apply "first aid" to keep the patient from harming himself. In such cases the therapist is justified in advancing his own arguments in order to avoid consequences of tragic dimensions. But even here the therapist stays within the world view of the patient and formulates his arguments within the value system of the patient. He never becomes a "missionary": he has to help believers within the framework of their beliefs, but he also has to let unbelievers find comfort within their particular nonreligious values.

Reducing the Symptoms

After a successful modification of the patient's attitudes, the third step in the logotherapeutic treatment usually takes care of itself: the symptom disappears or at least becomes manageable. In cases of the tragic triad, where the depression cannot be made to disappear, the new attitude helps the patient come to grips with his unalterable fate so he is able to bear it. The logotherapist cannot restore an amputated leg, but he can help the patient live with one leg without succumbing to apathy or despair, and without revolting against his fate in frustration.

The situation is similar in cases of severe psychopathic symptoms such as schizophrenia, endogenous depressions, paranoic abnormalities which cannot be cured at the present state of our medical knowledge. In such cases, too, a changed attitude may contribute substantially toward helping the patient make the most of his life situation. In his writings, Frankl illustrates with numerous cases how this is implemented in actual practice.

Orientation toward Meaning

After the symptom has been reduced, the prophylaxis can start: steps are taken to secure the patient's mental health for the future. The patient is guided toward meaning; all meaning potentials of his life and his particular situation are thoroughly discussed, enriched, and extended. The therapy aims at helping the patient clarify his values so that he remains protected from future existential frustrations. At the same time, the therapy aims at educating the patient to become capable of assuming responsibility for his life. The patient who feels responsible for his life is mentally healthy.

If the third step, the reduction of symptoms, has been successful, the patient experiences such a positive feedback from his new attitude that he tends to be open to a wider and richer meaning orientation. The therapist gradually becomes superfluous while the patient consciously takes control over his life now enriched in meaning potentials making him feel capable of steering in the directions he chooses.

Socratic Dialogue

In light cases of noögenic neuroses a simple modification of attitudes is often sufficient. The most useful contact between patient and therapist is the self-discovery discourse or Socratic dialogue. The therapist poses his questions in a way by which the patient discovers by himself a new attitude that he finds to be fitting to his situation. First, the therapist quietly listens while the patient is allowed to unburden himself and to present his problems. At the point, however, where the patient begins to expound his theories about his victimization by forces beyond his control, the logotherapist begins to take an active part in the discourse. Here is a significant departure from the client-centered therapy in which such interruption does not occur. The logotherapist does not accept theories in which the patient claims to be a pawn at the mercy of fate, though the facts may seem to warrant the complaint. Instead, the logotherapist insists that choice is always available to the patient, even if it may be only a choice of attitudes. If the circumstances cannot be changed, the attitude toward them can. Although the therapist is hardly authoritarian, he does hold a certain authority. To conduct a true self-discovery discourse, the logotherapist must be able to say "No," or "Stop, that far and no farther!" To accomplish the therapy, the patient is steered away from insisting that he is unable to change. This is an application of Frankl's distinction between the neurotic and the authentic mode of existence. The neurotic person, Frankl says, interprets his existence in terms of "that's the way I am, I cannot help it." Actually, however, existence should be understood as a choice of what one will be in the next moment; thus a person always is able to change for the better. It is in this spirit that Frankl often asks his patients, "Do you really have to take every nonsense from yourself?"

Here the logotherapist merely, but emphatically, assures the patient that patterns can be broken and that life has meaning even when it seems hopeless. The responsibility of breaking patterns and finding specific meanings is the client's. The task of the logotherapist is to educate the patients to take charge of their own lives. To accomplish this, the logotherapist has to pull his patients out of their existential vacuum and anchor them in a life that is rich with self-discovered meanings. In the course of this treatment, the therapist firmly says the "no" when the patient falls into the role of victim hindered in his noëtic development by fate.

The therapist will be successful only if he genuinely cares about his patients, without coddling them. The Socratic dialogue tends to be a struggle—first a struggle between therapist and patient, but eventually a common struggle in the search for meaning. Once the patient has found his focus and his direction, the therapist steps back, for he no longer has anything to add. To make this common struggle successful, the patient must give his trust. The therapist, however, must give his all: not only must he be a good psychologist and a good psychotherapist, he also must be and remain a human being. And he must regard those who come to him not only as patients and clients but also—in every moment of their consultation and treatment—as human beings. In fact, Frankl denies that the trend is directed toward an increasing "psychologization" of medicine; he believes that the trend is toward a progressive "humanization of psychotherapy," and that in the course of this process, the therapist rather than seeing in the patient a set of mechanisms will see, behind the disease, the suffering human being.

The Appealing Technique

Appealing to the patient may take the form of suggestion. Suggestion is not a preferred treatment in logotherapy but is appropriate where other methods have failed or cannot be used. I use it when the patient is too primitive, too young, too old, or too sick to achieve distance between himself and his symptoms by the Socratic dialogue alone. Only in those cases do I consider it permissible to suggest new attitudes to the patients rather than letting them find new perspectives by themselves.

Any appeal must be kept within the value system of the patient and never must go against it. Frankl, commenting on a case, explained, "The therapist simply verbalized what the patient already subconsciously knew. Is it not, ultimately, the task of psychotherapy to make unconscious knowledge available, so that the patient can manage it, and therefore become more aware of it?" (2, p. 33).

I am making use of suggestion on tapes, based on the methods developed in autogenic training. It is not necessary for the patient to be especially suggestible, but he must have a minimum of willingness to cooperate. Suggestion will be most effective with patients who are immature, shy, blocked, emotionally unstable, weak-willed, generally nervous, or regressive-infantile.

In contrast to paradoxical intention and dereflection, suggestion usually has no lasting effect and must be repeated from time to time. Because suggestions can be made on tape, they are easily repeated but must remain under the supervision of the therapist; wrongly applied, they can cause undesirable side effects.

Effective suggestions are made by a voice of the same sex using the I-form, or by a voice of the opposite sex using the you-form. If the patient is ego-centered and self-assured, he will want to educate himself rather than let someone else teach him, and thus the I-form is more appropriate. He will regard the suggestion as the voice of his own thoughts. If the patient is unsure and unstable and prefers to be led by someone else, it will be more effective to select the you-form.

Suggestions are used while the patient is lying down, and it is often advisable to precede them with relaxation exercises. Where the patient shows a definite desire to talk or abreact, it may be useful to include, before the relaxation exercises, a short period of free association. In any case, all tapes begin with a suggestion of a quieting down and end with a "waking up." The waking up must not be too weak because it is irresponsible to have the patient go home after a weak awakening. The therapist, when making the tape, must not deceive himself and underestimate the suggestion as too weak because the talking for the tape keeps him fully awake. I always test the tape on myself to see if the intervals between the formulations are long enough, and if the awakening phase is strong enough.

The formulations of the suggestions differ strongly from those used in paradoxical intention. Formulations in paradoxical intention are always vastly exaggerated because exaggeration is part of the therapeutic effect; they cause the patient to laugh at himself and thus help establish a distance between himself and his fears. Formulations for suggestion never are exaggerated, but must sound genuine, simple, and impressive. Their purpose is not to make the patient laugh but to make him identify himself with his own thoughts.

The contents of the suggestions, within the principles of logotherapy, are mostly aimed at training the will, to defy a given situation, to achieve new attitudes, or to guide the patient's thoughts toward new directions. It remains within the responsibility of the therapist to select the appropriate suggestion.

As far as the frequency of the suggestions is concerned, I have found it useful to have the patient listen to the same tape daily for at least four weeks. The subsequent tapes can be changed but should not differ too widely from each other. After half a year it may be useful to repeat the suggestive training.

For the purpose of logotherapy a slight suggestion is usually sufficient. But sometimes even hypnosis may well be indicated. In commenting on such a case, Frankl (2, p. 152) has pointed out that it is not justified *a priori* to reject hypnosis. As he sees it, hypnosis may rather serve as a vehicle eventually to restore a patient's existential freedom, and thereby to combat his noögenic neurosis.

References

1. Frankl, V. E. (1972). *Der Wille zum Sinn.* Bern-Stuttgart-Wien: Hans Huber.
2. ______(1959). *Critical Incidents in Psychotherapy.* Ed. Standal and Corsini. Englewood Cliffs, N.J.: Prentice-Hall.

IV

Medical Uses

The applications of logotherapy in the medical field come in "concentric circles." The inner circle covers noögenic neuroses. These neuroses, originating in man's spiritual dimension, require logotherapy as their specific therapy. Their treatment is discussed by Hogan.

The next circle takes in somatogenic and psychogenic neuroses. Originating in man's body or psyche, they may require medication or psychotherapy of various kinds to unblock the patient's access to the resources of his noös. Often the patient's spirit has been affected, in terms of low self-esteem, loss of meaning, or confusion about goals. In such cases, logotherapy can be applied as supplementary therapy, or—particularly in such cases as are described in the previous section—even as primary therapy using paradoxical intention and dereflection.

A still wider circle in which logotherapy is medically useful includes illnesses that challenge the spiritual core of the patient to take a stand to his sickness. Takashima, Jepsen, and Travelbee discuss the use of logotherapy by the internist, the dentist, and the nurse.

The literature is beginning to list still other specialists who find logotherapy useful in their fields. An example is the article, "Practical Aspects of Logotherapy in Neurosurgery," in *Existential*

Psychiatry, Volume VII (1969), by William Hyman, assistant professor of neurological surgery at the University of California, Irvine. Hyman stresses the use of logotherapy for metastatic cancer and for paraplegic patients. "Logotherapy might be employed after surgery, even if it was not effective before surgery in these drastic cases." Hyman warns against the neurosurgeon who would operate and "get on to the next problem. It would be far better if [the doctor] could impart some meaning to that patient or at least plant the seed of meaning that others could develop with the patient. Suffering has many facets: it can be given dignity; it can help set an example for others; it can be transformed into many opportunities."

There is, perhaps, a fourth circle where logotherapy can be applied in the form of therapeutic counseling. But counseling lies at the periphery of the medical field and uses logotherapy in many forms; it is therefore discussed separately in Section IV.

Treatment of Noögenic Neuroses

Timothy V. Hogan

Although Frankl's writings thoroughly explore the nature of man and his behavior, they leave to the therapist much freedom to help the patient overcome his noögenic neuroses.

Frankl defines noögenic neuroses as those that "originate in spiritual problems, in moral conflicts, or in . . . [the] conflict between a true conscience and the mere superego . . . [or] which result from the frustration of the will to meaning . . . existential frustration, or from the existential vacuum" (WM, p. 27).

This essay discusses the logotherapist's approach to noögenic neuroses. It accepts the assumption that, to feel fulfillment, man must search for meaning; and it investigates the methods by which a patient may learn how to go about this search and gain a sense of meaningfulness.

To begin with, we need to consider what it means to search for meaning. Frankl makes it every person's responsibility to glean from his understanding of life a personal set of values which in some way adequately represents what may be established as an objective set of values. He makes it a person's responsibility to understand what life is about, to grasp the meaning of death, suffering, work, play, love—the broad range of human emotion and experience. Searching for meaning, then, is to understand the world inside and the world outside oneself, and to establish one's personal significance within both.

Seen in this sense, a search for meaning is not only recommendable but inevitable. Even a person denying meaning will be confronted by it at some point during his lifetime. If his will to meaning is frustrated, a noögenic neurosis may develop. The therapist has the task to diagnose it, motivate the patient to make the efforts needed to overcome it and teach him how to conduct his search for meaning.

Diagnosis

The first task of the therapist is to diagnose the noögenic neurosis, as distinguished from the traditional types.

My experience has confirmed the existence of noögenic neuroses. They may be suspected if nothing in the patient's development would indicate any psychological causes for the neurosis. His parents were in no way depriving, overindulging, overprotecting, or rejecting. He has a healthy interaction within his family, with his peers, and in intimate relationships. But at some point in his life (frequently between the ages of eighteen and twenty-five, or in his late thirties or early forties, or as he approaches retirement and, later, death) he is called upon to consider fundamental questions regarding life, death, love, work, or suffering. He feels that he has to come to grips with his own personal experience and to terms with himself. At this "moment" (which may last a few minutes, days, months, or even years) he feels confused, bereft of love and kindness, alone, despondent, alienated, empty, without a sense of purpose and significance. He feels that life has no meaning. Nothing within him or his circumstances would justify these thoughts and feelings—no significant failure, death in the family, or other unhappy event. In many respects he behaves like a depressed person. However, in the absence of any precipitating event one cannot appropriately label the condition as reactive depression. The only "problem" seems to be that he is thinking a great deal. He is looking at his reality and is seeing the caricature of the sad, the unpleasant, the tragic components of life. He is conscious of the dimensions of his existence with all its limitations. There is nothing immature about such a profile, nothing hysterical, nothing typically neurotic. The person is attempting to understand himself and his reality better. He is in the process of spiritual growth, as a result of personal distress and suffering. Because he behaves so much like other neurotics, particularly those suffering from neurotic depression, his condition is frequently misdiagnosed. The determining factors distinguishing the noögenic from a psychogenic or somatogenic neurosis are found in the developmental history of the person. Occasionally a patient suffering from some other maladaptive behavioral syndrome, such as anxiety neurosis, hysteria, neurotic depression, may also suffer from noögenic neurosis. That is to say, he has a "conventional" neurosis based on his inability to cope with stress or poor biological predisposition to manage his life situation. However, once the neurotic condition itself is alleviated, the patient may still be left with symptoms of a noögenic neurosis; he may still feel alienated from his environment and may still be wondering whether there is any purpose in life. Many therapists will work with the conventional neurosis successfully but will find the patient still unresponsive and in distress when they feel the situation ought to have improved. The patient may be left in the throes of the noögenic neurosis and may need the additional intervention of a logotherapist.

Motivation

Once the noögenic neurosis has been diagnosed, the therapist may have to motivate his patient to make the efforts needed to overcome his neurosis. The patient is aware of his distress, suffering, and psychological confusion, but does not understand why he feels that way, nor what he ought to do about the problem. It is the responsibility of the therapist to make him aware why it is necessary to begin a careful evaluation of himself within his environment and to show him how the recommended procedures will help him.

In the early stages of the therapy, the client may feel skeptical about the feasibility of the treatment and wonder whether he should invest so much energy. The therapist must point out the necessity of the search but also the difficulties and problems which may ensue. The therapist must also show that he cares and is willing to help the patient overcome the difficulties although the ultimately responsibility of the search rests with the patient.

The Process of the Search

Once the patient has decided to embark on the search, the first task of the therapist is to listen to the patient and elicit from him meaning potentials which he is then encouraged to pursue. The patient may need to learn how to go about examining himself, his consciousness, his conscience, his behavior patterns and situations which in the past he found meaningful. He will need to learn to focus on his activities, his experiences—including his relationships with other people, and his attitudes in the face of unavoidable suffering. The patient is encouraged to list his assets and liabilities, and is taught the processes of self-examination, problem-solving, and decision-making.

Methods

The therapist will have to avoid the temptation to do all the examining, analyzing, and clarifying for the patient. It is usually more appropriate for the patient to do his own examining and to find his own explanations. The search for one's self and for the meaning of life often starts as a groping in the dark. If the therapist merely demonstrates how good he is at analyzing the patient's life situation, at clarifying his problems, and explaining his behavior, while the patient learns nothing other than to stand in awe of the therapist, then the therapeutic procedure leaves much to be desired. Neither is it advisable for the therapist to simply sit quietly watching the patient fall all over himself, making unfortunate mistakes, without any attempt to give assistance.

The therapist must judge each case on its own merit and help his patient in specific ways. He may begin an interpretation and then halt or stall, giving his patient the opportunity to carry on with the clarification process on his own; the therapist may hint at the best possible interpretation of the situation, or even come right out and tell how he sees it. A useful therapeutic device is comparing and contrasting. For instance, a patient who feels inadequate may be asked if he is as bad as someone who is obviously worse. The technique of silence is effective for patients who tend to become dependent, but silence must be purposeful. Silence may be useful when the patient asks the therapist to solve a problem for him, to provide an answer to a question. Also, the therapist should be ready to provide a positive reinforcement when a patient who lacks self-confidence comes up with a good insight into himself or of what is happening around him. The patient's attention should be drawn to the importance of tiny but significant happenings. For instance, if he spends fifteen minutes a day thinking about himself and his circumstances, and if he continues to do this for an extended period, he is accomplishing two things: he is persisting in a difficult undertaking, even if he cannot clearly see the payoff; and he is working toward an insight or toward a new appreciation of himself and his environment. It is the further responsibility of the therapist, at crucial times, to cast light on the therapeutic process: when a patient, who has been unable to see a particular situation or has been denying a feeling about himself, becomes unblocked or confronts the truth, the therapist may point out to him these facts and the achievement this represents.

Aims and Objectives

In his search for meaning a person faces two classes of goals: ultimate and specific. Ultimate goals, such as the decision to become a conscientious person or a mature Christian are motivational because they encourage the individual to carry on even when the goals become difficult. It is important to make it clear to the patient that ultimate goals are elusive and virtually unattainable. He may find that the harder he tries to become a mature Christian, the more immature he may feel and the less Christian he may find himself to be. Ultimate goals provide a focus, help a person to see the significance of his endeavor.

More important are the specific goals, which are immediate, intermediate, and long-range. A man's long-range goal may be to have a more harmonious relationship with his wife. To achieve this he may find it necessary to take some steps toward intermediate goals such as setting aside a time to talk to her or joining her in some activity. However, he may realize that he has to understand the nature of his marital situation, and especially his inadequacies vis-à-vis his wife with which he can deal on a short-range basis. He may become aware that he does not answer his wife's questions, never helps her with chores around the house, and does not respond readily to her sexual desires. His behavior pattern shows a lack of consideration for his wife. It will be useful to him to observe how often these behaviors occur, under what circumstances, what either positively or negatively reinforces them, so he can bring them under control. He will find it difficult to improve his behavior patterns systematically if he has not established some intermediate or long-range objectives.

Understanding Reality

Because a person's psychological and spiritual dimensions are related to his physical condition, the therapist may find it necessary to help the patient correct his physical shortcomings. Therapy may have to start with an appropriate program of physical health, including exercise.

Next, the patient may have to be encouraged to carefully evaluate himself and his environment, possibly at a certain time of the day. His thinking should include his problems, their clarifications, their possible solutions, and the decision-making process leading to the solution he has chosen.

But the search for meaning has to go beyond the intellectual. The patient has to learn to understand his feelings about himself and his environment. Many people learn only a few emotional responses—a certain stimulus always triggers the same emotional response: if someone becomes angry at them, they become angry in return. The patient has to be conscious of the range of his emotions. As he becomes more aware of his own feelings and those of others, he will find that his own emotional life is more discriminating.

As the patient becomes more aware of his thinking and feeling, he also becomes conscious of the reality of the spiritual, transcending qualities of life—of goodness and evil, beauty and ugliness, the importance of truth and the destructive power of dishonesty. These considerations will give him new perspectives and a sense of tranquility.

There is, however, a danger in reaching out for transcendence. A person, in his search for meaning, may become so transcending that he loses his grip on reality. Searching for meaning in no way implies this; on the contrary, it helps people cope with day-to-day circumstances—including suffering, guilt, and fear of death—as part of everybody's reality. Whether the individual is thinking more deeply, feeling more profoundly, or becoming more transcending, is appropriately measured by how well he is coming to terms with his day-by-day functioning. If he is becoming more productive, more insightful, more conscientious and responsible on a day-by-day basis he is experiencing more genuine meaning.

Evaluation Procedures

Most therapists will agree to supervision and collaborative arrangements, but few wish to have their therapeutic activities evaluated systematically. They continue some activities indefinitely, without reference to specific goals and their attainment. As a result, these activities may be lacking in effectiveness. Therapists, including logotherapists—perhaps because of their abiding interest in the human condition, perhaps because they are groping in the dark as they work with the patient and develop therapeutic procedures—tend to reject attempts to systematize their working procedure. It is as if they were saying that good therapy and critical evaluation are contradictory.

If procedures are not evaluated, however, both the therapist and the patient may become doubtful whether the procedures are effective. Periodic evaluations may show that established goals ought to be re-established and made more tenable for the patient; that applied procedures lack in effectiveness; or that the patient or therapist has more assets or liabilities than was previously determined. A regular evaluation procedure, built into the therapeutic process, is in the best interest of both patient and therapist because it will allow for a more effective relationship, in which some positive reinforcement may be possible.

Special Problems

Because the patient feels insecure and has met someone who appears strong and supportive, he may become dependent on the therapist. Such dependency could be in order for only a short period. The aim of the therapy is to make the patient autonomous in his searching and as responsible as possible.

When a therapist is strong, supportive, and understanding, and the patient feels in need of depending on the strength of another person, the danger exists that the patient will "fall in love with the therapist" (transference) and that the therapist will feel so flattered that he finds himself responding in kind and falling in love with the patient (countertransference). Such feelings are not immoral, improper, or uncalled for. In fact, they may indicate that therapy is taking place as it should. If therapist and patient can openly discuss the nature of their relationship, it will likely improve even further, so that both may profit from it. However, if the nature of the relationship cannot be scrutinized honestly, it can no longer be called therapy.

Another problem concerns the patient's relationships with friends and relatives. Before his therapy, these people knew what he was likely to do in some circumstances. Because of basic changes in his personality makeup and behavior patterns, however, the patient in logotherapy may become an enigma to his friends and relatives. For instance, a patient who has been docile and dependent within his family may begin to look at himself and his responsibilities, assets, and liabilities, and decide to encounter the members of his family more aggressively. This may be a surprise to them; they may even see it as undesirable.

There are a few fast rules that a therapist treating noögenic neuroses can follow. He must establish a relationship of caring with the patient. He must serve as an example of a person aware of his obligation to respond to the meanings of the moment so the patient can search for his. The therapist must be willing to improvise, to refrain from manipulating the patient, and to give him the greatest possible chance to assume responsibleness for his cure—that is, to find meanings according to his own values.

Living with Disease

Hiroshi Takashima

Logotherapy's emphasis on attitude has direct applications to a person's reaction to his state of health. When he is attacked by a disease, it is natural for him to instinctively struggle to get rid of it. This "fighting with disease" is a brave, but often a pathetic attitude. A person engaged in a grim fight against disease, where recovery is a reasonable hope, is like a distance runner doggedly keeping to his course, sustaining pain with tight lips and twisted face. Just as the winning post awaits the runner, so final recovery awaits the patient. Many diseases of the young fall in this class. The determination to fight the disease is important, especially when the condition of the patient is serious. It is medically established that such will power helps the success of the treatment.

However, the matter is different with the chronic diseases of the middle-aged and the elderly. Arteriosclerosis, diabetes, and chronic rheumatism are still basically incurable. In these cases a struggle with the disease will either turn the patient's life into a gloomy sequence of battles or exhaust him, aggravating the disease.

A seventy-three-year-old patient began to feel pain in both knees when he was sixty. It was diagnosed as a mild form of chronic rheumatism, for which he received medical treatment. In the following two years he tried various remedies, including such folk medicine treatments as acupuncture and moxa burning, but his condition did not improve. Eight years ago he came to see me, complaining, "My legs are incorrigibly stiff." I advised him, "Then spare your legs. Ride in cars. Use elevators and don't climb stairs. Today's medicine cannot cure your trouble; it can only ease your pain. Leave it alone. After all, you are an aged man. No wonder you have some pain in your legs."

He saw the point of my advice, Now he speaks almost cheerfully about his rheumatism and doesn't worry, even though I advise him paradoxically "to make a great effort to worry." He boasts, "My rheumatism is so sensitive to dampness in the air that it forecasts rain more accurately than the weather station." He has admirably mastered his condition. He says, "It would be wrong to think of curing it. Instead, I treat these little knees as friends. I have been a burden on them for seventy years. Now I have to be kind to them."

I have called this attitude "sho-byo" in contrast to "to-byo"—"living with disease" as contrasted with "fighting with disease." The meaning of the latter is obvious, but the former needs some explanation.

"Sho-byo" is a combination of two ideograms meaning "conformity" and "disease," but this conformity does not imply passivity or a merely nonaggressive attitude toward disease; it does not mean "nursing the disease." "Sho-byo" is a positive attitude of adjusting oneself to the disease. This paradox reflects the mode of thinking of Zen, but also the principles of logotherapy. The attitude accepts a disease as incurable, and puts it under control without making futile efforts to get rid of it.

Hypertension

A person approaching middle age often begins to worry about high blood pressure. If he goes to a physican and is actually diagnosed to have hypertension, he may lose confidence in his health and develop anxiety, which in turn further intensifies his hypertension.

What may happen to such a person is illustrated by a patient who several years ago was diagnosed as having a light case of hypertension. He became so worried about it that he gave up his work, which had been a source of great satisfaction to him, and started going regularly to the hospital for treatment. He nervously followed the rise and fall of his blood pressure readings, and made pressure-reducing drugs and tranquilizers his sole consolation in life. At the age of sixty-three he had a sudden stroke and died.

In contrast, here is an illustration of how "living with disease" can be learned as an attitude that opens up the patient to the possibility of leading a meaningful life.

A forty-three-year-old professor of German literature was told years ago that he had a condition of hypertension and was placed under medical care. Eight years ago he came to me, depressed about the prospect of having to spend the rest of his life in a dismal struggle with the condition, against which he had to take medicine more regularly than meals. My examination showed his blood pressure at 150 to 80mm. This, he told me, was lower than before because of his daily medicine and reducing diet. His condition was otherwise normal.

Hypertension, being a disease that can be controlled but not completely cured, is not an opponent one can defeat by struggling against it. The professor did not suffer so much from his hypertension as from his anxiety about it, and from his exhaustion as a result of fighting it. I explained this situation every time I saw him and advised him to come to terms with his disease and live with it rather than put up a fight. At the same time, I told him to discontinue taking medicine, provided he would further reduce his weight and take sufficient rest when tired.

Ever since I saw him eight years ago, his blood pressure has been close to normal and he is in good shape, both physically and mentally. He no longer is a sick man, but a man of health with only the handicap called hypertension.

In some cases it is necessary to use medication to lower the blood pressure, or to prevent a worsening of the physical condition but, in addition, the patient has to learn to live with his disease, to keep a nonaggression pact with it.

In November 1968, at the Conference of the Gerontological Sciences of Japan, I read a paper, "What We Should Learn from the Examination Data of Thirty-three Persons Healthy at the Age around 100." One point I emphasized concerned the problem of hypertension, twenty-two of the thirty-three Methuselahs were high-blood-pressure types (higher than 160 to 100mm), and nine of them had had high

high blood pressure since their middle age. Although nothing decisive could be deduced from so small a sample, the data at least suggested that persons whose blood pressure was high in their middle age, still have a fairly good chance of living to an old age with a condition they have accepted.

Whether hypertension is a genuine disease is a controversial matter. But since it is a statistical fact that after entering middle age life expectancy shortens in proportion to blood pressure and obesity, physicians regard hypertensive patients as subjects for medical treatment and guidance. It is not advisable, however, for doctors to identify high blood pressure as a sign of danger to life; in some cases, such a diagnosis may even create the danger.

The Taming of a Disease

If a person were placed in a cage with a small poisonous snake, it would be natural for him to fight and kill the creature. The same attitude is expected to fight a disease that offers the prospect of complete recovery. Suppose, however, there were an ox in the cage instead of a snake. An ox is a gentle animal, but it is big and trying to overpower it would be imprudent. It would be wiser to tame him. This is the proper attitude of "living with disease" that cannot be overpowered.

A model for fifteen years developed dizziness and stomach pains which were diagnosed as gastroptosis and low blood pressure. She made strenuous efforts to overcome her illness, taking medication regularly. Five years ago she came to see me, weary of the struggle with the disease. After extensive tests I came to the conclusion that her fits of pain and dizziness were not strictly pathological because they were not directly attributable to the irregularities in her blood pressure and the state of her stomach. They were, rather, the effects of the accumulation of mental and physical fatigue in a body predisposed to such irregularities.

I explained the situation to her by appropriate, if not quite proportionate examples: "A lion eats flesh and turns it into its own flesh, so the lion has a comparatively simple stomach and intestines. An ox eats grass and turns it into flesh so it has four stomachs and long intestines. Westerners mainly live on meat and the Japanese mostly on rice, so the Japanese have long digestive organs and a long esophagus. You say that you often have to work, posing for photographers for eight hours at a stretch, taking in nothing but a cup of tea. Then you say you become so hungry that you eat two large bowls of rice. Well, you can eat that much and still retain your slim waist precisely because you have gastroptosis; that is, an elongated stomach. So you hardly need to let the gastroptosis worry you. And your low blood pressure is not really a disease, either. If it were, you could not have stood such a hard-working life for fifteen years."

I directed her to discontinue taking medication, but also to take sufficient rest after work. She came to my office only twice more with the same complaint, but each time she could get over her illness by taking a mild medicine and a few days rest. She is now able to perform her job better than ever, leading an unexerting life, living with her disease.

Professor Rokusaburo Nieda of Waseda University, one of Japan's leading philosophers, once told me, "My friends say that they are glad to see me always as sound as a bell. If I were so inclined, I would inwardly grumble, 'Nobody understands me.' For I am congenitally weak in my stomach and my brain. So I make it a point not to be hard on these two organs and live without straining myself too much."

It is true that he has a weak stomach, but it is far from true that he is weak in his brain. This professor, who is thus taking care of himself, has mastered the art of living with disease. He lives as a man of health while having vulnerable parts.

Living with Cancer

In 1963 Jun Takami, one of Japan's most celebrated writers, underwent an operation for throat cancer. It recurred one year later and spread to the neck, the stomach, and the peritoneum. It had affected almost all parts of his body when he died two years later. During this period he underwent four operations, and his condition became critical five times; but he survived all these dangers and died a tranquil death hearing the long-awaited news that his project, the Modern Literature Museum, had at last reached the official ground-breaking stage. The project was to collect and preserve for posterity all available material connected with Japanese literature of the past hundred years. Takami had directed the project as its chairman.

Because he avoided a life of struggle against the disease, he managed to coexist with it and devote himself to the museum project. He knew that his disease was not a foe which he could subdue by fighting it. He said, "Cancer can bite my body but not my spirit."

What made Takami's death dramatic was his strong will power that enabled him, lying in bed and fully aware of the nature of his malady, to press forward with the project. From his death bed he sent a message to the people attending the ground-breaking ceremony, describing the establishment of the museum as "a once-in-a-lifetime grand dream."

Frankl, describing the life-prolonging, even life-saving effect of the defiant power of the human spirit, cites the example of the German classic author J. W. Goethe who worked for seven years in spite of his failing health, in order to complete his *Faust*. He died in March 1832, two months after he had sealed the manuscript that fulfilled his life's goal. He "lived biologically beyond his means."

Neither Takami nor Goethe engaged in futile battles against an unsurmountable enemy, but they worked to complete the tasks to which they had committed themselves, letting—so to speak—death wait at the threshold.

The case of a sixty-eight-year-old bill collector is another example of an attitude of living with disease. Suffering from cancer of the stomach, he underwent an operation but now is leading a serene life, fulfilling his duties as a citizen in the same way as before. "I leave everything to my doctor and I don't worry. Things are going well with me; I may even live longer than the average." As he speaks there is not a shadow of dread. Indeed, he has so happy an air about him that it is hard to believe he is suffering from a fearful disease.

Had he lost himself in a headlong struggle with the disease, he might have invited premature death by exhausting himself. But he knows better. The task to which he applies himself is not the impossible conquest of cancer but the surmountable issues of his life.

It is not always wise to wrestle with one's disease, especially if it is incurable. The attitude of "living with disease" is not a passive way of life. It is not a surrendering to the disease, not an acceptance of letting it rule one's life. It is a creative attitude of adapting oneself to the inevitable.

Dentistry

Carl H. Jepsen

Dentists and dental educators can benefit from the principles and working methods of the logotherapist.

In the two years I spent as preventive dentistry officer for the U.S. Naval Air Station North Island in San Diego, California, I had the opportunity to observe dentists with varying amounts of dental practice experience and representing various dental schools. Most competent were those who established a strong rapport with their patients. These dentists were spontaneous and sensitive, and recognized the individuality of each patient. One could sense a harmony as they functioned in response to the wholeness of their patients while treating them. On the other hand, there were those who loathed each hour in the dental office. They were dogmatic and rigid, and grumbled about their patients who "did not cooperate," and "should shape up or ship out." Several of these dentists frequently complained about back pains or headaches. They tended to be dissatisfied with the dental equipment of the clinic. Their assistants requested changed assignments. And often the technical quality of their treatment left something to be desired.

Focus on Techniques

One possible reason why well-trained dentists demonstrate this negative approach to their chosen profession is the reductionistic mode of teaching in most dental schools. Classes usually focus on teaching a technique. Rarely is the whole patient considered; seldom is the dental procedure integrated into the total health and emotional pattern of both patient and dentist; patients and dentists are regarded as objects. It is no wonder that after graduation many dentists view their patients as "the filling" or "the toothache" or "the extraction" or "the denture." The human aspect in providing dental care is neglected.

Dean Maurice Hickey, a dentist and plastic surgeon, told our class during our first week at the University of Washington, "You will be spending four years learning dentistry and acquiring an extensive new vocabulary. But the knowledge and skills you will amass will be useful only if you are capable of transmitting them effectively to your patients. The tooth is part of a dental arch, the arch is part of the jaw, the jaw is part of the mouth, and the mouth belongs to a person. You are treating people—whole people."

So much attention in dental curricula is being placed on the mechanics of dentistry that dentists have come to be regarded as super-skilled technicians. Only a total integration of these skills with knowledge of human transactions makes the dentist a true professional in the healing arts and sciences. Recently, the attempt has been made to provide this necessary knowledge in motivation, sociology, psychology, and human behavior. In this area of dental education logotherapy is germane and vital.

The Fear of Dentists

One of the most perplexing problems facing the dentist is the patient who avoids having necessary dental treatment because of fear. Many times, when such a patient comes for an initial examination, his posture, respiration, facial expression, and movements indicate his anxiety. He may say something like, "Please don't take this personally but I hate dentists." All his communication flags are flying signals of terror.

Each person's anxiety must be met at his own unique level. A dentist recognizing this anticipatory anxiety has several alternatives. He can acknowledge the patient's fear and assure him that everything will be done to make dental work as easy as possible. Often after a patient has had a chance to talk about his fear, it will ebb. If the patient has a paralyzing fear, however, the cycle of fright can be defused by paradoxical intention. Dentophobia is kindled by avoiding the dentist. Paradoxical intention helps the patient to desensitize his fright by exaggerating it, by confronting his fear.

When I ask a patient if he would like to overcome his fear of dental work, his answer usually is, "I'm sorry, doctor. I try not to be afraid; but the more I try, the more frightened I become. Yes, please help me." I ask the patient to talk about his fear, describe where he feels it, and how he experiences it.

I describe how other patients have used paradoxical intention and their own capacity of self-detachment to overcome their anxiety. I comment on man's capacity to come to grips with his fear through his sense of humor. Then I say, "Why don't you exaggerate your fear so that you can be my most frightened patient? Be my best trembler, allow your knees to knock until I can hear them; or try to faint spectacularly. Make it dramatic. This whole thing probably sounds unusual but try it. That's how the wind can be taken out of the sails of your anxiety." The cycle of fear can be broken if the patient can be made to see the humor even in a previously anxiety-producing situation.

It has been amazing to see the signs of fear melt away. The desensitization of the anticipatory anxiety of dentophobia begins. Tolerable and even relaxed appointments can follow. Building on each success, the patient can overcome his fear. Persons who have conquered their fear have become some of my most satisfied patients.

Modern dental equipment, use of local anesthesia (preceded by a topical anesthetic applied on a cotton swab so the injections can hardly be felt), and efficient assistance allow dental treatment to be quick and comfortable. Such treatment presupposes that the dentist is aware of how important his touch is—his gentle touch. Sometimes, of course, a sensitive area is contacted, a small discomfort might be experienced, or the patient may feel his mouth is extremely full during some procedures. Patients will tolerate these situations better when informed in advance. Surprise and deception in dental practice are both unsettling and unnecessary.

Thumb Sucking

Orthodontists know that finger and thumb sucking after age four can lead to malformation of the dental arches and malalignment of the teeth, dependent upon the intensity and duration of the sucking. Since thumb sucking after age four is an overextended and unnecessary habit, it should be discouraged. Paradoxical intention can help patients overcome thumb-sucking habits.

Erickson applied what he called the law of reversed effect in the hypnosis treatment of a sixteen-year-old girl who retained a thumb-sucking habit aggressively to act out her hostility (1, pp. 428–430). I have adapted his approach, without the use of hypnosis—essentially by paradoxical intention.

When a child persists in sucking his thumb beyond age four and his parents come to me for help, I ask them to discontinue berating the child's habit and to cooperate with me in a supportive attitude which says to the child, "You and Doctor Jepsen have talked about the harmful changes to your mouth that continued sucking will do. We know that he has suggested a way that will help you decide when to stop."

Weekly counseling appointments varying from five to fifteen minutes are scheduled for the child. Daily, timed thumb-sucking practice sessions are established. At first they are scheduled for ten minutes. Together we decide what time of the day the practice sessions will be scheduled. At each counseling appointment we talk about how this concentrated practicing is helping the child decide when he no longer needs thumb sucking. The duration of the practice sessions is reduced by mutual consent, with the child setting the pace. These practice sessions are for sucking without interruption and are continued so long as the child feels he needs them. When the youngster decides that this thumb-sucking practice is silly and unnecessary, he decides to quit the habit. Treatments last from two to eight sessions. The success rate has been 84 percent.

Additional factors can contribute to discontinuance of a thumb-sucking habit. One five-year-old girl's father offered to take her on a dinner date when she no longer needed to suck her thumb and was ready to tell Doctor Jepsen. She quit her habit after two sessions. Another five-year-old girl, however, decided to continue sucking her thumb indefinitely. She was influenced by her father's confession that he sucked his thumb until he was twelve and her mother's statement that she sucked her thumb until age ten. (The parents' malformation of their teeth attested to the fact). The child declared that we should "practice" again when she was six because she then would be "old enough to stop." Shortly after her sixth birthday she came to my office and proudly held out her thumb, saying she did not need to suck it.

Paradoxical intention can also help patients relax who had been unable to do so. In such cases, the patient can overcome resistance by exaggerating it. I usually advise them, "Resist your natural tendency to relax. And the more you resist, the more relaxed you become." Paradoxically, the harder a patient resists relaxing the more relaxed he becomes.

Dereflection in the Dentist Chair

The dentist trained in logotherapy can also apply dereflection. Often a patient's difficulties with new dentures are caused by thinking too much about them—hyperreflection. Most of these patients are retired people who have much time to think about themselves. They focus on each minor problem until wearing of the denture seems to be the most difficult experience they have ever had. Their intense self-evaluation works against them.

Dereflection in this situation requires more than telling the patient to "just forget about the denture and the problem will disappear." I will usually discuss how hyperreflection actually perpetuates and aggravates the troublesome condition.

These patients are invited to focus their attention on their accomplishments. Each successfully eaten type of food and each hour of holding a denture confidently with coordinated tongue and cheek muscles are celebrated as significant accomplishments. The goal, of course, is to eat and speak efficiently and comfortably. We focus attention not on negative thinking but on the positive joy of success in mastering the foreign body in his mouth.

Occasionally, I will confront a patient directly with a statement about his hyperreflection. One sixty-two-year-old man became certain that he would never sucessfully wear dentures when his teeth had to be removed to eliminate oral infection caused by periodontal disease. Healing took place uneventfully, but several weeks later he started calling for a series of appointments. Each time he came in, something needed adjustment. The dentures were too high or too low or too tight or too loose. Finally, in frustration, I reviewed the course of his appointments and realized that his true problem was not the dentures.

When he came in the next time, I engaged him in a conversation about gardening, which we both enjoy. We discussed our rose gardens and the forthcoming flower show. When I eventually asked him about the reason for his visit, he could not remember why he had made the appointment. I then explained how sometimes denture problems are caused by hyperreflection. I suggested that he try an experiment. When he had a problem with his denture, I advised him to work in his garden to take his mind off his new mouth piece. He took my suggestion. His next appointment was a regular recall checkup. He reported that miraculously everthing about his new dentures had improved.

I help my patients avoid hyperreflection when I write some types of prescriptions. When a patient has had a tooth extraction or oral surgery, I order a pain-controlling medication. Usually prescriptions of this type instruct the patient: "Take one or two tablets every four hours as necessary for pain." I change that to the following: "Take one or two tablets every four hours as necessary to maintain comfort." Instead of stressing possible pain and suffering, I stress the idea of continuing comfort.

Person-related Dentistry

The desirable efforts to provide more people with more dental treatment in our technologically oriented society holds the danger that dentistry will become more procedure-oriented and less person-related. The prevailing trend could lead to automaton dentists drilling, filling, and billing. This need not be so. More and better dentistry will be provided by combatting reductionism in both dental education and dental practice. Dentists do not need to be clinical psychologists; however, a strong foundation in human relations and psychiatry including logotherapy is imperative to providing dental care for people who are human beings, and only incidentally dental patients.

References

1. Erickson, Milton H. (1967). *Advanced Technics of Hypnosis and Therapy,* ed. Jay Haley. New York: Grune and Stratton.

Nursing

Joyce E. Travelbee

Nurses, for most of their professional lives, work with people who do not recover from illness. Aside from infectious diseases and some acute surgical conditions most illnesses are incurable. Most ill persons must learn to live with the effects of a long-term, indeed a lifelong, illness.

A curious situation exists. Most nurses are cure-oriented and derive great satisfaction from helping ill persons get well despite the fact that most ill persons do not recover in the sense of being cured. Because of their cure orientation, nurses generally tend to lose interest when caring for the chronically ill. When one listens to the manner in which nurses talk about caring for "chronics" one realizes the full impact of what this belief has done in terms of nursing care.

The approach to nursing care must be drastically revised if the health-care needs of people are to be met. Nurses must be educated to become active agents skilled in the methods of illness prevention and health promotion. In addition, nurses must assume an entirely different role than generally acknowledged today: they must be educated to become health workers who can assist ill persons not just to cope with the stress of illness and suffering but to find some meaning in these experiences.

In the area of assisting others to find meaning in illness nurses can use the concepts of logotherapy.

Contemporary American culture values youth, health, material possessions and productivity. A person who becomes old, ill, or nonproductive is generally viewed as pitiable. Americans have great difficulty accepting the sick role—indeed even accepting their human condition. Many act on the assumption that somehow they should be exempt from illness. One of the questions most ill persons ask themselves is "why did this have to happen to me?" They search for a blame object. Some blame God and believe they are being punished for past misdeeds. Others blame bad luck, hard work, or other people for causing their illness. The plaintive cry "why me?" results in nonacceptance of illness, and this can have fatal results. Most nurses have encountered persons with cardiac problems who refuse to follow medical advice or others with diabetes who refuse to remain on a diet or to inject themselves with insulin. It is not helpful to lecture individuals who cannot accept illness. Neither is it helpful to assume that if only the ill person knew more about his illness and the health measures he must take to control his symptoms, all would be well. Instead, what is needed is someone to assist the ill person to accept his human condition and, even further, to find some meaning in a situation that seems senseless.

Human-to-Human Relationships

How does a nurse assist a person to find meanings in the experiences of illness, suffering, and pain—meanings that can be used as life-enhancing? Most importantly, the nurse must believe illness and suffering *can* be life-enhancing. This does not mean she prefers illness to health; only that she is able to conceive of the possibility that these tragic experiences can offer a potential for growth and deeper maturity. After the nurse sees these possibilities she then must be prepared to undergo the difficult task of helping ill persons to accept the reality of their condition and to derive some meaning from their experiences. Ill human beings need to see a reason to live, in order to endure their condition. It is the unique function of the professional nurse to assist the ill person to find a reason to live. The nurse cannot give meaning to ill persons but can assist them to formulate meanings themselves that make sense to them. Each person has life tasks only he or she can fulfill and is uniquely responsible for performing them. When the ill person is made to see the tasks only he or she can undertake, the possibility of meaning is more likely to emerge in illness and suffering—or, in spite of them.

To assist persons to perceive meaning in illness presupposes that the nurse is able to establish a human-to-human, not a nurse-patient relationship. The nurse deliberately acts in such a way as to be perceived as a human being who happens to be a nurse. The nurse perceives the ill person as a human being who happens to be a patient. The word "patient" and its connotations are stereotypes that interfere with human-to-human relationships.

The nurse pays attention to all requests made by the ill person no matter how trivial, and assists him to be as comfortable as possible, both physically and mentally. The nurse relieves pain and discomfort whenever possible.

The next step is to elicit from the ill person his perception of the illness experience, that is, to discuss with him the whole problem of his attitude toward suffering. He may not need the assistance of the nurse. However, if the nurse discovers that he perceives his illness as a punishment, a senseless condition, or an inexplicable happening, she then proceeds to the next step.

She attempts to recognize feelings the ill person has about his illness. These feelings may include bafflement, depression, anxiety, anger, or rage. It is important to allow the ill person to express his feelings about his condition. The nurse always admits to him validity of his feelings, whatever they may be, never telling him he "should not feel that way." She agrees with his perception of his feelings. She offers support by listening when he grieves the loss of bodily functions, or when he becomes angry about his fate. She may offer support by such simple comments as, "It must be difficult for you. It has not been easy. You have suffered much." She always acknowledges the sufferings the ill person is enduring.

After a period of listening to the ill person's feelings, the nurse tries to assist him to find "the why to live for," and supports and strengthens this "why." This is done by asking him, his family, and his friends, about his dreams, hopes, unfinished tasks, life roles still to be fulfilled, work still to be completed, and so forth. Working with family and friends, the nurse discusses with them the problem of helping the ill person cope with the feelings engendered by his condition. She enlists their aid in helping him to still feel needed in tasks only he can accomplish or in relationships only he can fulfill. This devotion to the human problem of the ill person will make heavy demands on the nurse's time. Logotherapy thus challenges the nursing profession to reorient itself, and perhaps leave the menial tasks to other individuals while the nurse can concentrate on the vital activity of directing the ill person's attention to his resources of the spirit.

Some Cases

G., a longshoreman, injured his back while working on the docks. He was married and had two small children. His physicians had told him that he would never again be able to work as a longshoreman and that he would have to seek less strenuous employment. G. seemed angry at everyone. He blamed his union's lax safety standards for his injury; he was angry at his physicians because they could not cure him; he felt "all washed up at thirty;" he told a nurse, "I've always worked hard. Never been sick a day in my life. I always tried to take care of my wife and kids. Where did it get me? My family would be better off without me. I'm worth more dead than alive. If I died at least they would have the insurance money. Now, all they have are bills and a broken man."

G. was soon stereotyped as a "bad patient." He refused to follow medical advice and complained about the quality of care given to him. Nurses on the unit began to avoid him. They only went into his room when they had to perform some treatment. His complaints became more vehement.

It became apparent that a concerted nursing effort was needed to assist him. A plan of care was developed. Nurses were encouraged to anticipate his physical comfort needs. Instead of avoiding him they were to stop by and talk to him. I was asked to work intensively with him.

The first problem was to help him work through his anger. I encouraged him to vent his anger openly. I agreed with his perception of his condition. Whenever he expressed anger I made such statements as, "It must be rough on you. It must be hard to accept the fact that you can no longer do the work you were used to doing." I made no attempt to cheer G. at this point.

I talked with his wife whenever possible. She was a shy, reticent woman who worried about her husband and said that she did not know how to help him. In a moment of frankness she said, "I need him so much and I love him but I never seem to find the words to tell him. Why are the words so hard to say?" I made the suggestion that sometimes it was important to put thoughts into words. Three days later the following conversation took place.

G.: "I've been thinking about how much I have been griping to you. You must think that all I do is complain."

Nurse: "No, I don't think that. I think you were very angry, and you have every right to be."

G.: "I was angry and I still am a little. But I can still work. There are other jobs I can get. I don't feel sorry for myself any more. Besides, my wife came to see me last night." He hesitated and then said, "She told me she needs me. She doesn't care what kind of job I have. It's *me* she wants."

He was discharged from the hospital the following day.

Suppose, however, the ill person has no family or friends and there are no life tasks left undone, no roles to fulfill? Still there may be someone, no longer living, yet present in the person's memory, for whom he would be willing to endure the "how" of his existence. It may not be a human being. It may be, for religiously inclined persons, "the ultimate Thou"—God. Whoever this someone is, the important thing to ask is, "What is still expected of me?" The nurse discusses this question with the ill person. She may also use a retrospective approach by asking him to look back over his life, to remember his accomplishments and the fact that no one can remove from the world what he has been through or suffered. The ill person is given the impression his life has not been wasted—his existence is what matters.

A. was a middle aged woman stricken with multiple sclerosis. She was single and had been the sole support of her elderly parents who had recently died. She had loved them and grieved their loss. She missed them but admitted she was glad to be free of the responsibility of caring for them. She had planned to travel and make new friends but the rapid onset of her illness had interfered. When I met her she was hospitalized for neurological treatment. She seemed depressed and cried often. In the course of our conversations it became apparent that she believed she "had wasted her life." "I never had a chance to live like other girls," she said. "I was always busy caring for mother or father. The few friends I had drifted away. Now, I am forty-six and my life is over. I know I am very ill. I have nothing to look forward to and nothing to look back upon. What is the point of it all?"

A retrospective approach showed her that her life had not been wasted.

Nurse: "Suppose you had *not* cared for your parents. What would have happened to them?"

A. (after some thought): "I guess they would have had to go on welfare. They would have had to go to the free hospital for medical care. It would have killed my father. He was such a proud man."

Nurse: "You spared your parents much suffering by your sacrifices. Have they really been in vain?"

A.: "I don't regret what I have done. They had only me. They gave me life. In return I was able to give more years to their lives. It *does* count for something."

After several similar conversations, her depression seemed to lift and she no longer expressed bitterness. She began to make friends in the hospital. She realized that her life had not been wasted, that even in her present condition, life still expected something from her.

The Nurse's Role

The nurse's role is to sympathize, comfort, and where possible direct the ill person's attention toward meaning. The fact that he is able to bear suffering bravely should always be pointed out to him because his attitude is an important example to other persons in similar predicaments.

The nurse consoles while assisting the ill person to accept the reality of his condition. She acknowledges but does not emphasize the limitations of the ill person. Realistic hope must be fostered because with only a little hope a human being can do a lot. It is not easy to accept the loss of a body part or body functions, or to accept one's disability without being masochistic about it. Acceptance of disability, however, comes slowly and is not to be equated with enjoyment of suffering. There is much truth in statements stressing the necessity for ill persons to "accept disability" before undergoing rehabilitation. However, acceptance is not a permanent state. It comes and goes, and there are varying levels. Acceptance is certainly not to be equated with a cavalier attitude toward one's disability. Acceptance is rather a state of mind which is won, lost and rewon many times a day as a person works through his varying feelings about his illness.

The nurse does not submit ill persons to a disagreeable process of "moral improvement" without their consent. No one should be forced to find meaning in illness any more than one should be compelled to show to others more of his inner life than he feels it natural to show. The nurse does not submit the ill person to "uplifting lectures." Neither does she "jolly him along" by making light of his disability. This does not imply that the nurse must always be grim and serious. A sense of humor is helpful in nursing provided its expression is judiciously and kindly intended.

We may bungle in our attempt to help others; we may be awkward and inept. Our lack of knowledge, however, should not stop us from searching for ways to help persons undergoing illness and suffering. There are no magic words a nurse may utter to assist an ill person in finding meaning in illness. There are no marvelous panaceas—no easy steps to follow that will produce the desired result. Indeed, if we waited until we were experts we could never begin. We cannot wait. Ill human beings need help now with the attitudes they develop toward their illness. We cannot sit back and wait for major scientific breakthroughs that will magically eliminate illness and suffering. In a world where the only permanence is change, the undeniable fact is that human beings will undergo suffering, pain, and eventually death. Human beings need other humans to help them cope with their feelings about loss, disability, and illness.

If professional nurses accepted the function of helping ill persons with their attitudes toward illness, many so-called "nursing problems" would disappear. We would be more effective in helping ill persons to cope with the health measures they must take to control symptoms of illness. If we could use the hospitalization experience as a life-enhancing one, perhaps we could help reduce the readmission rate. So many times we discharge persons from hospitals only to have them return shortly, sicker than when they left. If we are able to accept helping others find meaning in illness as a legitimate nursing function, perhaps we could reduce the staggering load of suffering and despair that so many ill persons are forced to cope with alone. If we could just reduce the loneliness of the sufferer our efforts will not have been in vain.

V

Counseling

Logotherapy's greatest impact has been in the area of counseling, and each essay in this section provides a different reason for its usefulness.

The counselor does not deal principally with the mentally sick but with the mentally searching, and especially with those frustrated in their search. He deals most clearly with matters of the spirit, the logos; therefore, logotherapy is indicated.

In the past, spiritual guidance was available almost exclusively through religious channels. The emergence of the secular counselor is a result of the spreading existential frustration, the abundance of new findings by psychologists, the difficulty of religious counselors in absorbing and applying these new findings, and the increasing reluctance of persons to seek help in religious institutions.

Logotherapy meets the needs of our age in many ways. The religious counselor, as Tweedie explains, finds logotherapy more acceptable than most other psychological approaches. Crumbaugh shows that the secular counselor finds it a suitable method for those who prefer taking their spiritual problems to nonreligious advisors. Group counseling, now increasingly popular, can apply logotherapy, as Fabry demonstrates, to participants who need not merely to release their pent-up emotions but to become aware of their totality, including the resources of their spirit. Bulka shows how the basic philosophy of logotherapy can help marriage counselors and the partners themselves deal with marital dysfunction. The counseling of the aged, as Leslie argues, profits by the philosophy of logotherapy because a reorientation from success to meaning is therapeutic for the rapidly growing number of persons who face early retirement and longer life in a work-oriented culture. Finally, Brandon investigates the qualifications of logotherapy to help affluent, skeptical, science-oriented people to deal with man's eternal problem of how to make sense out of life in the face of unavoidable suffering, guilt, and death.

Religious Counseling

Donald F. Tweedie, Jr.

The demobilization of American society as a war machine after World War II seemed to release energies and aspirations for mobilization in a war against personal and social distress that had invaded its citizenry. This changeover brought about soul searching by the church regarding its commitment to this "social salvation." Funds were provided by foundations to evaluate counseling training in the curricula of theological seminaries. Widespread discontent existed with theological training that did not have immediate social consequences. Personal counseling with psychological sophistication was deemed necessary to complement, and in some cases to substitute for, the traditional preaching task of the church.

The federally funded, five-year study of the mental and emotional status of the United States published in 1961 (1) indicated that during the course of a year about one-seventh of the adult population experience a personal emotional crisis and seek professional help for its resolution. The church could not avoid its responsibility in trying to meet this pressing need, for the study also reported that nearly half of these persons would initially seek the counsel of a clergyman. Clergymen, who generally perceived themselves as relatively incompetent counselors, were further challenged by the report's findings that of the various kinds of mental-health professionals they were considered the most satisfactory counselors for personal problems.

Churchmen, feeling a sense of vocation to meet the mental-health requirements of their parishes and communities at large, were looking for an appropriate model. The available models of counseling were found wanting. During this time of social and ecclesiastic ferment in the postwar years logotherapy appeared on the scene.

Logotherapy did not become the only option as a model for churchmen as counselors, but it appealed to many because of its high potential for meeting their needs.

The Image of Man

There may be some doubt whether a counselor's method of psychotherapy follows from his view of human nature, but he will feel more secure when he has one. The Freudian view of man, especially its focus on erotic impulse, seemed by and large ineradicably alien to the most generous biblical anthropology. The view of man as a machine which appeared to be the premise of behaviorism, was even more unsuitable. Thus the two views of personality that had emerged from the young history of psychology were at worst directly opposed and at best inadequate for the purpose of the Christian counselor. The "third force" which moved into the situation—the theory of Carl Rogers—was vaguely structured but at least offered an emotionally Christian view of man. The "client centered" man was human and without guile. The churchman counselor could relate to him without the necessity of any particular psychodiagnostic finesse or any elaborate analysis of the learning environment. For many clergymen, however, Rogers' man was too optimistic a model, and too secular—untouched by either sin or sanctification. Rogers had abandoned his earlier vocational goal of the Christian ministry because he did not find the Biblical view of man an adequate concept for the counselor.

The logotherapist sees man as having an essential and primary spiritual dimension. The image of God in man is neither an object of denial nor a victim of reductionism. Instead of being inexorably determined by internal and external forces, man is free. He has the power of contrary choice and is held responsible for his choosing. To understand and cure man's ills, he must be understood in his spirituality with its potentials for transcending his physical and psychological dimensions. These messages from a prominent and articulate scholar-psychiatrist were gladly heard by churchmen.

Therapeutic Goals and Values

The church counselor also had to find a satisfactory definition of mental health and therapeutic goals. The reduction of tension and the attainment of a light-hearted happiness seemed a dubious hope. Such goals seemed strangely alien to human creativity and Christian conduct. Such end products of psychotherapy, while not necessarily negative, were simply not appropriate as universal goals. Finding some redemptive values in suffering seemed a significant task demanded by our Christian heritage. Not peace of mind, but strength of mind was the mark of mental health.

Logotherapy once again seemed to fill the gap. It presents the process of psychotherapy as only peripherally an ego massage or a soothing of the spirit. The healing consequence of changing the focus of one's commitment from self to others and the realization of values in inexorable suffering are primary challenges of logotherapy. These goals helped make the therapeutic task more appropriate to the calling of the churchman.

A Religious Context for Counseling

One of the thorny problems for the churchman in meeting the call to be a counselor was the general mood of contemporary psychotherapy. The mainstream of clinical counseling, as well as the text and the context of the training facilties, were a secular enterprise. Religious values were avoided and religious genius, in the sense of William James, was regarded as a grave symptom.

Logotherapy seemed a more compatible approach to counseling. It is comfortable with religious terminology and religious goals. The title of Frankl's first theoretical book to be translated into English was *The Doctor and the Soul.* Its original German title, *Aerztliche Seelsorge,* is even more unabashedly religious in tone: "Medical Ministry" or "The Medical Care of Souls." The term *logotherapy* also struck a responsive note to churchmen. Even those who knew little Greek knew that, "In the beginning was the Logos." Frankl's intention may have been to relate his theory to a more classical and philosophical Greek context, but the outcome jibed with the need of churchmen for the possibilities of counseling as a Christian enterprise.

On the other hand, there was some anxiety about religious counseling being "too religious." It was one thing for the counseling context to have Christian character and another to set it up as an evangelistic enterprise. The shades of Freud were still alive in the religious community. The religious literature which presented psychotherapy as a nondirective altar call tended to be disregarded. Logotherapy seemed to resolve this conflict, too. It calls for a clear distinction between churchman and therapist. Psychohygiene is the intention of the counselor, though the possibility of an "accident" of religious conversion or spiritual growth are well within the limits of logotherapy. Although logotherapy is not a specifically religious practice, it regards man as a religious being and is available as a tool for religious counselors. This distinction has its problems but it was a boon to many clergymen.

It was also important for the church counselor to avoid an identification of sinfulness and emotional illness. Churchmen, in general, reacted negatively to the approach in Mowrer's concept of "Sin, the Lesser of Two Evils" (3). For the most part, this indictment of the emotionally disturbed person as a devious sinner seemed more than common sense and Christian theology required. Logotherapy, while often asserting the negative consequences of violating one's conscience or the social mores, avoided Mowrer's extremes and thus drew the approbation of the average church counselor.

Logotherapy with its openness to religious values, vocation, and terminology seemed complementary to the work of the ministry. It met an important need for the clergyman to meet the task demand of the mental health problem. In addition, Frankl had made a satisfactory discrimination between the medieval "cure of souls" and the modern "care of souls."

Style of Counseling

Much of the popularity of Rogers's approach to counseling and psychotherapy had been the implication that anyone could do it.

While comments about the need of intensive training and careful research were made, they seemed more of a sop to the psychotherapeutic and academic establishment than a matter of necessity. Rogers's method was free from psychodiagnostic considerations and complex therapeutic decisions, had few warnings of danger to the novice counselor, and implied that love, listening, and learning to be an emotional reflector were the secrets of success. Most clergymen felt they could use this method. It was in line with the theme of the "priesthood of all believers."

Frankl presented logotherapy as a medical discipline, insisted on a skilled diagnosis differentiating somatogenic, psychogenic, and noögenic neuroses, and introduced the logotherapist as a highly trained professional. Yet, logotherapy was perceived as a generally nonmedical method which would well fit into the repertoire of skills of the average clergyman with some clinical experience.

The counseling style of Carl Rogers had a serious defect in its application by the church counselor. It seemed as time-demanding as psychoanalysis. In the literature the excerpts from tape recorded sessions frequently spoke of the "sixty-seventh session" or the "hundred and third session." This seemed impossible to schedule for the busy pastor or priest. Frankl's presentation seemed a godsend in its short-term characteristic. Clinical anecdotes in the logotherapeutic literature, indicating the remarkable effectiveness of one or two sessions, were intriguing. A survey of the session frequency of the patients in Frankl's clinic during a two-year period averaged slightly less than eight. These were cases of cure or improvement to the point that professional counseling was no longer indicated. Clinical problems of years in analysis were apparently cured in brief sessions with the logotherapist. The recovery from emotional ills did not require an intensive and extensive historical survey of the development of the client's personality nor a long-range experience of retraining positive emotional responses, but rather an existential attitude. No matter how long a person had been going in the wrong direction, the task of the logotherapist was merely to get him going in the right one. This was an attractive feature to churchmen.

Churchmen historically are primarily preachers. Something about the appellative mode of logotherapy blends with this heritage. The direct challenge and confrontation is more akin to the ministerial style. The inhibitions of psychoanalytic passivity and client-centered nondirectiveness are alleviated in logotherapy. One of Frankl's anecdotes focuses on this spiritual confrontation. When asked to distinguish between psychoanalysis and existential analysis, he retorted, "In psychoanalysis the patient lies on a couch and tells the therapist things that are difficult to tell; in logotherapy the patient sits up in a chair and is told by the therapist things that are difficult to hear!" Leslie's book (2) was designed as a case study method in which the methods of logotherapy and the preaching style of Jesus were compared. These factors of logotherapy seemed to fit the function of the ministry.

An Intellective Style of Counseling

A final dimension of the clergyman's need for a more appropriate model for his counseling refers to theological style and method. Logotherapy, with its emphasis upon meaning and its philosophical approach to the betterment of man's miseries, accords well with the church counselor who has emerged from a tradition of cognitive need, expectation of apologetics, and exegetical process. He expects it to be helpful for someone "to give a reason for the hope that is within him." The rational analysis of the hopes and expectations of suffering man, as well as a methodological investigation of the meaning and values of his living, deeply embedded in logotherapy, accord well with the clergyman. The logotherapist, like a competent theologian in his Biblical studies, does not impose his own values and meanings but attempts to draw them from the patient's own experience. Both are convinced that life is deeper than logic, but also agree that reason ought to guard the heart.

The literature of existentialism, especially in its theological dimensions, from Kierkegaard to the present, has been significant for the churchman, but also abstruse, and, for many, only marginally comprehensible. Logotherapy has been a refreshing exception to this. It is clear in the presentation of its theory and therapy.

However, for the pragmatic American mind, a theory must not merely "make sense," but also offer a program of action. Although much of the imported existential literature seems content to make analysis of human existence an end in itself, even when it refers to pathological modes of personality development, logotherapy provides a clear course of action for the counselor. A practical existential approach which serves to mediate both thought and action is a valuable possession for the church counselor.

A few caveats are in order. I do not mean to imply that the relationship of logotherapy and Christianity is in any way official or universal. Anyone with even a casual acquaintance with the pluralistic character of the American church would recognize that this could hardly be true. Nor would I want to imply that logotherapy has not been significant in Jewish or other religious and nonreligious circles. My observations rather would indicate that the Church, awakened to its responsibility to provide "action for mental health" to a large degree has found a satisfying theoretical and practical model in logotherapy.

References

1. Joint Commission on Mental Illness and Health (1961). *Action for Mental Health.* New York: Science Editions.
2. Leslie, Robert (1965). *Jesus and Logotherapy.* Nashville: Abingdon Press.
3. Mowrer, O. H. (1961). *The Crisis in Psychiatry and Religion.* Princeton: Van Nostrand-Reinhold.

Exercises of Logoanalysis

James C. Crumbaugh

The concept of meaning can be demonstrated by some elementary developmental psychology: The newborn infant enters a bewildering world in which he is totally insecure. He understands none of the stimuli which impinge upon him, and they are therefore all threatening. He perceives a loud crack, a flash of light, and a rapid repetitive ping, and cries helplessly because he cannot connect them, and therefore cannot see meaning in them. The child of six has learned to perceive this pattern as a summer thunder shower; he no longer cries but may feel uneasy because he understands little of the nature of these stimuli. The adolescent has gained some understanding of them but may still be anxious because he cannot control these forces. Not, of course, that the adult can: he has simply learned to protect himself from harm, and his anxiety has been reduced. He perceives the relationship of these stimuli as one with which he can cope. He has succeeded in his search for meaning in the pattern.

As the individual develops from infancy, he gradually perceives more relationships and thus meanings. His natural tendency is to try and fit more relationships into larger and larger relationships in an effort to comprehend the totality of nature. In this task, however,

Portions of this chapter are adapted from the author's book, *Everything to Gain: A Guide to Self-Fulfillment through Logoanalysis,* Chicago: Nelson-Hall. 1973. Reproduced by permission of the publisher.

he is doomed to ultimate failure: No matter how intelligent he is and how educated he becomes, he arrives at a point beyond which his comprehension is inadequate to grasp the meaning of the total picture. Thus he has an unsatisfied need which creates "existential anxiety," resulting from his inability to deal with the ultimate meaning of existence. This anxiety can be reduced only by a "leap of faith," to use Kierkegaard's term, in assuming an unknown design—what Fabry calls "an awareness that, in spite of apparent chaos, there is order in the universe" (2) and what Frankl calls "suprameaning" (MS, p. 187).

Many persons can tolerate the ambiguity caused by failure to make this leap of faith in ultimate meaning, and they may even function efficiently in adjusting to life problems; but they will still have existential anxiety, because their fundamental need to find meaning in life will be only partly met. If they are emotionally suited to living in this state of ambiguity, they can still find personal meaning in a world of chaos which they perceive as a product of chance. But for most people, this is difficult or even impossible; as a result, they may be frustrated, insecure, and anxious.

A Framework of Meaning

When a person has formed a framework of meaning (and everyone does this to a certain degree), he finds his own identity—a place for himself as Somebody—within this framework. If he has not found an adequate and personally satisfying position on the broader questions of universal meanings, he will have difficulty in establishing this personal identity, for he will have an inadequate foundation for it. And even if he has answered for himself the broader questions, he may still find it hard to place himself in a meaningful position as Somebody in the scheme of things as he sees them.

This is where the logotherapist can help. He cannot find meanings for his client, for no one can do this for another, but he can guide the searcher in the avenues of exploration, encourage him during periods of discouragement, and point out hope when the quest seems fruitless.

The successful application of logotherapy will elicit an awareness of a job to be done, a challenge that makes the struggle worthwhile.

Logotherapy assumes that there is design and purpose in the universe and that man is more than a passive mechanism responding to the environment through conditioning. It assumes that human life has an ultimate though unprovable meaning in which each individual shares. The individual has an obligation as well as the privilege to search for his own unique destiny and thus to fulfill his personal need to find a meaning in life. Logotherapy denies the mechanistic view of man which reduces him, in the final analysis, to *nothing but* a machine.

Logotherapy's view of man leads to another assumption: that man, as a spiritual being, is free to make choices which are not mechanistically determined. This view contrasts with determinism, which is a corollary of mechanism. Logotherapy does not deny that limits of choice are set by heredity and environment, but it asserts that within these prescribed limits every person has an area of freedom to choose the attitude which he will take toward the preconditions. Thus man is a spiritual being because he is free; only man can freely choose his own attitudes.

Without these two assumptions—the existence of ultimate meaning and the freedom to choose one's own attitudes toward set conditions—there is little motivation to search for meaning in one's personal life. The search for meaning is still possible even without these assumptions, but it becomes a matter of "going it alone" in a strictly mechanistic universe. The logotherapist must guide the client in establishing his own philosophy, even if the latter has no idea what a philosophy is. The thinking of the client must reflect his own initiative and not the stereotypes of society, and certainly not those of the therapist; therefore, treatment must primarily motivate the client to become conscious of what he really believes about life.

The word *therapy,* however, does not imply that the client is necessarily mentally ill. Frankl considers the existential vacuum to be a human condition. Only when it combines with clinical symptoms does it become what he calls a *noögenic* neurosis, which research has shown to be present in perhaps 20 percent of a typical clinical population (3). Logotherapy is therefore applicable to a broad spectrum of problems, only a portion of which involve mental illness. Frankl feels that therapy of the mentally ill should be restricted to a psychiatric setting, while counseling of all others may properly be conducted by a variety of helping professions. It is for this form of counseling that I have suggested the term *logoanalysis,* to imply applicability to the broader spectrum (1).

Logoanalysis

The first step of logoanalysis is to help the client to expand his conscious awareness and to stimulate his creative imagination, so he can evaluate himself and his potentials within as large a totality as he is able to conceive. The goal of logoanalysis is to open vistas that enable the client to see new solutions to problems and open up new avenues to meaning, in place of the feeling of hopelessness. The search for meaning is seen as the hunt for the thousands of pieces of a jigsaw puzzle. There always will be many parts missing—the failures, conflicts, and troubles with which the client is faced. In some cases, he may be able to find some of the missing pieces, but some he may never find, which may lead him to conclude that his life is meaningless and not worth living. The logoanalyst must lead him to shift his attention from the holes in the picture to its over-all design with all its shapes and colors.

Logoanalysis must guide the client to evaluate himself realistically in honest self-appraisal of where he stands and wishes to stand in the totality of his life. He is encouraged to make an inventory of his assets and hopes, his liabilities and shortcomings. I have devised six lists that are used throughout the analysis:

1. Life-long aims, ambitions, goals, and interests going back as far as the client can remember, including those he no longer considers important.
2. The strong points of personality, physical and environmental circumstances, "good luck"
3. The weak points of personality, failures, "bad luck"
4. Specific problems that cause his conflicts
5. Future hopes (this list may overlap with the first list above but emphasizes the future while list 1 includes past ambitions)
6. Future plans, immediate and long-range

During the course of the analysis the client is encouraged to add to and subtract from these lists as he changes his self-appraisal. Eventually he is asked to summarize his progress.

Logoanalysis, like logotherapy, helps the individual systematically explore all human values for the particular areas where he can find maximum personal meaning.

Logotherapy stimulates the individual to explore each of the three types of values—creative, experiential, and attitudinal—to find his own personal meanings. Here every logotherapist must develop specifics, because Frankl leaves the system intentionally generic in this respect. However, logotherapists who come, as I do, from a background of experimental psychology are likely to desire some standardization of specifics. Admittedly, these will be subject to continuous experimentation and modification, but procedures that prove effective in some cases can be recorded and maintained until better ones are found. A given case will usually respond well to some of these but not to others; and since there is no way to determine this in advance, a number of them must be tried out with each individual. Each therapist will develop empirically his own set of procedures. This is a professionally healthy situation, as from these divergent approaches a common foundation of sound technique will eventually come that works better than any of the individual approaches alone.

Frankl may have had this point in mind when in his address at the first of his annual seminars in logotherapy at United States International University in San Diego, he said, "Logotherapy is not a closed system but open to both the cooperation of other scientifically established approaches and to its own evolution. As I see it, logotherapy is still in the process of development. Logotherapy does not exist as yet, but you will create it. I have only laid the groundwork."

In line with this aim I am offering my own methods of inducing the exploration of values, in the expectation that some methods will prove useful to other logotherapists, and that some may suggest other original variations helpful in particular cases. All these devices induce the client to think through all possible values in each of the three value areas and to adopt the ones which can have meaning for him. A selection of those devices which have so far proved useful to this therapist is presented below. Many others are used (1), and new ones are constantly being added. They are called "exercises" in that they require specific acts or mental responses which elicit associations in the various value areas, and thereby furnish practice in perceiving meanings in each of these areas.

Creative Values

1. A sense of personal identity.
   a. If you had to identify yourself in *one* sentence, what would you say of yourself? Write five sentences that would identify you, starting with one which would furnish the best identity, then the second best, and so forth.
   b. Write, in order of importance, five sentences which you *wish* you could truthfully write to identify yourself.
   c. What keeps you from becoming the person you would like to be?
2. Three wishes.
   a. If you had three wishes, what would they be? Write them in order of importance.
   b. What basic human need does each wish satisfy?
   c. By what possible means can you fulfill each of these needs?
3. The meaning of life in one word.
   a. Select one word which best expresses the meaning you would *like* life to have. (Examples: A wife said, "husband," an actor, "applause," a student, "wealth.")
   b. Name the value which lies behind the word you choose. (The wife might say, love or security or companionship; the actor, popularity, fame, or bringing happiness to others; the student, security, fun, or independence.)
   c. Think of possible activities which could fulfill this value.
4. Writing your own epitaph.
   a. Write the epitaph which you would prefer for yourself. (Example: Robert Louis Stevenson wrote, "Home is the hunter, home from the hills; the sailor home from the sea.")
   b. What life value underlies this epitaph?
   c. What activities could help you to fulfill this value?
5. Analyzing the most important meaning in your life.
   a. If a murderer offered to let you live provided you could give him one good reason why you *should* live, what reason would you have?
   b. What life meaning underlies this reason?
   c. What can you do to fulfill this meaning?

Experiential Values

In art, examine some paintings, sculpture, or photographs; listen to music—rock, folk, or opera; read a poem, story, biographical sketch, or play. Then, record the meaning each suggests to you.

Similarly, in science, visit a laboratory, museum, or planetarium; and arrange to look through a telescope, microscope, fluoroscope, and the like. Then record the meaning each suggests to you.

Attitudinal Values: Facing Unalterable Circumstances

Think back over your life to some unalterable circumstance, and record how you handled it. Did you adopt an attitude that there was a meaning and purpose in the event even though this could not be demonstrated? As you now look back, what possible purpose could have been present?

These are merely samples of the exercises used in each of the three basic value areas. The client is led to understand that they have no magic in themselves but are only devices to stimulate thinking. From this thinking, it is hoped, will grow an awareness of a set of meanings which is uniquely his own, and which can furnish a new sense of direction and purpose in life.

Commitment

One step in logoanalysis remains to be discussed. In many respects it is the most important and certainly the hardest. It is the final step the client has to take when his system of values has come into focus—commitment.

Commitment is a matter of motivation. It is the complete dedication of a person's total being—his energies, his mental and emotional resources—to the fulfillment of the meanings he has found. Like many other aspects of motivation, it is difficult to analyze, and therefore difficult to accomplish by objective techniques. I have no exercises for it. The exercises for exploration of human values are basically exercises in perception, which have been intensively studied by several generations of psychologists and are much better understood as a process.

If we postulate the will to meaning as man's basic motivating force, it should follow that, as a person perceives attainable meanings, he should be motivated to achieve them. In practice, however, he may perceive such meanings, yet show much resistance to committing himself to their achievement.

A basic reason for this failure in commitment usually is a lack of self-confidence. Perceived meanings lose their strength when the person feels insecure and inadequate. It is, therefore, important to pay attention to his level of self-confidence and strengthen his self-concept. Because this takes time, gaining self-confidence cannot be postponed until the client is ready to commit himself to a course of action; self-confidence should be a featured part of logoanalysis from the beginning. I have used for this purpose an exercise called "Act as if . . .," a continuing procedure that runs simultaneously with the other exercises. It requires the client to do that which he fears most—to imagine that he is the self-confident person he would like to be and to set aside regular periods during which he acts as he thinks this adequate person would act. In time he gets to feel as he acts, and then he is no longer acting.

Acting-as-if is a good preparation for commitment, but there is no direct means of establishing it. It is up to the ingenuity of the counselor to stimulate commitment in interaction with his client. The basis for this stimulation is the quality of the relationship between the two—what the existentialist calls the encounter.

When a client has found meanings and genuinely committed himself to attaining them, the work of the logotherapist is done. But the work of the client has only begun. Its completion will require the rest of his life. Finding meaning is never a homeostatic mechanism which can be satisfied once and for all and which thereafter leaves the individual complacent, unmotivated, and inactive. The will to meaning is, rather, a dynamic mechanism which never reaches completion. Its satisfaction consists not in the finished task, but in the experience of progress toward its attainment.

This is the state in which the successful application of logotherapy—or logoanalysis—will bid the client goodbye. He is now on the road. It is up to him to complete the journey.

References

1. Crumbaugh, J. C. (1973). *Everything to Gain: A Guide to Self-Fulfillment through Logoanalysis.* Chicago: Nelson-Hall.
2. Fabry, Joseph B. (1974). Application of logotherapy in sharing groups. *Religion and Health.* April.
3. Frankl, V. E. (1967). Logotherapy. *Israel Annals of Psychiatry and Related Disciplines* 5 (2): 142–155.

Sharing Groups

Joseph B. Fabry

Ideally logotherapy, with its emphasis on personal uniqueness and individual responsibleness, is based on a relationship between two human beings, the counselor and the client. It is the task of the counselor to motivate the client to search for meaning, and provide opportunities for him to select new ways of finding meaning, through the doors the counselor opens before him.

This approach runs counter to the popular trend of encounter groups, where "encounter" often is understood to mean a clash in order to release blocked emotions, and "group" often turns out to mean pressure on the individual to conform to the patterns of the group or the directions of the leader—one *has* to be angry, or loving, or "relevant," one *has* to play certain games or pretend to have certain feelings. Other aspects of encounter groups that go against the principles of logotherapy include the practice of "acting out" emotions such as aggression or anger. This may provide relief but fails to give the participant the opportunity to make use of his human potential—his spiritual resources, including his "freedom to change something in the world for the better, if possible, and to change himself for the better, if necessary" (3, pp. 75–76). Frankl is also critical of those encounter groups in which the participant is encouraged to observe himself, "endlessly to discuss whatever he furnishes from within himself," and in general practice hyperreflection which may result in neuroses or at least reinforce a neurotic attitude toward himself. Encounter groups may invite "hyper-discussions" which may become "more and more a substitute for the meaning of life" (3, pp. 81–82).

Although I have seen participants become "addicted' to groups and, in their search for encounters, neglect their search for meaning, Leslie (5), Crumbaugh (1), Holmes (4), and others have shown that groups can be useful vehicles for the logotherapist. In the "sharing groups" I have conducted in universities, growth centers, churches, and social-service organizations, I make it a point to announce that the group is "not for the mentally sick but for the mentally searching." In these groups the participant remains the center of inquiry; pressure toward confrontation is avoided; encounter is interpreted to mean positive relationship between leader and participants, and among individual participants; emotion is allowed to be unblocked where this is wanted by the participant, but emphasis is placed on his noëtic resources—his goal orientation, his ability to relate to others, and his awareness of a will to meaning. The participant is helped to see his human nature not only as *nature,* with all its physical and psychological limitations, but also as *human,* with all its potentials available to him in his healthy, noëtic core.

Sharing groups then, are not for "patients" but for persons who feel in need of self-direction and meaning. My groups are intended to help participants reorient themselves more positively, clarify goals, break the grip of failure, and find meaning in their lives within the framework of their own value systems.

Touching, hugging, or role playing may come up spontaneously but are not planned as techniques. An atmosphere of trust is developed where participants will risk granting others a look at themselves not only as they are but as they wish to be. The emphasis is not on mere mutual "self-expression" but on "self-transcendence" (3, p. 74). No one is forced to speak about matters he does not wish to discuss; he is free to pass up any question that is directed toward him; but if he decides to answer, he commits himself to honesty. The purpose of the sessions is to help the participant become aware of the healthy part in him, and to expand his human potential. I often start the session by asking everyone to write down the things he likes about himself, and also what he dislikes, with the assurance that, if he so desires, this will remain private information. The participants are asked to reveal only what they feel comfortable to share with the others. The emphasis is on the positive aspects of the person, what he has found meaningful in the past, his goals, his visions of himself; but he is given the opportunity to admit failure, loneliness, and the need to reach out for help, and is aided to see his choices in overcoming roadblocks, traps, and unwanted patterns.

Thus, a sharing group amounts to a genuine dialogue which enters the dimension of meaning-logos, rather than to a "mutual monologue." This type of sharing group goes somewhat beyond those described by Leslie (5), who sees the function of the leader as "not to solve problems nor understand their origins but simply to acknowledge them, encourage full expression of them, and relate them to observed patterns of behavior; to provide support where needed, pursue tentative expression until the real emotion is revealed, and protect members from attack; to challenge the group and its members toward growth, point out learning as it is experienced, help self-understanding and understanding of others; and help people feel accepted as they are, without hiding the darker side."

Doors to Meaning

Doors to meanings can be opened in several ways. Participants need to be assured that any feeling of emptiness, the existential vacuum, is no disease but merely shows that they are human: only a human being searches for meanings, has doubts, and feels frustrated if he cannot find them.

Participants also need to be shown that finding meaning requires patience and can usually be achieved only in small steps. If a person has decided that his life goal is to be a great physician, he has to start out by giving his most careful attention to the patient at hand. Finding meaning is like stepping into the dark with a small lamp; by holding high the lamp, a person can see a small circle around him. He is encouraged to take one or two steps in the direction he chooses, and to hold up the lamp again. With patience he may reach his goal.

Participants must further be shown that meaning can be found not merely in activities, paid and unpaid, and in experiences (art, nature, human relationships), but also in the attitude taken in situations of life traps. One participant expressed one possible meaning to be discovered in those traps by saying: "The meaning of suffering is to understand the suffering of others, so you can help." Another example is provided by the survivor of concentration camps who wanted to convince others that such inhuman treatment of humans must never occur again, but no one would listen. Eventually he said: "The meaning of suffering is not to change others; its meaning is that it changes *you.*" Meaning can be found by a person even on his death bed, as a young man illustrated to a group: "When grandpa died it was he who cheered us up when we visited him. We kids never thought much of the old man, but he taught us a lesson we'll never forget—how to die with dignity."

Truth, Choice, Uniqueness

In the deepening climate of trust, members of sharing groups can be led to see several areas in which meaning suddenly may illuminate their life. I shall mention five such areas. The first is the discovery of a truth about themselves; not a truth told them by someone else, but by personal insight. The truths hidden behind a person's masks unblock his noëtic core and tell him that it's all right to admit weakness, reach out for help, and admit failure, anxiety, and anger which he had so carefully sealed that he did not even admit them to himself. But the leader must watch out that the person stops his unmasking, as Frankl warns, when he reaches his healthy self; otherwise he will tear off not only his masks but his truly human motivations—his love, his honesty, his ideals. If he reduces love to a sublimation of sex, and conscience to a mere superego that has to be obeyed, he will have surrendered the essence of his meaning potential; fulfillment through love promises more than just orgasm, while the meaning potential of the conscience lies in a person's freedom to make decisions in matters that crucially concern him.

Choice is a second area of meaning potential. A sharing group helps the participants realize that, in spite of all physical, psychological, and environmental limitations, every person has a core in which he does have choices; to be aware of that center of choice in him may make the difference between a meaningful and a meaningless life.

The participant is encouraged to list the choices he has, to escape an unwanted situation or reach a desired goal. Others in the group can help, not by making the decisions for him but by recalling how they have chosen in similar situations. But more important than helping a person in a trap to make a choice is to make him aware that he actually has one. A participant in a group of counselors recalled how he had been phoned by a man about to commit suicide. The counselor told him, "All right. You have a choice. Either you can kill yourself, or you can come to my office and we can talk things over." The man stammered, "I do have a choice? I . . . didn't think I had any." He came to the counselor who commented, "Once a person realizes that he has a choice, he can go ahead to find a solution."

In situations of unavoidable suffering, the choices are limited to those of attitude. This is also true of the way we decide to consider our past. A person cannot alter the facts of his past, remove childhood traumas, undo mistakes, or change his early environment. The choice here consists of either letting past mistakes drag him down or allowing a lesson to come through the experiences; he may use childhood environment and traumas as excuses for present failures, or as challenges to be overcome. What needs to be transmitted is logotherapy's view of transitoriness (PE, p. 30): the past is not seen as a horror chamber but rather as a treasure chest of achievements. Beautiful experiences cannot be relived but can serve as assurance that something similar may happen again. A woman who had found meaning in her college studies and had married could, at the age of 45, not become 18 again but she could take advanced courses in college. Another woman, age 60, twenty years back had had a religious experience that had illuminated her life with meaning, but the experience had faded, and no return to the same church had rekindled it. She kept searching because she knew she had the capacity to feel the way she had once felt; and her search, rather than a new "conversion," gave direction and focus to her life.

The third area in which meaning can be found is the individual uniqueness of the person. Most people who are suffering from an existential vacuum feel replaceable in their work, their community, even in their family. If a person is prompted to recall moments of fulfillment, he will remember incidents of personal human relationships and creative activities. Only *he* could relate to a friend just the way he did; only *he* could make a poem just the way he wrote it. One of my students said, "To sit in a class of 500 is no achievement; but I know if I don't go and help Tom (a youngster in a deprived neighborhood) with his homework, no one else will." Similarly, a professor of zoology said, "In science today, everyone is working on the same problems, but when I make collages from pebbles and driftwood, I know that no one would make them just the way I do."

Responsibleness and Transcendence

Logotherapy stresses two more areas in which meaning can be found. They are less comfortable than the three mentioned, but they need to be emphasized in sharing groups. Everyone likes to find the truth about himself, make decisions, and feel unique. But logotherapy reminds us that freedom is not likely to bring meaning if it is not exercised responsibly. This message is not always accepted cheerfully by the group participants, especially the young. They sense authoritarianism behind the demands for responsibility—an attempt, as one young man expressed it, "to sneak the Puritan ethic in by the back door." Another resented the observation that "to always have a task to fulfill is therapeutic." Logotherapy, however, distinguishes between responsibility which is given to us as a duty, and responsibleness which we assume ourselves as a self-chosen commitment. In the past, the task prescribed to us by an authority figure—a father, a priest, a king—was meaning-fulfilling, but increasingly the guidelines of authority are questioned and resented. Where duties are rejected, a self-chosen commitment must replace responsibilities with responsibleness. This, however, many people find difficult to accept; they wish to "do their thing," but freedom without responsibleness degenerates into arbitrariness (WM, p. 49).

Closely connected with responsibleness is the fifth area of meaning potential—self-transcendence. Participants in sharing groups have to be led to see that meaning often comes with a commitment that transcends personal interests by acting for the sake of something or someone outside of ourselves. They will remember that in meaningful moments in the past they included at least one other person in their "selfishness." Intellectually they know that this is what they "ought" to do—the entire pressure of religion and morals being on the side of transcendence, and yet it requires an effort to motivate someone to reach out. In universal stress situations self-transcendence comes naturally—in cities under air attack or after an earthquake. The young find self-transcendence in the ecology movement; they are beginning to see that the entire earth is in a universal stress situation, and that the meaning of the moment for mankind is to help each other in order to survive.

Such considerations are far too theoretical for most participants in sharing groups. They have to be led, by personal recollections of instances, to see that life does not owe us pleasures but offers us meanings. If the participants become conscious of these offers and respond to them, pleasure and happiness will come automatically as by-products. Group members also have to be led to see that a person's goal of living is not the elimination of all tension but living in the "healthy" tension field that is unavoidable in his search for meanings, goals, and potentials.

To translate such philosophical concepts into a group experience that will motivate its members is a challenge to both leader and participants who are invited to share responsibility for the success of the group, just as they are encouraged to take responsibility for their lives. The participants are most strongly motivated by the atmosphere of caring in the group and by the example of other members who may have overcome a problem with which someone in the group is still struggling. Together they explore the truths about themselves, their choices, their uniqueness, their responsibleness, and the outreach beyond themselves.

It has been objected that the logotherapist uses an intellectual approach. This is true only insofar as he makes use of the totality of all human resources, including the intellect, the psyche, and the spirit. But it is the inclusion of the spirit that distinguishes the logotherapist from most of his colleagues. His emphasis on the human capacity to reach out for meanings, goals, and ideals draws the participant's attention to the positive aspects of his life while not neglecting the tragic realities of his human predicament. One group member said, "I went to many therapists to find out what was wrong with me. Here, for the first time, I realize what's right with me." The group focuses on what pulls a person toward goals rather than on what drives him to satisfy a need. The participant finds himself in an environment where he can express his hopes as well as his fears without being knocked down. The primary aim of the group is not to adjust a person to society but to allow him to be himself despite the limitations society—and life—has placed on him. The emphasis on choice makes him aware that he can act against some conditions of society with which he disagrees, and that meaning will come from taking up such causes. But logotherapy also shows him that meaning possibilities are still available where change is not possible. In such a group the leader is an integral part in the common search. He serves as an existential example in his pursuit of meaning rather than as a "healer."

Preliminary Surveys

A survey of 82 participants in sharing groups showed that one year later 46 said they had found new directions; 38 of the 46 asserted they had learned to formulate their own meaning orientation. The most important discovery, 35 participants said, was not a specific meaning but the awareness that meaning existed and was available for their discovery. Asked what they found most valuable in the group, 14 listed the step-by-step approach to meaning, 12 their awareness of choice, 10 their recognition of their uniqueness, 6 the emphasis on responsibleness, and the rest, the general philosophy of logotherapy. Almost two-thirds, 52 participants, had found comfort in the idea that the existential vacuum was not a symptom of an approaching neurosis, but rather a challenge to fill it with meanings.

A second survey checked the long-range effect of the groups on interpersonal relationships. As a result of the group experience, most participants said they had learned new things about people's behavior (53 yes, 6 no) and listened more when people talked (43 yes, 18 no). For 43 the experience had a significant influence on how they felt about themselves, while 21 found no such influence. Almost half the participants said that the group experience had brought significant changes in their lives (25 yes, 29 no). Here is a breakdown of how participants felt affected in their relationships with others outside the group:

Get along with:	*Better*	*Worse*	*Same*
Spouse	17	2	17
Children	18	0	22
Boss	6	1	19
People in general	31	0	20

Written comments indicated that a significant number of the participants found that important insights about themselves and others had come as a result of the group experience "on the way home from the meetings," talking to a spouse or a friend who had not attended the group, or "by thinking about it."

References

1. Crumbaugh, J. C. (1973). *Everything to Gain: A Guide to Self-Fulfillment through Logoanalysis.* Chicago: Nelson-Hall.
2. Fabry, J. B. (1974). Application of logotherapy in small sharing groups. *Religion and Health.* April.
3. Frankl, V. E. (1973). Encounter: the concept and its vulgarization. *Journal of the American Academy of Psychoanalysis* 1 (1): 73–83.
4. Holmes, R. M. (1970). Alcoholics Anonymous as group therapy. *Pastoral Psychology* 21: 30–36.
5. Leslie, R. C. (1970). *Sharing Groups in the Church.* Nashville: Abingdon Press.

Philosophical Foundations for Marriage Counseling

Reuven P. Bulka

The counselor facing clients in marriage and love difficulties has now at his or her disposal a great variety of techniques, tests, "games," and exercises.

These techniques, however, according to logotherapeutic beliefs, are likely to bring lasting results only when directed toward the ultimate goal of helping the couple find meaning in their relationship. This essay presents some of the concepts that are oriented toward that end by seeing love as a truly human phenomenon.

Logotherapy on Love

Logotherapy sees love as a vital component of human expression. Truly human love, as truly human life, exists in the spiritual dimension, and is a spiritual relationship between individuals.

Logotherapy emphasizes the responsibleness of the individual to life, his being responsible for the fulfillment of meaning. This responsibleness is based on each person's uniqueness and on the singularity of each moment of his or her life. Each individual is unique, and each of the moments of life can be lived only once, can never be retrieved. The imperative to act flows from the responsibleness rooted in the unique individual capacities combined with the singularity of the moment. It is a responsibleness not to waste the self or time. In Frankl's words, "each moment is irrepeatable and each person irreplaceable." And, more specifically, "Love is living the experience of another person in all his uniqueness and singularity. . . . In love the beloved person is comprehended in his very essence, as the unique and singular being that he is; he is comprehended as a Thou, and as such is taken into the self" (DS, pp. 106–107).

Uniqueness implies the realization that the partner is irreplaceable. In human love the partners are not concerned with what the other "has"; instead they focus on what the other "is." What each one "is" is unique and cannot be duplicated. Singularity stresses the value of each moment in the love relationship, which can be lived only once. The awareness of the partner's uniqueness and each moment's singularity serves as a guarantee never to neglect or take the other for granted.

The Meaning of Love

To Frankl, love is "the ultimate and the highest goal to which man can aspire" (MS, pp. 58–59). It presupposes the capacity of the lover for self-transcendence, which enables him or her to concentrate on values and being outside the self instead of yearning for self-realization or self-expression. In order to love, one must transcend the self toward another being or cause. "Man is never concerned primarily with himself but, by virtue of his self-transcendent quality, he endeavors to serve a cause higher than himself, or to love another person. Loving and serving a cause are the principal manifestations of this self-transcendent quality of human existence that has been totally neglected by closed-system concepts such as the homeostasis principle" (3, p. 44).

Love facilitates the mutual self-transcendence of both partners. It opens up a new world of values and gives to the partners a heightened receptivity to these values.

Self-fulfillment is self-defeating when inner oriented. Instead, it is the outgrowth of an orientation toward transcendence. Love contains its greatest meaning in this context, for it opens up the world of possibility and effects its actualization. Frankl believes that by making the beloved person aware of the inherent potential, the lover helps the beloved make these potentialities into actualities.

Love triggers an upward spiral which causes both partners to attain heights otherwise unreachable. The loved one wants to be worthy of the lover, to grow more and more in the image the lover holds. Each one, in a manner of speaking, outbids the other to be worthier and thus elevates the other. In a good relationship, the partners "bring out the best in each other," just as in a bad relationship they bring out the worst.

Frankl emphasizes that although love can give meaning to life, a life without love is not meaningless. Meaning is unconditional, and love is an effective means to meaning, but other avenues can also lead to meaning fulfillment. Meaning is realized not merely through what is given or denied, but rather through the attitude and approach taken. An unhappy love experience can start a process of self-investigation leading to true fulfillment. Meaning is never in anticipation: it is recognized retroactively through the quality one sees in each situation.

Sex and Love

Frankl's theory on the role of sex in the love relationship follows from his contention concerning the pursuit of pleasure: "Actually, man does not care for pleasure and happiness as such but rather for that which causes these effects, be it the fulfillment of a personal meaning, or the encounter with a human being" (2, p. 101).

For the healthy person, pleasure and happiness are side benefits of meaning fulfillment. If sex is considered the pleasure aspect of the love relationship, then one's primary concern is love itself, the spiritual core of the other. Arousal is stimulated by the body, but love itself is not directed toward the body; it is directed to the other's being.

In human love, sex is not an end in itself. "For the real lover the physical, sexual relationship remains a mode of expression for the spiritual relationship which his love really is" (DS, pp. 112–113). The sexual act is the symbolic immersion in the totality of the partner, and opens up an ultimate togetherness.

For Frankl, sex is really human sex only when it is the expression of love. Love is a primary phenomenon, not an epiphenomenon of sexual drives. It is not sex which brings love; rather it is love which has, as its unique language, sex.

When sex is anything less than expression of a deeply rooted relationship, the partner is reduced to a mechanistic source for the satiation of the sexual appetite. The partner becomes a mutual means to an end, and all physical communication becomes a desecration of individual dignity.

Within this framework, a love relationship does not disintegrate when sex is impossible. If love is primary, and sex a mere expression of that love, then, in situations where renunciation is called for, love remains unabated.

Love and Marriage

Marriage does not follow necessarily from the presence of love, but love is the most important precondition for marriage. If love is the recognition by each partner of the unique potentiality of the other, then marriage is the mutual agreement to meet the world of values as a committed whole, and to complement each other in the actualizing of these values. A partner trespasses the agreement of matrimony when indulging in a diversionary act which neglects and negates the other. Since marriage is commitment to infinite possibility, there is no moment in the union which does not afford the opportunity to realize values, or to fulfill the potential meaning of two lives spent together.

Willful disregard of the singularity of the union manifests itself in many forms, each destroying the exclusiveness of the bond. In this respect, the marriage partners may be guilty of the same deviances that abound in the everyday confrontation with life, namely the failure to realize all possible values. Awareness of this ought-is gap is a healthy state of being, because it at once acknowledges what might have been and what can still become.

The dynamics of fidelity in the framework of logotherapy work in a specific direction. "Certainly, fidelity is one of love's tasks; but it is always a task only for the lover and can never be a demand directed at the partner'' (DS, p. 123). Faithfulness cannot be demanded, it must ensue as the mirror reflection of each partner's commitment.

This ideal of love and marriage is not the norm, even though it is philosophically sound and clinically justified. For many, marriage involves union with a type, easily found and easily replaceable. ''Today's average man takes this type of woman for his erotic ideal because she cannot, in her impersonality, burden him with responsibility. The type is ubiquitous. Just as one chorus girl in the revue can be replaced by any other, so in life this type of woman is easily replaceable. The chorus-girl type is impersonal woman with whom a man need have no personal relationship, no obligations; a woman he can 'have' and therefore need not love. She is property, without personal traits, without personal value'' (DS, p. 115).

The very nature of such a relationship invites its breakdown, for infidelity follows from impersonality. Frankl has also pointed out that where the quality of love is missing, it is compensated by quantity of sexual pleasure.

Logotherapy Applied

Logotherapy's theory of life and love appears to be highly moralistic and idealistic, almost unattainable for mere mortals. Logotherapeutically trained counselors have found, however, that what appears to be moral preachment is really empirical wisdom of the heart, retranslated from its phenomenological context into the language of the man in the street (5, pp. 131–132). It may seem beyond the reach of ordinary people, but the demand for such reaching, if it comes from one's own spiritual unconscious, is therapeutic. In fact, Frankl calls his idealism ''the real realism'' (5, p. 83). ''Humane humans are and will probably remain a minority, but it is precisely for this reason that each of us is challenged to *join* the minority'' (5, p. 84).

Logotherapy examines what is necessary for humans to achieve a state of health. The will to meaning is the primary motivational force not because moral law so dictates but because the human being is healthy when oriented toward meaning. The authentic striving for meaning eventuates in pleasure and self-fulfillment automatically and holds off existential frustration or ''nöogenic neurosis.'' The ideal human is a healthy spiritual being, and logotherapy derives from the ideal. Therapy often bridges the gap between the real and the ideal, or changes the static thinking of the patient to an outward, future-oriented frame of mind.

Marriage illustrates how the failure of an ideal leads to the breakdown of the real. The human love relationship cannot be grounded in the striving for self-fulfillment, or even in the mere fulfillment of the other. In the I-Thou relationship, "this dialogue defeats itself unless I and thou transcend themselves to refer to a meaning outside themselves" (WM, p. 8). Just as the individual is fulfilled tangentially through the actualization of values, so the dual individuality of the marriage couple fulfills their selves through that which is outside them, the objective world of meanings and values.

In this ideal relationship, sex is the language of love, as natural and automatic as speech. But, as to happiness deriving from sex, Frankl cautions again and again that "happiness cannot be pursued, it must ensue." "The more sex is made an aim, the more likely it is to fail. The more a male client tries to demonstrate his potency, the more he is likely to become impotent; and the more a female client tries to demonstrate to herself that she is capable of fully experiencing orgasm, the more liable she is to be caught in frigidity" (4, p. 10).

The approach of logotherapy in cases of sexual dysfunction is to put the matter of sex into the proper perspective.

> A young woman came to me complaining of being frigid. The case history showed that in her childhood she had been sexually abused by her father. However, it was not this traumatic experience in itself that had eventuated in her sexual neurosis, as could easily be evidenced. For it turned out that, through reading popular psychoanalytic literature, the patient had lived all the time in the fearful expectation of the toll that her traumatic experience would some day take. This anticipatory anxiety resulted in both excessive intention to confirm her femininity and excessive attention centered upon herself rather than upon her partner. This was enough to incapacitate the patient for the peak experience of sexual pleasure, since the orgasm is made an object of intention and an object of attention as well, instead of remaining an unintended effect of unreflected commitment to the partner. After undergoing

> short-term logotherapy, the patient's excessive attention and intention of her ability to experience orgasm was "de-reflected," to introduce another logotherapeutic term. When her attention was refocused toward the proper object, i.e., the partner, orgasm established itself spontaneously (MS, pp. 194–195).

The logotherapist is likely to use dereflection and proper intention to counter sexual dysfunction. Another logotherapeutic improvisation might be to permit the patient every sexual access to the partner except intercourse itself, for "medical" reasons. The patient is thus dereflected from the sexual performance because he is not intending it. The logotherapist will not be surprised when shortly thereafter, as is likely, the patient will apologetically admit that the doctor's orders were not heeded, that the sexual act flowed naturally and could not be stopped. Sahakian and Sahakian (6) suggest that in the technique of dereflection Frankl anticipated by many years—in fact, in 1947—the sex therapy approach of Masters and Johnson.

What is true of sexual dysfunction in the narrow sense is true of marital dysfunction in the wider sense. In exploring the reasons for the high divorce rate in America, Weiss (7, p. 8) says that "to a greater extent than seems true elsewhere in the world, we Americans seem to cherish our right to the unimpeded pursuit of happiness, no matter how much sorrow that pursuit may engender."

Beyond this, Americans heavily accent the realization of the inner potential for growth, development, and expression, what could be termed the "ethic of self-realization." It seems increasingly that some aspect of this ethical position is given as a reason for impatience with marriage. And "in several instances in which the pursuit of self-realization did not itself produce the separation, it seemed nevertheless to have contributed to marital strife" (7, p. 10).

Is it possible that the high rate of divorce can be traced back to a philosophy? And, from a clinical view, is it possible that marital problems can be cured through a reorientation toward a different philosophy?

Allport (1, p. 97) once asked, "May not (sometimes at least) an acquired world outlook constitute the central motive of a life, and, if it is disordered, the ultimate therapeutic problem?"

Given Allport's approach and Weiss' views regarding the increase in marital breakdown, it would appear that many cases of marriage difficulty are rooted in a disordered philosophy. Logotherapy's philosophy of self-transcendence as opposed to the "ethic of self-realization" seems as logical a curative for the disordered marriage as its technique of dereflection is a curative for disordered sex.

References

1. Allport, G. W. (1961). Comments on earlier chapters. In: *Existential Psychology,* Rollo May, ed. New York: Random House.
2. Frankl, V. E. (1966). Self-transcendence as a human phenomenon. *Journal of Humanistic Psychology* 6(2): 97–106.
3. ______(1968). The task of education in an age of meaninglessness. In: *New Prospects for the Small Liberal Arts College,* Sidney S. Letter, ed. New York: Teachers College Press.
4. ______(1974). The depersonalization of sex. *Synthesis,* Spring, pp. 7–11.
5. ______(1975). *The Unconscious God.* New York: Simon and Schuster.
6. Sahakian, W. S., and Sahakian, B. J. (1972). Logotherapy as a personality theory. *The Israel Annals of Psychiatry and Related Disciplines* 10(3): 230–244.
7. Weiss, R. S. (1975). *Marital Separation.* New York: Basic Books.

Counseling the Aged

Robert C. Leslie

Logotherapy can make an important contribution to old people by shifting the emphasis from "old" to "people." The body may deteriorate, the psyche may suffer in our youth-oriented culture, but the spirit (noös) remains intact. Just as it cannot get sick, so it cannot get old. Every person, up to the final hour, retains his or her uniqueness, the capacity to make choices, and a will to meaning. The full human being remains, even though earning capacity, eyesight, hearing, or strength may be impaired.

Opening New Fields of Meaning

Many aged persons feel that life has ceased to have meaning because meaning no longer is available in the area where it had been dominant: the retired person has lost the meaning of regular work, the aged mother the meaning of bringing up children, the surviving spouse the meaning derived from marriage. It is the task of the logotherapist counseling the aged to help them realize that meaning potentials beckon in many other areas not closed to them, and, indeed, offer new unexplored opportunities.

In our culture personal identity is so tied up with vocation that a person's sense of meaning is related to his job. If in retirement the opportunity of pursuing a vocation is no longer available, it is easy for a person to lose his sense of meaning. The retired person needs to learn to define his values and goals. It may be necessary for the logotherapist to reorient old people away from a focus on success that has dominated their mature life toward meaning in a wider area than they had found in their career. Many were considered, and considered themselves, machines for the making and spending of money; and now that the machine is out of order and beyond repair, and success is not possible, life seems empty. The logotherapist may have to make his clients see that life may be empty of success, but never of meaning. The meanings of the moment have shifted to new areas: the old person has now the opportunity to correct old follies, deepen compassion, free himself from competitiveness, and learn—not to prepare for a career but for the sake of learning.

The logotherapist can help his client see old age as a time not of stagnation but of potential inner growth. Ideally, the therapist can prepare his client for old age long before the magic 65th birthday; better still, the person, using the principles of logotherapy, can prepare himself. A good time to start a hobby in preparation for retirement, it is said, is in junior high school.

Hobbies, however, hold meaning for the elderly only in rare cases. There is nothing wrong in collecting stamps, playing cards, or sewing dolls. Retirement is certainly the time when a person can indulge in all sorts of activities he was unable to do because of the pressure of routine, and the logotherapist can even help such a person rediscover hobbies long abandoned. But the old person needs to be reminded that his goal is not to keep busy but to find meaning; he now has the opportunity to find meaning in areas he may have neglected, including intellectual pursuits, creativity, human relationships, and devotion to causes. Rather than trivialize his existence with an overemphasis on hobbies and games, the retired person can now use his accumulated wisdom and experience for what he considers important. He has to learn to use leisure not primarily for entertainment and recreation, as he did during his working years, but for life-filling, meaningful pursuits. The aged person may have to be helped to shift his search for meaning from activities to experiences. In retirement, he is more likely to find meaning in people than in things. This switch may be difficult to make. Although the working person finds meanings also in his relationships with his co-workers, the emphasis is on the product, the activity, even his mere physical presence at a certain place at a certain time. In finding meaning in human relationships (experiential values), he does not enter a new field but the emphasis changes: to take a child to a circus, to visit a sick friend, to talk to a neighbor were previously incidental relationships; now they hold the promise of becoming the center of meaning.

Such a switch requires a new goal orientation, a transcendence of personal interests, and an awareness of uniqueness—all tools found in the tool shed of the spirit. The logotherapist redirects the client's orientation from success to meaning; he demonstrates that self-transcendence—helping others—is a source of satisfaction; and he motivates his client to discover his unique qualities that make such help possible. His uniqueness may lie in skills he has learned, in insights he has accumulated, in the time at his disposal which, far from being a liability, may be used as an asset. Most important is the example he can give to others who are also retired. No one can help a retired person overcome boredom and self-pity better than a retired person who leads a full life.

In my counseling I have found the aged receptive to the idea that they can learn to be more effective in human relationships. Many visit ailing friends. With little training, old people can learn new skills that will make their visits more than social calls. I urge visitors to stay in the areas of the friend's concern. If the friend says, "Things are not going well," it is more helpful to let him talk than to say, "Things will be better tomorrow," or to change the subject. I warn the visitor against trying to solve the friend's problem for him. I encourage the visitor to help his friend clarify his own thinking with the expectation that he can find his own solutions. When people are talking about problems, they are not asking for answers. Giving them advice only starts the "Yes but" game. "I've tried it but . . . ." The excuses are many: too old, too expensive, no transportation.

The Element of Choice

Sympathetic listening, however, does not mean inactive listening to endlessly repeated complaints. The biggest contribution the logotherapist can make to persons in restricted situations—convalescent hospitals, homes for the aged—is to draw their attention to the choices they still have. Such persons are inclined to be critical of their situation, the food, the care. I tell the visitors that they themselves have a choice: to listen to the recital of the same grievances, or to apply logotherapy. After listening for a while, they can say, "Yes, I know there are lots of problems in your living here and we have talked about them. I was glad to hear what they are, but I'd be interested in what you are doing with them, how you respond to them." I don't know any better approach to help patients than to dereflect their attention from their grievances and at the same time to make them aware that there is something they can do. The visitor cannot provide solutions but he can help his friend feel optimistic about his own capacity to better his situation. The visitor can express confidence based on real experiences of his friend, remind him of past achievements and of his successful handling of difficult situations, and then throw his influence on the side of his friend's constructive handling of his present life. "I know what you have done," he can tell his friend, "I know you can find a way if you put your mind to it, and I'll be interested to know how it comes out."

The visitor can help his friend list alternatives but needs to resist the temptation to make the choices for him. He gently leads his friend to see the one choice no one can take away from him under any circumstances: the choice of changing his attitudes in situations when the facts no longer can be changed—the facts of deteriorating eyesight or the death of a friend. In teaching the aged how to get a clear perception of another person's situation, the logotherapist not only helps the patient who is being visited but also helps the visitors to find meaning. I have seen an old person find meaning in his newly discovered skill in human relationships which prompted him to visit not only his friends but strangers to whom he was referred by organizations such as the Retired Senior Volunteer Program (RSVP).

Some old people no longer can find meaning in their activities and find it in human relationships; others go the opposite direction—from relationships to activities. Examples are women whose children have grown up, divorcees, and widows. These women have spent most of their adult lives in fulfilling relationships with their nuclear families. When the nucleus breaks up, life as they knew it collapses. A woman in this situation often realizes on her own what a logotherapist would lead her to see: that meaning for her may now lie in activities—she goes back to college, seeks a new career, or takes on voluntary work.

To help the aged find their own uniqueness as an antidote to their feeling of uselessness, the logotherapist may have to fight the stereotypes that society, and indeed the aged themselves, have accepted: that they are helpless, have a poor memory, always complain, and live in the past. Nobody needs to accept the label of a stereotype; he has his own strong points and shortcomings. Some shortcomings must be accepted, others can be disregarded, and some even turned into assets. One 77-year-old woman was on the verge of suicide because she saw herself as a burden to her family. She had been given to understand that her stories about the past were tiring, and she had crawled into her shell. But the counselor found that her grandchildren were interested in knowing something about their own roots. So grandma, the only living link with the past, was made the "family historian." She wrote the family history, and her oldest grandson made a cassette tape on which she voiced incidents of her early childhood. She became so interested in the life of her parents that she went to the attic and looked up old diaries, letters, and souvenirs, and eventually took a trip from California to Rhode Island to find out more about her ancestry from church records and tombstones. When she found among their ancestors soldiers of fortune, gold diggers, and even a pirate who had been executed, the grandchildren urged her to find out more. The last eight years of her life were filled with her "research," and she died in the midst of planning a trip to Scotland to follow a lead about another branch of the family.

Use of Groups

It is useful to suggest to the aged to think back over the past and note down the moments that gave them their greatest satisfaction. When they talk about these moments, the thought naturally comes up: How can some of that satisfaction they once felt be recovered and continued in the present?

Such inventory-taking is profitably done in groups. The memories of one participant trigger similar experiences in others. The participant, in the presence of others who can respond to what he said, will extend his recollecting a bit further. The group leader keeps the accent on the positive values—the successful choices and even the disappointments from which meaning emerged only in hindsight. The tendency to feel sorry for themselves because the past is over can be overcome by the thought of "the full granaries of the past wherein [a person] has salvaged once and for all his deeds and his joys and also his sufferings. Nothing can be undone, and nothing can be done away with" (MS, p. 191).

To elicit meaning in the aged, the group allows its members to share their experiences. Sharing promotes their feeling that they are not useless things on shelves or people who have nothing to contribute and must be entertained. Entertainment, in the form offered in many homes for the aged—bingo games, child-like birthday parties, or lectures by experts—is helpful, but the greatest gain comes in groups where the old people are their own experts. The most successful groups are those where the participants can capitalize on the resources within the group and where leadership emerges from the group itself.

Every person is the most qualified expert in one field: his own life. As a chaplain in mental hospitals and as a group leader in churches I have set up study groups in which the material presented—a Bible story, a poem, a news event—was a means for encouraging participants to relate their own experiences. The purpose was not to pour in a lot of information but to elicit responses to the stimulus of the material. From the story of Jesus's visit to Mary and Martha, for instance, came associations of times when companionship was wanted, when a person was tired from giving out all the time and wanted to take in, when he was exhausted from routine work and needed a quieting atmosphere surrounded by loving people. The participants need to realize that what is expected of them is not an understanding of a book but a sharing of whatever is stirred up in their memory. In teaching pastoral counseling I try to impress on the students that their primary job is not to bring information but to create a climate in which sharing can take place.

In sharing groups, especially those for the aged, the group is primarily not a means but an end. Friendships are formed, self-knowledge gained, a more positive self-image established. These are ends in themselves even if the group was established to accomplish a specific purpose. One group in an old-age home was formed in response to a hospital request for bed slippers. Few slippers were ever delivered, but the group went on meeting in response to the desire for companionship.

Sometimes, however, a group enhances a sense of identity that encourages participants to move on to outside activities. The Retired Senior Volunteer Program in Berkeley, California, needed helpers in convalescent homes. They found it easier to get volunteers living in retirement housing where they had met as a group in preparation for their work than from among single individuals living alone. Occasionally, the inward and outward purposes blend. A group of ladies, aged 62 to 90, meet every two weeks in the Oakland Jewish Community Center to sew clothing for orphanages. They do little sewing at their meetings but there is much chatter followed by private visiting. Nevertheless, an enormous amount of sewing is being done by the participants at home and, for some of the ladies, this work is a major incentive for living. "They crave the appreciation of the group," the group leader commented. The relationship between the internal benefits from the group experience and the benefits from outside activities resulting from the group has been illustrated by Elizabeth O'Connor (1).

Churches and other organizations can also help the aged by including some older members in their working committees. Here the healing effect comes as much from the satisfaction of being one of the group as from being asked as an individual who has something to contribute.

A group can provide a major motivation for old people to seek meaning. It offers the example of participants who have overcome obstacles that are still bothering others in the group, it promotes supportive friendships, and it presents a meaningful activity through the group itself. The group helps participants to shift their attention from feeling old to feeling as human beings who incidentally happen to be getting on in years. One participant reported an experience he had in Vermont when he visited a 103-year-old woman who operated an apple orchard. The visitor admired her apples, and she offered to pick some for him. When he protested, she said, "I'll get the boy to pick a few." The "boy" turned out to be her 97-year-old nephew. By her attitudes, the woman was a logotherapist without knowing it.

References

1. O'Connor, Elizabeth (1968). *Journey Inward, Journey Outward.* New York: Harper.

Approaching the Tragic Triad

Owen Brandon

Logotherapy rejects the use of religion as a therapeutic tool; it denies that a neurotic reaction to life can be cured by the expedient of religious instruction or spiritual direction. It stresses the difference between the aims of psychotherapy and those of religion: Psychotherapy is to help a person restore his mental health and as a by-product he may find faith; religion is to help a person find faith and occasionally, as a by-product, he may also find mental health. But religious experience and mental health are not necessarily the same. These are valid distinctions, yet the psychotherapist in relation to his patient and the minister in relation to a member of his church are at times in similar situations and deal with similar problems.

Religion is concerned with the major problems of human existence: the meaning of life; the nature of ultimate reality; man's relation to the universe; suffering; good and evil; right and wrong; man's relation to man; and the issues of death. No universal agreement exists among the great religions on these matters; but, in the main, all have these basic concerns. It is at such points of concern that human beings break down: when life has lost its meaning or when a meaning for life has never been discovered; when they face ultimate responsibility, under the strain of suffering; when guilt burdens them in their relations with other persons; in the face of death, and in the hour of bereavement.

Patterns

A man in his late forties, a prominent member of a local church in which he was Sunday School superintendent, no longer felt worthy to hold that position and wished to resign. This led to a series of counseling sessions during which other problems not manifestly related to his religious profession came to light. It surprised him to realize that the feelings of unworthiness began shortly after he had missed a chance of promotion in the firm for which he worked during the week. A younger man had been promoted "over his head," and this made him feel "done for," "unwanted," "out of the running." He had hoped for promotion in spite of secret fears he might not succeed in a higher position. He had hoped in vain and felt despondent and frustrated.

As the counseling session progressed, this pattern of hope and fear, disappointment and frustration became apparent in a succession of episodes throughout his life. He could recall such a pattern in childhood, in response to his mother's frequent assertions that he was "no good at anything." She must have been an impatient woman who little understood the aspirations and hopes of her child.

All through his life he was saying, "I want to, but I cannot, because of . . . ." "I want to do what other children do, but I cannot, because I am no good at anything." "I want to be promoted in business, but I cannot be, because there is a younger and better man to be given the position." "I want to be a good Christian and an efficient Sunday School superintendent, but I cannot, because I am unworthy."

As soon as he began to see this pattern, light began to dawn. He realized that by living through the hope-fear-disappointment-frustration pattern over and over again, he had never found a positive pattern by which to live. So he was encouraged to transform the negative "I want to, but I cannot, because of" into the positive assertion, "I want to, and I will, in spite of." The "in spite of" part is most important, for he had come to realize that difficulties and limitations would always confront him; but now he was determined to overcome them. This challenge provided him with a new meaning, suitable for a man who had reached the limit of his wordly ambitions, yet had a useful period of life before him. He took his new zest for life back into his office and continued Sunday School work with renewed enthusiasm. Some time later he was promoted in his firm, though to a position demanding less responsibility than the one to which he had formerly aspired.

This process of breaking the pattern has an important place in logotherapy. Every person develops some pattern for living which prompts him to act in predictable ways. He may be vaguely aware of the pattern and may make occasional abortive attempts to break or change it. Intellectually he knows he does not like it but feels unable to change. Or he may know intellectually that he could change the pattern but lacks the motivating power to effect the change. Others are less aware, or totally unaware, of any pattern. The pattern emerges only through reflection—perhaps in a series of counseling sessions.

There are three essentials to help the person break and reverse an unwanted pattern.

The first essential is a person's realization that there is a pattern. And with this discovery he may become aware that the pattern reflects the basic meaning he has been giving to life.

The second essential is for the person to consider the pattern as objectively as possible, and to try to understand what he has contributed to its emergence. By gaining distance from his pattern, he comes to appreciate the significance of his attitudes toward fear, jealousy, self-seeking, or any other dominant attitude. He comes to accept the fact that by his own attitudes he has contributed to the pattern. This acceptance often is the most difficult part of the process. At first he may say, "Yes, that's the pattern all right, but why did it happen to *me?"* But that very question might bring him up with a jolt; he may see it as perpetuating the pattern.

The third essential is the person's determination to change his reactions, reverse his attitudes, and break the pattern. This reversal of attitude is the final phase. The person has to be helped to adopt positive attitudes toward life. Hence the formula suggested to the man in the story above—from "I want to, but I cannot, because of" to "I want to, and I will, in spite of." It was the difference between his saying "No" and saying "Yes" to life.

Some people are helped by a formula such as this, others by the creation of a mental image. A young man complained that he felt imprisoned by the circumstances of his life and work, yet did not have the strength either to accept the situation or to alter it. Ostensibly his problem was dissatisfaction with his everyday job. He did not dislike his work, but he disliked the place where he worked and found it difficult to get along with his coworkers. In a series of counseling sessions, as deeper problems became apparent, he noticed he used the word "imprisoned" a number of times and in significant contexts. This pattern of liking and disliking, satisfaction and dissatisfaction, with the emphasis on the negative alternatives, had occurred before. It was, as he came to see and express it, "history repeating itself." But he made a deeper discovery—he discovered himself. He saw that disliking and feeling dissatisfied were his own reactions to the circumstances of life, which he had been accustomed to accept as inevitable.

As he had often used the word "imprisoned" he was encouraged to form a mental picture of himself behind prison gates—gates that were not locked and from which, if he wished, he could free himself. He arrived for the next counseling session with a pen-and-ink drawing depicting himself behind those prison gates. This, he said, represented himself as he had been; but now he had made the discovery that he was more *imprisoned within* than by the external circumstances of his everyday life. Then he turned the paper over, and there he had drawn a picture showing the prison gates open and himself as having walked out into freedom. That experience helped him face the problems outside.

The "Value" of Suffering

Life is not all success, however, and room has to be allowed in our understanding of life for the meaning of suffering.

Suffering is an integral element of human existence. Pain acts as a warning system on the physical plane. Inability to feel pain is a symptom of illness, not a sign of health. Pain in any part of the body indicates some malfunction. Without the twinge of pain there would be no awareness of danger to health, and therefore no possibility of cure.

Of course, we ought to reduce suffering where possible. No good purpose is served by enduring avoidable suffering. But a vast amount of suffering, seemingly pointless, has to be accepted by its victims, and alleviated as far as possible by those who have the power to help. Some of today's unavoidable suffering may be avoidable in the future as scientific investigation uncovers causes and cures; but it is likely that a residue of suffering must always be regarded as inevitable, such as the pain in the process of decay and dying. Also, so long as man lives, there will be various forms of emotional suffering, such as sorrow, grief, and anxiety.

The logotherapist sheds light on the meaning of suffering by showing that it is the individual's attitudes which determine whether he is enriched or embittered by it.

Two elderly blind ladies lived alone within half a mile of each other. They had been much alike in circumstances and general outlook before going blind. They were members of the same church and had similar interests. Their reactions to blindness, however, contrasted sharply. The one revolted against her fate: "Why me? What have I done to deserve it?" Her friends and neighbors were kind and attentive, but she was so engrossed in her own misery that she never seemed to appreciate their thoughtfulness; and as the years passed she became hard, bitter, complaining. She resisted, but never succeeded in overcoming her disability; rather, she seemed to be increasingly at variance with herself and her lot.

The other woman was altogether different. When it first seemed evident that she would go blind, she made a conscious resolution to accept the fact and triumph over it. She learned Braille, began to take an interest in work being done for the blind, and accepted blindness as a new experience. She seldom mentioned her blindness, and never referred to it as an affliction. On one rare occasion she told a friend, "Since I have been like this I have learend so much. The world is a different place. Sounds mean more to me now than they did before: I appreciate music more than I did; people's voices mean more to me; and I recognize people by the sound of their walk. And somehow—I cannot explain it—I feel nearer to God."

Life is a mystery, but the word "mystery" has several meanings. It can mean something unknown and unknowable. Given a mystical or religious connotation, it can mean something which once was hidden from man's understanding but now has been made manifest. Or the word can convey the idea of an open secret—something which can be discovered if duly sought.

In logotherapy life is a mystery in this last sense. The meaning of life is not always easy to discern; and as the years pass, and one's circumstances change, new meanings have to be formulated from time to time. But without some meaning, life cannot be lived in its fullness. Each person has to find his own meanings; and the surest way to find them is to recognize life for what it is, respond to its demands, become involved in its activities, and accept the responsibilities—and the limitations—it imposes. The vital difference between the two blind women was that the one had come to terms with herself in her new situation and the other had not.

Guilt

Both pastoral counselor and psychotherapist are familiar with suffering of another kind—the pain and anguish of a troubled conscience. Conscience is that element in a person that weighs and judges his thoughts, feelings, and actions according to his own standards. It is the instrument of self-judgment.

Conscience is an emotionally loaded word. It *stings.* A humorist remarked that most people follow their conscience as they would follow a wheelbarrow—they push it where they want it to go. Yet many people at times are pushed, harassed, and driven by their conscience. I think of the man who was happily married, successful in business, well liked, and who appeared not to have a care in the world. But secretly he was tormented by memories of past indiscretions, and at times he would be overwhelmed and go away and cry. I think also of the woman who for years made herself miserable because of an unhappy memory of something she should have done but had left undone. She could do nothing to alter the situation, but continued to dwell upon it and never forgave herself. The positive way to deal with a troubled conscience is to analyze the situation and act accordingly.

Three kinds of guilt feeling are distinguishable—fantasy guilt, situation guilt, and real guilt. Fantasy guilt is imagined. A little girl heard her mother say to a friend, "When she (the child) was on the way I really wanted a boy." The remark stung the child. She began to feel guilty and to blame herself for not being a boy. Situation guilt implies some degree of culpability. A person unwittingly transgresses some unimportant by-law. Technically he is guilty and, if discovered, might have to pay the penalty. But only by a long stretch of the imagination could he be considered morally at fault. Real or true guilt implies a genuine failure to achieve an authentic standard of behavior. In this sense it is value guilt—the outcome of a subjective feeling that some desires and actions are wrong because they conflict with the chief aims of the self.

A guilt-ridden person needs to come to terms with the reality of the situation as well as with his own conscience. Is he suffering from fantasy guilt, situation guilt, or real guilt? If there is doubt about the nature of the guilt feeling, it needs to be investigated further. If it arises from a sure knowledge of wrong done to another person, it must be acknowledged and, so far as possible, rectified.

Repentance requires humility. Sincere repentance is a healthy exercise. The basic meaning of repentance is a change of mind, a transformation of outlook, a change in the direction of one's life. True repentance arrests the disintegrating process within the self resulting from devastating guilt feelings. It reverses impulses, breaks tensions, resolves conflicts, unites the self within, makes the person whole, and directs the life forces toward worthwhile ends.

Every experienced psychotherapist and pastor knows the intractable nature of some forms of guilt feeling, especially where the sufferer is unable to forgive himself or is dominated by unwarranted fears. Fear is both a cause and a form of suffering.

A woman parishioner, in a private interview, said, "I am afraid. I don't know why, and I don't really know what frightens me, but I am afraid. At night, or when I am alone, I sometimes get a dreadful feeling which I can hardly describe but which I am sure I shall not be able to stand much longer." She said this feeling was not new, she had been afraid for years, but now the fear seemed to be intensifying. She added, "I am scared. I have prayed about this and asked God to take away the fear, and I have asked his forgiveness, for I think that it must be a sin to be so afraid." She was assured that fear is not a sin and was encouraged to give up praying about it. She was told, "Praying is likely to make the problem worse. You cannot stifle fear. What is needed is understanding. If you feel you must pray about it, ask to be given insight and understanding. Ask to be enabled to see what it is you fear." Some weeks later the parishioner came to a further interview relaxed and radiant, saying, "I followed your advice, and now I know what I feared. I was afraid of fear. Now I am no longer afraid."

In several carefully selected cases, Frankl's paradoxical intention has been found helpful. If a person is fearful because he must make a speech in public, he is prodded to say to himself, "I'll show these people how nervous I can be. I can shake like a leaf. When I rise to make that speech I will shake as hard as I can." By thus adopting a lighthearted attitude toward his fear he is able to detach himself from it, to view it objectively, and thus to overcome it. In the counseling situation this technique is to be used selectively and with great care; but I have known it to be of value in several cases where the problem has been simple fear or imagined guilt.

Death

The final fear for many people is the fear of death, and here again the problem is within the purview of logotherapy.

Death is the one certain, universal fact of life. Death cannot be avoided: it must be faced. In a sense, we begin to live when we are prepared to die. Death is a lonely, solitary experience. However tenderly a dying person is supported by others, he has to depart alone. This may appear tragic, but it need not be. For the dying person it can be a triumph. Once more, it is his attitude that is all-important.

Many people fear death, while others go through life without seriously contemplating it: thus, when they come to die, or when they are bereaved through the death of another, they are ill prepared for the experience. Some people seek to cope with death by trying to minimize it so as almost to deny it. Their very phraseology is as a cloak to hide the reality. They say, "If anything happens to me . . . ." Yet it is not *if,* but *when;* and it is not *anything;* it is *death.* Such phraseology tends to build a barrier between a person and the frank acknowledgment of death as an issue of life.

Life can give meaning to death, and death can give meaning to life. A person's view of what happens after death, or whether indeed there is any life after death, seems immaterial; though if he believes in personal survival and ongoing existence in a future life, the meaning of death ought to be that much clearer. But even if death is the end and there is no hope of survival for the individual, death can still be an incentive and inspiration to life, because it limits the time span within which meanings must be found.

Logotherapy, although not a religious system, has much to offer to those whose ministry is the work of pastoral care—it helps us to search for meaning even in situations of suffering, guilt, and death.

VI

Problems of Youth

The problem of meaninglessness is most acutely felt by youth. The young suffer more than other age groups from a confusion about values and goals, and the emptiness that comes with an insistence on freedom without responsibleness. Youth is the time when basic decisions toward meaning must be made—the choice of a career, a life style, a mate, a family. Preliminary studies indicate a low meaning score for people of high-school and college age. In a three-generation survey in the San Francisco area by Diana Young, the parents scored highest, even if divorced; the grandparents second, even when retired or sick; and the youngest generation lowest. Another study by Augustine Meier in Eastern Canada revealed the lowest meaning score for the 17 to 19 years age group, followed by the 13 to 15 years age group. Purvis explores the nature of logotherapy's appeal to youth.

Logotherapy speaks to the young on many levels. It helps juvenile delinquents reorient themselves toward meaning (Barber), offers a method of treatment for emotionally disturbed children (Macaruso), and warns against reductionism in education.

Logotherapy may have an unexpected impact in other areas of concern to youth. One such area is sports. Not enough research is available to justify a full essay, but some remarks will indicate a possible new trend in mental attitudes toward sports in schools and training centers.

The Olympic Committee showed an awareness of this trend when it invited Frankl to a symposium held in 1972 at Munich. He stressed his belief that the healthy person requires the tension that comes from the challenge to stretch toward his potentials. Sports is a healthy way to create such a tension. Only a human being places hurdles in his path in order to jump over them, and climbs mountains simply to see if he can do it. If challenges to probe one's own limitations are eliminated, as it happens in affluence, the young person may create unsafe or socially unacceptable tensions, such as defying authority or seeking thrills through the likes of drugs and fast cars.

If this interpretation of the therapy of sports is correct, the main purpose of sports is not to beat someone else but to challenge one's own capacity. Frankl told his Munich audiences of athletes and coaches, "Try to give your best and you are likely to wind up as a winner; conversely, the more your main intention is defeating competitors, the more liable you are to lose. You then become tense rather than remaining relaxed."

This is a hypothesis still to be tested. There are indications, however, that it is valid for some individuals in certain situations. Upsets in tennis have been explained by the surprise winner against a top-seeded opponent by such remarks as "I had nothing to lose. I didn't expect to win, just wanted to play the best game I could." Austria's Ilona Gusenbauer achieved the world record in the women's high jumps, as she explained in an interview, by her attitude, "I must not tell myself that defeating others is a must." Some coaches are testing the idea that a similar appeal to a team may be more productive than the traditional demand of "Fight! Fight! Win! Win!" The members of the Austrian national soccer team left the field discouraged at half time when they trailed the Hungarians 0:2. They came back in high spirits and tied the score after their coach had told them he would not blame them for losing provided they would truly give their best, whatever the outcome. Baseball coach Robert Korzep told a logotherapy class at the United States International University in San Diego that he successfully applies paradoxical intention to players in a hitting slump. He suggests they tell themselves, "I don't give a damn if I never hit that stupid little ball the rest of my life. I'll show everybody by how many yards I can miss." It seems, this coach reported, that "this technique may be useful.'' Warren Byers, a high-school swimming coach, in an unpublished paper written for the same class, reported the use of dereflection, by focusing the swimmer's attention away from winning and toward swimming his own race. The same technique also prevents athletes from becoming nervous before the meet, being unable to sleep and digest properly. As a side effect, Byers reported, acceptance in the high-school swimming team improved the scholastic performance of previously uninterested students, and prompted others to give up drugs, although—or because—continued membership on the team required much extra work. ''Educators should concern themselves with providing meaningful challenges,'' he declared. ''My swimmers show me that today's young people are not afraid of hard work; in fact, they are hungry for this very thing.''

This brief presentation is not to suggest that logotherapy is about to bring about revolutionary changes in sports, but merely that it offers approaches to the problems of the young in many unexpected fields that need to be explored more fully.

A Philosophy of Youth

George C. Purvis, Jr.

The problems of youth are the problems of man, only more intense, demanding, complex, and critical. Logotherapy, as a philosophy as well as a therapy, offers an answer to the central problem of youth—the awareness of man's transition from essence to existence. Essence is the nature of a thing; the eternal, unchanging realm; the world of ideals; perfection. Essence is what something is intended to be, pure potentiality. Existence, on the other hand, is the reality of "being," with all its imperfections of the real world; the world of matter, time, space, change, and flux; the world as man experiences it—his environment, consciousness, freedom, responsibility, history, procreation, and death. Existence is the world where the potential of essence is actualized, and the questions of values and meanings are asked.

The adolescent awakens to a developmental state radically different than childhood. He senses a demand to act, freely and responsibly, which brings a new sense of anxiety. The physiology of puberty demands physical, sexual awareness and response. Adolescent psychological development often demands an emotional roller-coaster trip. Sociological demands from peers push the youth to extremes in learning how to handle acceptance (and closeness) and rejection (and distance). "Society" demands that the youth deal with authority (both appropriate and inappropriate). In his parental relationship he faces the conflict between dependence and independence.

In the midst of all these experiences, the adolescent begins to feel his freedom and responsibility as personal, undeniable facts—he must decide how he will respond to this knowledge. He knows that he knows!

And he knows "good and evil." He is aware of value as an objective reality, not invented subjectively but discovered as a universal. This awareness means that his response-ability becomes qualified—influenced, colored, measured, "normed," "standardized," "judged."

The adolescent wants to understand what is happening in and around him, and to respond to his life situation. He sees himself not merely as a passing object controlled by internal chemistry and external social forces but also as an active subject who can choose a stance toward the self and the world.

That is to say, during adolescence the will to meaning begins to emerge. The adolescent begins to ask questions about the meaning of his life. These questions are usually more emotive than cognitive—another manifestation of his intense identity crisis. This search for meaning is an attempt to make his life "livable." He assumes there must be a purpose in all his turmoil and tension.

The Basic Mistake

Here the youth is likely to make his basic mistake: he may mistake the unbridgeable tension between essence and existence for another tension which he can and must deal with—the tension between who he "is" and who he "ought to be."

The tension of the essence-existence gap is expressed in the question, "Who am I?" which the adolescent is beginning to ask himself. He knows *that* he is; he knows it from his growing pains. But the question, "Who am I?" is basically one of essence: "Who am I essentially? Who am I ideally? Who am I intended to be? Who am I potentially?" The cliché of the youth "trying to find himself" is true. Every youth begins adolescence with the desire to find himself, his ideal self. This is where the basic mistake originates. Man knows his essential nature as a possibility, and his existential nature as an actuality. He faces the problem of how to live with the tension of living actual existence and not being able to reach potential essence.

But there is another tension which is less frustrating: the tension between who he is and who he ought to be. Both the "is" and the "ought" lie entirely in the dimension of existence. The ideas of who he ought to be are affected by his evaluating the world around him, his comparing himself to others, his observing a variety of lifestyles expressing different values, and the influence of his family, peers, and society. The most powerful contributing factor in the youth's experience of tension between the "is" and the "ought" is his conscience. Frankl sees man's conscience as a human phenomenon which empowers a person to see the meaning of the moment in its uniqueness. Conscience deals with both the "is' and the "ought" and always in the real, objective world. It tells a person what meanings he can actualize in the human dimension of time, space, and personal relationships.

The basic mistake of youth is to equate the two different tension fields: the one between essence and existence; the other between the "is" and the "ought." The adolescent wants to "find himself"—both his essential self and who he ought to be. But these two goals lie in two different dimensions. His essential self is pure potentiality, a concept to be thought about, while the "ought" exists in the real world. The youth can find who he "ought to be" only in the context of the world as it exists and as he responds to it—by looking at himself, relating to himself, evaluating himself, taking a stand toward himself. These responses can never lead him to his essential self.

The mistake of youth, therefore, is dimensional. To the adolescent, because he is driven and pulled in many directions, tension is tension. But since these two basic tension fields lie in different dimensions of human experience, the youth will experience an unbearable, destructive tension if he equates the unbridgeable gap between essence and existence with the gap between who he is and who he ought to be. Man cannot live with the despair that the "is" cannot move toward the "ought." He must be able to believe and experience that what he is can become what he ought to be, in specific, unique, successive life events. According to logotherapy, "it is the meaning of meaning to set the pace of being" (WM, p. 51). In this sense the "ought" is an expression of meaning and the "is" an expression of being.

Because the adolescent cannot bear the frustration of being tantalized by an essential self that can never be actualized, he tries to escape the tension. He cannot live with the belief that, for him, meaning can never set the pace of his being.

Three Escape Routes

There are three ways to escape the tension. The first is a denial of any tension—an attempt to return to the womb, to escape reality. It is a denial of essential humanness because it is a denial of consciousness. The primary symptom is withdrawal. The youth denies that the external world has any influence or demand upon him. He refuses to participate in the realities of life. The results are disastrous, and can ultimately lead to psychosis or suicide.

The second way for youth to escape the unbearable tension is by totally identifying with essence, and denying the part of reality that is experienced (spiritually, mentally, and physically) as existence. One symptom of this attempted escape is extreme idealism, the identification with utopian ideologies. This attitude may take the form of fanaticism, political or racist. Or it may take the form of fundamentalism. Many youthful expressions of fundamentalist religion today—both Eastern and Western—are examples of youth trying to escape the real world. They become toally identified with religious dogma which they consider "pure" essence. Religious fantasies, language, and rituals dealing with the realm of essence (an expression of magic) become a hiding place from the ambiguities of existence. Religious fundamentalism is an attempt to achieve "certainty" at the expense of existential honesty, that is, of being human within existing reality. Another symptom of this second escape attempt is idealistic romanticism. Many early marriages may express the desire to be absorbed into the partner. Complete identity with the mate is to be a way to avoid existential awareness. The result is often painful for the young couple when they see that romantic love does not abolish the basic tensions in life.

The third escape route is the opposite of the second. Here, the young people become totally immersed in existence, with no awareness of essence. They are determined not to let essence make any demands upon them, since they "know" that essence can never "really" be actualized, "I can never reach perfection, so I'll just do what I feel like doing." Rejection of the ideal and total identification with existence lead to sensualism, as in sexual promiscuity. Pleasure becomes an end in itself, and the sexual partner becomes a means for escape. Other examples of entirely living in existence are compulsive playing, busyness, or work. These physical activities demand immediate energy, and avoid holding still long enough to consider essence.

Much of the misuse of drugs also is an attempt to identify totally with existence. The young person avoids the pull of essence as a part of reality by using drugs to "create" essence in his own mind. He attempts to manipulate meaning by manipulating his own body chemistry. Logotherapy rejects the validity of this invented meaning. The person who is intoxicated by drugs "finds subjective meanings, but they are not the objective meanings in wait for him, to be fulfilled by him" (1, p. 48).

If the young person gravitates to the pole of existence, the consequence is boredom, apathy and, as an extreme result, nihilism, a dangerous expression of the collective neurosis of our day, "nihilism is not a philosophy which says there is only nothing, *nihil,* and therefore no Being; nihilism is that attitude toward life which says that Being has no meaning. A nihilist is a man who considers Being, and above all his own existence, meaningless" (PE, p. 121).

None of these escape routes works because the youth's manipulation of essence and existence does not abolish the tension field between the "is" and the "ought." He is still in a bind. Only now he feels a greater sense of meaninglessness because the consequences of running away from the original tension have intensified it. Avoiding tension, however, is not desirable. Logotherapy maintains that man's basic aim is not an inner equilibrium and the reduction of tensions. "I deem it a dangerous misconception of mental health that what man needs in the first place is homeostasis. . . . What man really needs is a sound amount of tension aroused by the challenge of a meaning he has to fulfill" (PE, p. 83).

Homeostasis may result in the existential vacuum. The person today, doubting traditional values, "not knowing what he must do, not knowing what he should do, . . . often does not even know what he basically wishes to do" (1, pp. 41–42). This uncertainty may lead to three dangers: conformism, totalitarianism, and noögenic neurosis deriving from despair over the apparent meaninglessness of life.

Logotherapy's Answer as a Philosophy

Logotherapy's first answer to the problems of youth comes through its philosophy. The logotherapist can correct the mistaken belief that essence is equivalent to "ought," and existence equivalent to "is" by showing that there are *two* tension fields, in different dimensions. The tension between essence and existence lies in a vertical dimension transcending the human, whereas the tension between the "is" and the "ought" lies entirely within a horizontal, the human dimension.

Thus, the logotherapist gives a new option to the adolescent who believes he is in a destructive tension field with no escape. He shows that the is-ought gap can be bridged because this tension field lies fully in the dimension of the real world. The "ought" is a real possibility; it is not mistaken as "pure" potentiality. A youth can become the person he believes he ought to become, but not all at once, or once and for all. There will always remain a gap between who he is and who he ought to be, but both lie in the same human dimension.

This human (noëtic, spiritual) dimension where meaning is found is where the youth "finds himself" as he actualizes unique meanings in the objective world. His will to meaning is not frustrated by a dimensional mistake about reality. Now he can have a relationship with the objective world rather than denying the tension, escaping to "pure" essence, or becoming indifferent to essence by exploiting existence for pleasure.

However, awareness of his human dimension does not eliminate all tension. It is not another form of homeostasis. Though a meaningful life is now a possibility, it is not a certainty. Man must still live with his freedom and responsibility. He has to decide, from moment to moment, how to respond to the meanings offered to him by the situations of which his life consists, although he never can be certain to have found the right answer. This, however, is a livable tension—not a tension of the vertical dimension that causes despair in the youth because he believes he cannot become who he "ought" to become. In the human, horizontal dimension, despair has been eliminated, though tension remains. This tension arises from the real possibility that the youth *can* become who he ought to become. The tension no longer is a frustration, it is a challenge.

Logotherapy's Answer as a Therapy

Logotherapy's second answer to youth is through its therapy. Here, too, the logotherapist functions in the human dimension where it is possible, but not guaranteed, for youth to find meaning. The therapist does not dispense meaning as a cure-all. He must consider the idealism and impatience of youth. He must challenge his client to discover meaning moment by moment, and in the wholeness of life's experience. He must remember that the youth is in a critical period, looking for direction. The problem of vocation and mate selection are examples of basic questions a young person cannot "evaluate" in a cold, analytic atmosphere. "The crucial agency in psychotherapy is not so much the method, but rather the relationship between the patient and his doctor . . . [their] 'encounter'" (PE, p. 144). An aloof, analytical therapist will only further frustrate his client's will to meaning, if the latter is suffering from an existential vacuum. If an anxious or depressed youth is made to feel like an object, a thing to be analyzed, he is likely to turn away from professional sources of help.

Certainly, the logotherapist has no exclusive claim to the importance of the personal encounter in therapeutic relationships. But he does have more responsibility for personal encounter because his therapy is primarily creative rather than analytical. The logotherapist must be careful that his personal statements about meaning, and his affirmations of value, are not subtle ways to manipulate the youth—to "give" him answers.

It is true that no method of psychotherapy is free from values. Every therapist transmits his value system to his client. Logotherapy makes this fact explicit. It is forcing every helping profession to admit the realities of values, especially in personal relationships. To be unconscious of the value system operating in one's own lifestyle is to be "controlled" by unconscious, and therefore unchosen, values. When the logotherapist confronts the youth with the fact that some values are objective possibilities to be realized in the real world, he is not at the same time forcing those values upon the youth. To bring values into the consciousness of a client is not to force values upon his conscience.

Logotherapeutic intervention, far from negating the youth's freedom and responsibility, directs him away from his escape routes and toward his human dimension where he can find self-fulfillment. Outside the human dimension, freedom becomes necessity (at the pole of essence) or license (at the pole of existence), and responsibility becomes legalism or nihilism, respectively.

This active confrontation is not a necessary therapeutic function for all youth. Some are already living in the human dimension, and not trying one of the escape routes. Rather than intervention, their need may be the supportive, creative aspect of logotherapy. This is where logotherapy becomes more educational in its "healing through meaning." Here, the therapist responds to a youth who is already asking the questions about the meaning of his life and can apply logotherapy's philosophy in a therapeutic way.

> As a kind of first aid in such cases—despair over the apparent meaninglessness of life—it seems to me necessary to show these young people that their despair is nothing to be ashamed of, but rather it is something of which to be proud. It is a human achievement because it is a prerogative of man not only to quest for meaning, but even to question it—to challenge the meaning of life. It is right if young people have the courage to do this. However, they should also have patience enough to wait until, sooner or later, meaning becomes clear to them, rather than commit suicide immediately out of an existential despair. (1, p. 43)

Even though logotherapy is educational, it does not heal through "teaching." The life style and personality of the logotherapist are important in challenging the youth to get on with the task of living a meaningful life. Neither the logotherapist nor the teacher can give values to the students.

> The only thing we can give is the personal example of our own dedication to the great cause of research, science, and truth finding. . . .

> Nor are logotherapists and teachers moralists who give meaning to others. The only thing we can tell [the individual] is that life has a meaning, never ceases to have a meaning, that life retains its meaning to the last moment, literally to the last breath. . . . From these individually discovered meanings, new values and morals may develop. Sooner or later morals in the old sense will give way to a new concept of what is good and what is bad. Good will be defined in terms of what promotes the fulfillment of the meaning of a being, and what is bad will be defined in terms of what blocks the meaning-fulfillment of a human being. (1, p. 57)

When working with an adolescent, then, the logotherapist acts as "spiritual midwife"; he helps the youth complete his transition from essence to existence by "delivering" him into the human dimension. The therapist does this by challenging the youth to be responsible for fulfilling the meaning of his own life. Here, logotherapy is "education toward responsibility."

Implied in logotherapy's task of educating youth toward responsibility is the task of value education. The logotherapist, not being a moralist, helps the client to realize values by stressing the necessity to sharpen his ear to the weak voice of his conscience.

> In an age such as ours, that is to say, in an age of the existential vacuum, the foremost task of education, instead of being satisfied with transmitting traditions and knowledge, is to refine that capacity which allows man to find unique meanings . . . A lively and vivid conscience is also the only thing that enables man to resist the effects of the existential vacuum, namely, conformism and totalitarianism. (WM, pp. 64–65)

The logotherapist, then, helps the youth who is often guilt-ridden because of a neurotic conscience, develop his true conscience. This is possible, not because the therapist has *the* true conscience model, but because he has *a* true conscience model. The therapist focuses not upon his own conscience, but upon the values that "pull" him into the fulfillment of meaning. The hierarchy of values is not found on any handy chart—the therapist still cannot become a moralist, but he is not without value orientation to relate to the youth.

This creative, nonmoralistic nature of logotherapy offers a challenge to anyone who works with youth. Logotherapy, it is hoped, will never develop into a narrow discipline of therapy or education, but rather will permeate other helping professions. If a young person is to find answers to his problems, he will do so most quickly and genuinely through a community of "logos." He is not likely to find self-fulfillment in isolation, nor in the vague crowd called the "mass," nor in groups that escape to essence or existence. The young person can best "find himself" in his relationship to an *accountable community.* This may begin with only one other responsible "thou"—but it is the beginning of logos for that youth.

To say that logotherapy should permeate society is not an ideal in the realm of essence. The need for logotherapy to create a more accountable community is an "ought." For values and meaning are not private possessions—they are public, and the human family is responsible for the transmission of life's meaning.

References

1. Frankl, V. E. The task of education in an age of meaninglessness. In *New Prospects for the Small Liberal Arts College,* S. S. Letter, ed. New York: Teachers College Press.

Juvenile Delinquents

Louis S. Barber

In 1966 the United States President's Task Force on Juvenile Delinquency found that 223,000 juveniles were under probation supervision, at an estimated cost of $75,916,000 per year (4). But the process of probation, as practiced in most institutions, in the vast majority of cases not only fails to rehabilitate the juvenile but contributes to his further delinquency or subjects him to a victimization process within the institution:

> Official action may actually help to fix and perpetuate delinquency in the child through a process in which the individual begins to think of himself as delinquent and organizes his behavior accordingly. That process itself is further reinforced by the effect of the labeling upon the child's family, neighbors, teachers, and peers, whose reactions communicate to the child in a subtle way a kind of expectation of delinquent conduct. (4)

The lack of meaningful rehabilitation by adult and juvenile rehabilitation and correctional facilities throughout the United States is evidenced by the admission of many state officials that incarceration in most instances does not rehabilitate the convicted individual. Massachusetts and California are in the process of closing most of their correctional facilities. However, a controlled environment for some offenders will be needed for some time. Wholesale closing of institutions without tested alternatives holds the potential for a national disaster, in the form of an increasing crime rate and a reaction, with devastating effects, on criminal justice.

This essay describes one juvenile rehabilitation facility which has experienced an extremely high rate of successful rehabilitation—greater than 80 percent. This success is attributed to a highly integrated and eclectic model, drawing from many fields, including the concepts of the humanistic and behavioristic schools of psychology and a method of systematic planning (3). However, for the purpose of this presentation I have attempted to isolate those aspects of the program which can be attributed directly to the concepts of logotherapy.

Logotherapy at Twin Pines

The value of logotherapy for rehabilitation lies in its basic assumptions that the human dimension enables man to reach out beyond himself and make aspirations and ideals part of his reality; that he primarily seeks not pleasure but life tasks, and that the deepest pleasure comes from accomplishing these tasks; that man is free to make choices about his activities, experiences, and attitudes, and that his freedom allows him to change himself—to decide not only what kind of person he is but what kind of person he will become. Each individual is seen as unique, and when he loses his sense of uniqueness he is less likely to be aware of his will to meaning. His uniqueness can be used to make choices which, to be meaningful, must carry responsibleness—to himself, to others, to causes, to the requirement of the moment.

Logotherapy came to Twin Pines High School with an administrative change in 1964—a new school principal and a counselor trained in humanistic psychology. The school's purpose has been to provide meaningful educational experiences for boys, ages 15 to 18, incarcerated at Twin Pines Ranch, a Riverside (California) County Probation Department rehabilitation facility. Each boy is committed to Twin Pines Ranch by order of a superior court judge. In this presentation, both the school and the ranch are viewed as part of the same program, as one therapeutic environment.

With the new school administration came a new concern about the effects of the institution on the self-concept of the individual student; also a new emphasis on responsibility for all students in the program, and on meaningful experiences in all its phases—academic, vocational, and interpersonal. One goal was to return uniqueness to every boy in the program.

Before his commitment at Twin Pines Ranch the typical youngster had experienced a lack of goals, frustration, despair, failure, and criticism. The experiences at Twin Pines Ranch are diametrically opposed to those of his earlier life. The ranch has neither fences nor locked dormitories. Each boy is counseled, by staff members and other boys in leadership positions, that responsibility for what he becomes is his, and no one will force him to change his beliefs or to conform.

The new arrival is introduced to the other boys and the staff during a special ceremony at lunch. The introduction is made by a fellow student, one who has assumed increased leadership responsibility, and closes with the statement, "We welcome you to Twin Pines and remind you that this is the first day of the rest of your life."

Responsibility for the construction, care and maintenance of all buildings is placed in the hands of the boys as a major part of their education. Half of the school day is occupied by specific vocational training.

Responsibility for attitudinal value changes is placed in the hands of the boys. As a youngster begins to take hold of his life, he is given responsibility for some other new boys in the program so that he sees life's meaning through a degree of self-transcendence. Leadership roles must be earned and are granted only when a boy asks for the additional responsibility. This responsibility is given only when those in authority are sure the individual asks for leadership because his attitude is positive toward his fellow students, not because he desires power.

The academic phase of the educational program is individualized. A boy progresses in school according to his ability and effort. The emphasis is on accomplishment, not on length of time spent in class. The teacher's role is primarily that of tutor, not lecturer. The program attempts to dignify education by making school a status part of a boys program. For example, night study is a privilege granted to the student only after he has been in the program for three months, has shown a desire to assume responsibility for his schooling, and has demonstrated that he is not destructive toward himself or others. A student may take only one academic subject at a time until he has proved his ability to absorb individualized instruction; then he may take a second class provided he has maintained at least a B average. He may apply for all-day academic school after seven and a half months at Twin Pines, if he has decided to remain in the program to graduate from high school, and has indicated by his behavior a sincere positive attitude toward himself, the program, and his fellow students.

The vocational part of the school program is designed to help students develop skills and knowledge in vocational areas. Each job undertaken has value and is needed as part of the total program. Vocational training is given in masonry, carpentry, electricity, plumbing, auto mechanics, cooking, agriculture, laundry service, garage services, and welding. The program includes four classroom hours of on-the-job work and one classroom hour of vocational theory each day.

Academic teachers are selected for their ability to work with students in a supportive manner, motivate student growth, and change their attitudes and behavior. Vocational staff members must be skilled tradesmen.

Goals of Twin Pines

Twin Pines aims at the rehabilitation of adjudicated delinquent boys and their return to society as both meaning-oriented individuals and fully functioning adults. Specifically, the objectives are:

To help the student acquire the academic skills necessary to function at grade level or beyond, as determined by standardized tests.

To build trust and respect for all members of the treatment environment.

To provide the student with the opportunity to assume responsibility for his rehabilitation and his life.

To assist him in learning to accept fair rules and regulations, distinguish between fair and unfair rules, and develop alternative methods for dealing with differing social situations.

To build his self-confidence and acceptance of others.

To provide a meaningful educational program for each student based upon his unique personality and ability.

To make school a pleasant and rewarding experience without threat of failure or punishment, geared to the student's ability and designed for his success.

To make academic competition a personal goal within the individual rather than turn students against one another by external control.

To enable the student to attend both high school and vocational classes and see the relationship between education and future vocational goals.

To develop the student's creative values, his attitudinal values concerning self-control and self-improvement, and acceptable social values dealing with peers, adults, and authorities.

To teach basic academic skills and independent thinking so that the student can solve problems by himself.

To assist him in becoming a fully functioning person and build his self-concept so that he may realize his own worth and that of others.

I conducted two studies which provide information on how meaningful rehabilitation was undertaken.

One study (1) investigated changes in self-concept during incarceration; the other explored changes in students' attitudes toward a "will to meaning" measured by The Purpose in Life Test (2).

The first study showed that the Twin Pines rehabilitation program altered the self-concepts of the subjects in a positive direction at or beyond the .01 level of significance for fifteen of the sixteen measures tested and at the .05 level for the sixteenth measure; and that the program tended to produce a more normal population than was true of the population before treatment. The study concluded that the program was highly effective for therapeutic rehabilitation; that a therapeutic environment, eclectic and pragmatic in nature, based upon the client's decision to take control of his behavior and responsibility for his choices, significantly altered his self-concept; and that it offered a meaningful, realistic rehabilitative program for those who had been judged as delinquents in need of rehabilitation.

The second study indicated that Twin Pines, as an example of a logotherapeutic environment, influenced the will to meaning of incarcerated boys, in a positive direction. A group of 15 students, Anglo-White, Mexican-American, and Black, were given the Purpose in Life Test (2). Their initial test scores were from 58 to 109, with a mean of 86.13—well within the range showing a lack of clear meaning and purpose. Six months later their scores had climbed to 93 to 124, with a mean of 103.46. Although only three students scored above the 112 level indicating definite purpose and meaning, all of them had progressed significantly toward that goal.

Three Case Histories

The following three case studies illustrate the effect of the Twin Pines program in kindling the individual's will to meaning. Each study reflects one of Frankl's valuing areas—attitudinal, experiential, and creative.

Case Study Reflecting Attitudinal Values

Norman Socio-ethnic background: Black lower class
Father: Absent from the home
Mother: A long-time welfare recipient
Place in family: Eighth of 16 children
Birth Date: 1948
Entered Twin Pines: 1965; Released: 1966
I.Q. (CTMM): 78

School file. Anti-social behavior. Frequently truant, many fights. Several suspensions and finally expulsion because of leading an attack of Black students on a white school-bus driver. Full file of negative reports from teachers.

Probation report. Norman has been unable to make any adequate adjustment to his school or community. He is beyond the control of his mother. After the unprovoked attack on the bus driver and Norman's expulsion from school, the school district filed a complaint with the Riverside County Sheriff's Department which led to Norman's arrest and placement at Twin Pines.

Twin Pines narrative. Norman entered Twin Pines High School with a low reading test score (2.3). Placed in diagnostic classroom. First objective: to change student's negative self-image, and thereby effect a change in his feelings toward others. He is highly defensive and easily provoked. Appears to have good athletic ability although he was never allowed to participate in high-school athletics because of his poor academic grades and low marks in citizenship. Shows interest in masonry and has been assigned to masonry as a vocational choice.

During the first few months at Twin Pines, Norman was a constant problem for both probation and academic school staff. He did well, however, in masonry where he seemed to have natural ability.

During the summer Norman continued to function below normal standards but was not removed from the program and was realistically praised for his vocational skill.

In the fall Norman joined the football team and did well enough in his academic studies to be allowed into an exploratory science program based more on field experiences than on the classroom work. In football Norman showed his natural ability to lead others and play a role as a team member. In his first football game he was expelled for unsportsmanlike conduct—having kicked an opposing player and cussed out the referee for calling him on the play. He was, however, not removed from the team. Norman's head coach was a Black, a former high-school all-American football player. Later in the season Norman was made defensive co-captain with responsibility for coordinating the defensive team. These two factors (in the principal's opinion) were responsible for changing Norman's image of himself and his role as a member of society: he was able to identify with a member of his own race who exemplified the highest qualities of citizenship and was given responsibility for others as well as himself.

During the baseball season Norman played regularly on the first team, alternating as an outfielder with another boy. During an early game Norman missed a fly ball which resulted in a decisive run being scored. Later in the game he was replaced by the other boy. Norman, with tears streaming down his cheeks, related to the school principal that he didn't mind being taken out of the game, but he hated letting the team down. He played the entire season and was selected by his teammates as the most inspirational player. Norman later commented that it was the white boys on the team who had voted him the honor.

At his own request, Norman remained at Twin Pines four additional months to complete his high-school education. He lettered in three sports, became a good student of masonry, and raised his reading skills above the seventh-grade level.

Follow-up study. Upon release he received additional help from the Riverside County Office of Economic Opportunity and began training at a local junior college. Some months later, after he was taken off probation, he withdrew from the college; he had received a "D" in one of his academic subjects and was suspended from the football team. As of January 1972 he has had no further contact with the law for any known violation, but his whereabouts at this time are unknown to the Riverside County Probation Department.

Case Study Reflecting Experiential Values

Mike — Socio-ethnic background: Anglo-Saxon, middle class
Parents: Mother and father divorced
Place in family: Second of three children
Birth Date: 1948
Entered Twin Pines: 1965; Released: 1966
I.Q. (CTMM): 93.5

School file. Emotionally immature and upset by parents' separation. Physically small, always trying to be the "big man." Constantly causing problems in class by talking out without permission.

Probation report. Mike has created numerous problems in his neighborhood and at school. He has been reported several times for being a voyeur (peeping Tom), and vandalizing his neighbors. Mike ran away from his home in June of 1965. The deputy probation officer recommended Twin Pines Ranch for placement after a psychological report showed Mike's feeling of hostility toward his parents and school and a deep-seated dislike for himself due to feelings of inferiority caused by his physical size.

Twin Pines narrative. Mike was placed in the regular school program, and in masonry as a trade area. His masonry instructor was concerned because Mike's size might pose physical difficulties for him. However, although weighing only 114 pounds, he could handle a wheelbarrow full of cement weighing 80 pounds or more as well as any of the other boys. During the first months Mike was frequently involved in minor incidents because of his "daredevil" behavior. His school progress was good, as he found that in his academic work he was not competing with anyone.

During the winter he transfered from masonry to agriculture where he was able to take advantage of a natural interest in science. During that winter Twin Pines was flooded. The bridge from the main campus to the agricultural area was washed out. The stream, which was twenty to thirty feet wide and from eight to ten feet deep, was impossible to ford. Mike, either because of his daredevil nature or concern for the hundred head of cattle stranded without food on the other side of the stream, climbed a tree which hung over the stream, tied a rope to a limb and swung "Tarzan-style" to the other bank. He stayed with the animals all of that day and night and part of the next day.

From this experience on, Mike continued to grow in his concept of self-worth and his ability to handle most of his personal problems. He requested permission to remain at Twin Pines in order to complete his high-school education.

He left Twin Pines a high school graduate. His I.Q. score had increased almost 19 points, to 112.

Follow-up study. Mike enlisted in the United States Army in 1967. As of January 1970 he was serving as a paratrooper with an airborne division. He has of this date had no known further violations.

Case Study Reflecting Creative Values

Henry — Socio-ethnic background: Mexican-born
Place in family: Second of 13
Father deserted family; mother ill
Family on welfare
Date of Birth: 1948
Entered Twin Pines: 1966; Released: 1967
I.Q. (CTMM): 94

School file. Dislikes school, has no goals. Is a chronic discipline problem. Has been suspended several times for fighting. Is highly belligerent. Irregular attendance.

Probation report. Henry has committed a variety of unlawful acts: a series of minor offenses including petty theft and shoplifting; one known incident of grand theft (auto) and one known burglary. The recommendation to place Henry at Twin Pines is based upon several incidents which indicate that he is beyond the control of his mother and developing a life style of increasing criminal behavior.

Twin Pines narrative. After Henry was tested with a general aptitude battery, he began working in the welding shop. This activity provided him with a creative value that showed him the meaning potential of his life. In his high-school experience, no meaningful relationship had ever developed with the school's staff. No attempt had been made to show him a way out of his dilemma. Most important, no method had been provided for him to learn a trade that would enable him to make a living.

In the welding shop Henry worked with an instructor who had been a professional welder. In Henry's welding program he attended four periods a day in vocational class work and one period of vocational theory. Because of his ability, Henry was increasingly called upon to repair and build needed equipment and parts, none of which was to fulfill a project, but which was necessary for the functioning of the working ranch program. He helped and supervised the creation of I-beams to support the roof of an auto-shop building, and also created an A-frame which lifted all the I-beams, exceeding more than 2,000 pounds. The A-frame was attached to the bed of a large truck and is still in operation today.

Some of Henry's academic class work was coordinated with his vocational interests, but many subjects were not. He completed all state requirements for high-school graduation.

In his vocational program Henry received the Twin Pines outstanding student vocational award for his work as a welder. He was made foreman of his welding shop. With help from the school vocational coordinator, Henry began working in a welding shop in Riverside.

Follow-up study. Henry is working as a welder in Los Angeles, is married, and has a child. He has had no further contact with law enforcement since his release from Twin Pines in 1967.

Logotherapy has much to offer the rehabilitation planner at a time when the need for therapeutic rehabilitation centers in the United States is urgent. A significant correlation exists between the self-concept of the individual and his value structure, and the key to successful rehabilitation often lies in changing the offender's self-concept and his process of valuing. Logotherapy's attitudinal, creative, and experiential value categories provide a logical foundation upon which to build a meaningful rehabilitation program.

References

1. Barber, Louis S. (1972). Changes in self-concept among delinquent boys in a therapeutic community. Unpublished Ph.D. Dissertation, United States International University.
2. Crumbaugh, James C. and Leonard T. Maholick (1959). *Purpose in Life Test.* Brookport: Psychometric Affiliates.
3. Kaufman, Roger A. (1971). System approaches to education: Discussion and attempted integration. In *Social and Technological Change: Implications for Education.* Eugene: Eric Clearing House on Education's Management. Published by the Center for the Advanced Study of Education Administration, University of Oregon.
4. U.S. President's Commission on Law Enforcement and Administration of Justice (1967). *Task Force Report: Juvenile Delinquency and Youth Crime.* Washington: Government Printing Office.

Treating Emotionally Disturbed Children

Mario C. Macaruso

Driving home from my office on a hot afternoon, I heard the sirens of police cars, ambulances, and fire trucks converging on a burning house. Firemen rolled out hoses, attached them to hydrants, spouted water, raised ladders. In all this programmed activity, no one made any effort to seek out the cause of the fire. Their mission was to put it out as quickly as possible and save whatever could be saved of the still unburned portion of the house. As I watched, I thought about the technique I have used with school children who are referred to me for character disorders, truancy, poor reading, or school phobias.

Mike, age 7, was referred because of his destructive behavior at school. He ripped pads and books, and broke chalk, crayons, and especially pencils. His older brother dominated him, and his father's attitude was that a boy had to learn to take care of himself. The classical analytical formation would suggest an unresolved hostility conflict directed toward both his father, the authority figure, and his brother with whom he had an unresolved sibling rivalry. Whatever the source of Mike's problem, the usual analytical therapy did not change his destructive behavior. Fortunately, he manifested his hostility toward things rather than people. In therapy I attempted to do the exact opposite of what he was forbidden to do. Gathering up a few dozen pencils and a few pads, I took them into my office and commanded, "Mike, here's a lot of pencils. I want you to break them all, first in half, then in quarters, and even smaller if you can." Mike looked at me quizzically, a smile curling his lips. He broke a few and said, "Is that enough?" "Oh no," I replied. "You have to break them all, and when you're through we'll get another dozen, a hundred, a thousand." At this point Mike's eagerness to break pencils waned. When I prodded him to break more, he blurted out, "That's the stupidest thing anybody has ever asked me to do, and I won't do it." Then we both broke out laughing, thinking how stupid it had been to break all those pencils in the past. The following week the teacher reported that Mike was no longer breaking school objects and was amazed at the change. It had been an application of paradoxical intention.

Tommy, a twelve-year-old boy, dreaded going to Junior High; he withdrew completely when his gym teacher scolded him for having long hair and threatened to send him to the girls' gym. Tommy developed strong psychophysiological reverberations. He was obsessed by the phobia that he would faint if he went even near the school. A physical examination showed him in good health, and the advice of the physician to buck up and forget about fainting only served to reinforce his obsession. There was clinical evidence that Tommy, an only child, had been protected from childhood on and at times would develop headaches and stomach problems when confronted by an unpleasant decision. His mother was quite gullible in this respect, and Tommy became skillful in manipulating her. His father's occupation often kept him away from home, so his mother was his major influence. When I told Tommy that the examination confirmed our opinion that he had no physical problems, he became only more despairing because he saw no cure for his fainting. After several weeks of cutting classes, his mother and I persuaded him to ride with me near the school. Before we approached the school I ordered him to faint, to go into the deepest faint he could and to stay there. He was puzzled by my insistent order. I pleaded, threatened to faint for him if he didn't, and stopped the car to make it easier for him to faint. Tommy looked at me with an expression between mirth and wonderment and said, "What's the use of trying? I can't do it."

We had several more sessions, each one closer to the school. Every time I implored him to faint I noted more amusement and less anxiety.

Finally Tommy said, "I can go back to school now. If I think I'm going to faint I'll tell myself to do it, so I'll find out that I can't." The immediate goal—getting Tommy back to school—was attained. Conferences with the school staff made them accept Tommy's "mod" look, and Tommy's father was persuaded to spend more time with the boy.

Paradoxical intention appears diametrically opposed to behavior modification which tends to suppress the deviant behavior for a more socially accepted one. The wellsprings of paradoxical intention are more deeply internalized: the phobia, obsession, or compulsion is figuratively uprooted rather than covered by some other behavior.

The principles of paradoxical intention are sometimes used in nontherapy situations. A father told me that he cured his six-year-old son's resistance to going to bed at 9 P.M. by agreeing to a "contract" to let the boy stay up all night. The youngster was flushed with victory in winning this major issue with his father. At 9:30 the youngster yawned, but his father reminded him of the contract. At 10:30 the boy was curled up before the television set fast asleep but was awakened and ordered to stay awake. The more the father insisted that the child must not sleep, the more the youngster pleaded with his father to let him go to bed, which the father refused to do. When the tears welled heavily in the boy's eyes another contract was negotiated. The boy was permitted to go to bed on one condition—that he never again balk at the time established by the parent. The father reported years later that from that time on going to bed had no longer been a hassle between himself and his son. What the father had done was to aid and abet the negative behavior in his son to a point of exaggeration.

New Directions in Schools

Arthur G. Wirth

"Men will happily tolerate great discomfort, discontinuity, and frustration if—and only if—they are working for some purpose, toward some end, which they consider wise, true, exciting and meaningful" (3, p. 181). These lines were written at the opening of the savage sixties by Keniston, a perceptive observer of American youth. He noted that the vocabulary of social commentary was dominated by terms like alienation, estrangement, withdrawal, indifference, dissatisfaction, noninvolvement, neutralism—"the *direction* of cultural change is away from commitment and enthusiasm to alienation and apathy."

Despite the brief flurry of hope when President Kennedy called people to join him in a new reach for greatness, the sense of meaninglessness spread among the many Americans facing change and experiencing the erosion of authority and of ancient belief systems. There was no way to escape the traumas of the sixties: the bitter confrontations over race with brutal lynchings, the burnings of the cities, the witnessing on television of the assassination of inspired leaders, and the hated killings in ten years of war in Southeast Asia, compounded by the fraudulence of high government officials.

A generation had grown up suffering from the "collective neuroses of our times." As children they sat in front of television sets watching a parade of violence, fictional and real, interspersed by shabby untruths of the advertisers. As they grew older they heard successive warnings of impending global disaster—population explosion, pollution of air, water, and land, an energy crisis. As young men they confronted relentless efforts by their government to conscript them for a war they detested. We had produced the first generation of Americans to grow up with an enfeebled optimism for the future.

Such events caused bitterness in young and old. As we crossed into the seventies the nation's journals reported an epidemic of mental depression. The afflicted suffered from feelings of hopelessness. Tens of thousands resorted to the pseudosecurity of alcohol and hard drugs. Others, more fortunate, found doctors who prescribed newly discovered pills. Any help was welcomed but more was needed than pills or therapy. The compelling task was to regenerate institutions so the young could find life worth living.

The Failures of Education

Outside the family the school is the institution that most engages the time and energy of the young. If we are to produce a generation which takes joy in living, the nation's teachers will have a vital role to play. It would be pleasant to report that educators are ready to pick up the challenge, but in an age when men have lost a consensus about who they are and what they might become, it is too much to ask that teachers have a clear vision of their task. Yet, the nation's educators received a heavy blow in Silberman's findings that the dominant feature of the nation's schools was mindlessness (5).

One of Goodman's essays on life in the U.S. may help us understand Silberman's conclusions. In weighing the country's future Goodman described the decisive question as "whether or not our beautiful libertarian, pluralist and popular experiment is viable in modern conditions" (2, p 274). He identified the challenger to that humane tradition as the Empty Society of mindless productivity and a cost-accounting concept of technocratic efficiency. He felt the Empty Society had become predominant. In education this emptiness expressed itself in feckless recitation and quizzing on textbooks, new primarily in their form and gloss. "Getting an education" meant "taking courses" without engaging oneself—with the purpose "to get ahead." More schooling meant more dollars, and all A's would get you a free ticket to the ballgame. Teachers were paid to "cover ground," and quantitative evidence of coverage could be demonstrated by the neat columns of figures in the blue-lined grade book. For many, confidence in the school was in direct proportion to "wins" of its football and basketball teams. The system worked, though, in roughly sorting out numbers according to the technocratic needs of the corporate bureaucracies. The most prominent idea now coming out of Washington is to apply the "systems analysis" scheme, used by industrial giants, to students, teachers, and administrators. Segments of knowledge are engineered in instructional packages, and quantitative measurements on standardized tests are to yield scores to establish performance ratings. The taxpayer then is supposed to know he has gotten his money's worth.

No plan I have seen so far includes provisions to weigh its psychic costs. To reduce feelings of alienation and self-estrangement does not appear a promising course to follow.

But the other America—the libertarian, pluralist, populist America—is still alive. From it comes fresh efforts to counter mindlessness by humanizing learning, and by using tools and techniques to help persons become more authentic and autonomous—more capable of taking responsibility for their own learning and actions. Perhaps the most important priority for teachers who wish to take a stand is to get their own lives and work in order. The quality of the teacher as model is crucial now when many youths feel alienated from their studies and estranged from the generation of their parents. "What you are speaks so loudly that I cannot hear what you say."

A serious encounter with logotherapy and its image of man can be a source of strength for both teachers and students who wish to live fulfilled lives in our time of turmoil.

Logotherapy and Education

As readers of this volume know, the logotherapist helps his patients overcome meaninglessness not by giving them formulas for happiness or success but by asking them to face up to their duty as human beings. To be human means to have the capacity and responsibility of creating values. The individual overcomes despair and finds meaning by what he does, what he experiences, and how he handles the unmanageable, tragic situations in life. If a person's primary concern is "What can I bring to this moment—this situation?" he can live with a sense of respect for what is represented in himself and all other men. While living from this base of self-acceptance he may free himself from the enervating need to please others and to pursue "success" compulsively as defined by the social system.

A person's essential task, then, becomes simply to be what he can be, to do what he can do, to honor what he sees through his own eyes, and to say truthfully what he perceives—to live authentically. He must resist influences that pressure him to live otherwise. The basic task is always present—and always within his capacity.

If the young are bewildered by chaos and violence in the world, the way to help them is not by preaching moralism. They will learn in their education that it is possible to live with meaning by experiencing teachers who demonstrate authenticity in the quality of their lives and work. The life styles of teachers and schools are contagious. If teachers are cynical, bored, and defeated the young will get the message, no matter how many literary classics they are required to read.

This point is made by Huston Smith: "Consider first the teacher's life impact. There is no way to assume that meaning will increase in children's lives during their school years, but the best hope for its doing so is to have them sharing time and space with teachers in whose lives meaning runs strong enough to be contagious" (6, p. 71).

The mindless quality in classrooms derives largely from the insipid "right answer" game in which teachers elicit monosyllabic answers to questions of who? what? when? where? The circle cannot be broken until teachers work from some other models.

Logotherapy provides a clue by saying that man basically is a being reaching out for meaning to fulfill. So why not work from a style of learning in the formative years which coincides with man's essential nature? We do have a relevant American philosophy of teaching and learning. The concept of teaching as meaning-seeking in a climate of trust is the ideal in Dewey's educational theory. It is caught in Dewey's technical definition of education as "that reconstruction of experience which adds to the meaning of experience, and which increases ability to direct the course of subsequent experience"

(1, p. 91). An experience is educative if it makes a difference in the way one sees oneself or one's world. Teaching in terms of this guideline can eliminate much of the pointless busy work.

Education as Meaning Seeking

There is no neat formula for teaching in this way. We may note, however, some characteristics of a teaching style that is consistent with it.

The teacher, for example, must have done more than "take courses." He must have thought his own way into the significance of his subject matter. He must be a continuing scholar so he can free himself from a text. Then he can be alert to the questions of his students, and from these he may get inquiries under way to guide them. On occasion, students may see perspectives he had not discerned. To share the probings of a dedicated teacher is to learn the disciplined skills of question raising, hypothesis projecting, and data collecting necessary to test truth claims against experience. To discover the possibility of integrity under committed teachers is to have first-hand evidence that authentic truth seeking is possible.

More than intellectual rigor is required. The teacher must be present as a person to his students. Caring and concern are essential in a climate of trust. To free a student from the feeling of being manipulated as an object, he must experience occasions when a teacher will really see and hear him, and will be flexible enough to let him move with an interest of his own. Such a teacher will take off his masks and be a human being among other human beings who happen to be students. This does not mean that he will smother his students with sentimentalism. He will make all his resources available to his class—his knowledge, experiences, books, creativity, and feelings; but he will not overlook that the students themselves present a vital resource and will, therefore, encourage each student to contribute the unique knowledge and experience he may have in the subject under discussion.

The teacher committed to meaning seeking will experiment with his teaching style to learn how to shift responsibility for learning to the learners. He will become a facilitator rather than a taskmaster. He will move in the direction of helping individuals or groups to define their own goals and to devise means for reaching them.

Becoming responsible and authentic requires each individual taking responsibility for the choices he makes. The meaning-seeking teacher, therefore, will give students practice in making value choices both in their conduct and in questions to be discussed. If, for example, a class has agreed to behave a specific way to take a bus trip to a museum, and if the agreement is broken, the trip must be terminated. This is in the tradition of Rousseau's principle of discipline through natural consequences. To practice value choices is also possible in academic study. On a given issue, such as whether public tax support should be given to religious schools, the teacher may tell students to identify polar positions on a continuum; then work with them to explore alternatives between the extremes. Each student takes a personal position with an understanding of the consequences.

The grading system can be a hurdle to autonomous selfhood. The attention of the student easily gets diverted from taking responsibility for his own learning to competing for "marks" and the favors of the teacher. There are alternatives. When teachers begin with collaborative planning and goal setting they can include student participation in evaluations. Ideally, evaluation should help the student see to what extent his goals have been realized. Evaluation helps him gain realistic understanding of what he knows and doesn't know. Honest confrontation of these facts is important for nurturing responsible selves. Grading, however, is another matter. Using marks to pit students against each other in competition for high standing on test score curves tends to hurt rather than help relationships. If grades must be assigned, the teacher can at least be frank about his policy, or see if students wish to participate in arriving at grades for the course. The problem, however, is not simple because competing values are at issue. Teaching in a climate of trust requires genuine concern for each individual but society's institutions require evidence of competence. We have to live with some problems until circumstances change or until our own experiments yield happier solutions.

Humane Education

I am aware that many teachers work under conditions which make a mockery of human efforts at teaching. But unless we clarify for ourselves the directions we ought to pursue and commit ourselves to achieving what is possible, we will be at the mercy of regimentation or succeeding waves of spurious fads. It is also true that we usually have more room to experiment in traditional settings than we care to admit. We often shy away from our own innovations because we fear failure.

In the sixties discontent with the limitations of standard schooling became widespread. A variety of alternatives emerged, some out of efforts to apply new technology to education and others out of the desire to humanize learning. Change, however, does not necessarily mean improvement. Access to a wider range of alternatives is salutary, but the effects of the alternatives must be weighed critically.

The new technology in the form of teaching machines, programmed instruction, and performance-oriented measurements patterned after system-management techniques in industry, may free teachers from drill and drudgery. But if "competency-based instruction" gets attached to monolithic testing procedures, with teacher effectiveness rated in terms of how well students score on standardized tests, then students and teachers may become victims of a new technological tyranny.

Educational alternatives aiming at humanizing learning may also fail if they strive only for an ill-defined "freedom." Aimlessness and chaos can produce their own kind of tyranny, so that no one has a chance to learn. Yet, alternative schools have opened important new options in education.

They have tended to limit groups to sizes which permit face-to-face living and planning. They prefer to place themselves in out-of-school settings so students and faculty can have a voice in deciding how to furnish their learning-center home. Students participate in designing individual and group learning projects. They draw on places and people in the larger community as learning sources. Our daughter, for example, who is now in an alternative public high school, planned and completed an extensive project on nutrition—readings, activities, and simple experiments. This was done under the guidance of a nutritionist at a near-by hospital. Alternative schools can become communities for learning where role differences between teachers and students are reduced and communication can take place at a level which does not seem possible in larger, more bureaucratized schools.

Limitations on Science

Logotherapy plays a role in still another issue of educational theory: the issue of what limitations should be accepted in the definition of man as it is developed by the sciences.

Science is the great transformer of our time. Education, like all other institutions, has been profoundly affected. One of the fundamental influences has been its effects on our image of man. Mechanistic behaviorism, the prestigious school of social science, works from the reductionist doctrine that man is "nothing but" a conditioned organism. He is "beyond freedom and dignity," to use Skinner's term. Behaviorism holds simultaneously two contradictory propositions: that all of man's actions are environmentally determined, and that he should choose to abandon some social practices and create new arrangements supportive of his needs. Despite the contradictions, the potent message which comes through is that man is no more than a conditioned organism.

This mechanistic ideology which teaches that free choice is an illusion undermines the idealism of the young and their aspirations to initiate reforms. In Frankl's terms, the young are taught that man, "in the final analysis is nothing but the battleground of conflicting claims of an id, eg, and superego, or . . . the mere outcome of various conditioning processes . . . that human existence is solely to be explained in terms of either the machine model or the rat model . . . then you should no longer be surprised . . . when people finally behave like automatons" (7).

A recent encouraging development, relative to Frankl's position, has been the broadening of research models beyond the mechanistic framework. One of the American leaders in this development was Abraham Maslow. Trained in the John Watson tradition of behaviorism, Maslow later began to practice as a therapist and became interested in understanding the conditions that make for productive, mature persons. As a knowledge seeker he examined the concepts and tools available from his behaviorist training and found them of little value for the questions he wanted to investigate. As he put it, "If the only tool you have is a hammer it is tempting to treat everything as if it were a nail." Maslow acknowledged that research of value can be conducted within the dominant mechanomorphic model. But he rejected that model as the sole system for studying human personality. "I believe mechanistic science . . . to be not incorrect but rather too narrow and limited to serve as a general philosophy." He came to the conclusion that the first obligation of science is to confront all reality as man experiences it—to describe, to understand, to "accept" all that is. He maintained it was a cardinal sin to deny reality, or to refuse to confront parts of it because they are not amenable to the best honed tools at hand (4).

The debate in psychology has significant implications for educational theory and practice. Educators cannot help being affected by theories of human learning and by explicit and implicit assumptions about the nature of man. Fortunately we are not confronted with a sharp either-or choice. Behaviorists and humanistic psychologists provide insights about learning from different perspectives. Educators reflect the pluralism in psychology by generating from the behaviorist viewpoint ideas like programmed instruction and behavioral objectives in curriculum building; and from the humanistic theories come proposals for "open classrooms," for dealing with affective learnings, and for improvements in interpersonal communication.

Frankl challenges the predominant reductionist doctrine that man is "nothing but" a conditioned organism. His image of man as the "responsible self" contains rich suggestions for education and other institutions. His philosophy is designed to help men escape from depression, apathy, and defeat and become autonomous persons who accept responsibility for acting on the world, experiencing it more deeply, and accepting the inescapable with courage.

References

1. Dewey, John (1916). *Democracy and Education.* New York: MacMillan.
2. Goodman, Paul (1965). *People or Personnel; Decentralizing and the Mixed System.* New York: Random House.
3. Keniston, Kenneth (1960). Alienation and the decline of utopia. *American Scholar.*
4. Maslow, Abraham (1966). *The Psychology of Science.* New York: Harper and Row.

5. Silberman, Charles (1970). *Crisis in the Classroom,* Part II. New York: Random House.
6. Smith, Huston (1965). *Condemned to Meaning.* New York: Harper and Row.
7. Smith, Huston, and Viktor Frankl (1963). Value dimensions in teaching. Transcript of a TV dialogue. Pasadena, Calif.: The Religion in Education Foundation.
8. Taylor, Harold (1960). In *Unitarian Register.* Midsummer.

VII

Addiction

Addiction is a complex problem consisting of components that have their origins in body chemistry, psychological drives, and sociological pressures. Logotherapy's contribution to possible solutions lies precisely in the complexity of the problem. Because logotherapy sees man as a totality, it cautions against solutions that lie exclusively in chemistry, psychology, or sociology. And it stresses as most important a largely neglected component, the addict's spirit and his human resources. It stresses the humanity of the addict who is seen—and is helped to see himself—not as the helpless victim of his body chemistry, drives, and peer pressure, however real and strong these may be. These factors have to be dealt with as well as present scientific knowledge allows; but, as Fraiser and Holmes indicate in their essays, the crucial step is to motivate the addict to change his pattern. Motivation to change, as Lukas points out, may be triggered by the addict's realization that he has reached a point below which he does not want to go, or through people who care, or through the example of others who successfully have overcome their addiction. All these motivations are being used by such organizations as Alcoholics Anonymous and Synanon. Logotherapy's contribution is its affirmation that man's prime motivating force is his will to meaning, that he has choices, and that he can, within limitations, take on the responsibility to be in charge of his decisions. Much research needs to be done about addiction; but it is clear that labeling someone "hopeless," a fiend, a criminal, or a psychopath will only serve as a self-fulfilling prophecy. If the logotherapist, or anyone else, is able to orient the addict toward a goal that he himself sees as meaningful, the first step toward health will have been taken.

Alcoholics

Robert M. Holmes

The problem of alcoholism is physiological, psychological, religious, cultural, and philosophical; and any effective treatment must take this multidimensionality into account.

Since logotherapy sees man as a physiological, psychological, social, and spiritual being, it treats the whole person. And since logotherapy assumes that man's most important dimension is the noëtic, it approaches him through this dimension.

The alcoholic dramatically illustrates logotherapy's claim that the fundamental human quest is for meaning and that the basic human problem is the existential frustration of meaninglessness. "Fundamentally, the alcoholic is not sick because he drinks, but . . . he drinks because he is sick, and then becomes doubly sick," wrote Wise (6, p. 37). The "sickness" from which he suffers is the existential vacuum. Beyond all psychological explanations for alcohol addiction (an authoritative father, an overprotective mother, conditional acceptance, emotional rejection, etc.) and beneath all physiological explanations (metabolic imbalance, deficiencies of the pituitary-adrenal-gonadal triad of endocrine glands) I have often found, as the major frustration, the inability to find meaning. Nature, abhorring a vacuum in the psychological sphere of reality as much as in the sphere of physics, rushes in with deceptive remedies to fill the emptiness—all manner of busyness, addictions, artificial thrills, and ill-placed commitments. But all such frantic efforts toward hyperactivity fail to obscure the central issue, man's frustrated quest for meaning. As surely as we fail to understand who man really is, so we fail to meet his real need until we meet him at the point of his existential frustration and help provide an authentic content for his existential vacuum.

So fundamental is man's noëtic dimension that for many, alcohol is an attempt to provide a religious answer to a religious problem. William James recognized this relationship.

> The sway of alcohol over mankind is unquestionably due to its power to stimulate the mystical faculties of human nature, usually crushed to earth by the cold facts and dry criticisms of the sober hour. Sobriety diminishes, discriminates, and says no; drunkenness expands, unites and says yes. It is in fact, the great exciter of the Yes function in man . . . It makes him for the moment one with the truth. Not through mere perversity do men run after it . . . The drunken consciousness is one bit of the mystical consciousness.(4, p. 377)

Alcohol is a spurious answer to the religious quest, but the quest itself must be taken seriously. Hence the appropriateness of logotherapy—a psychotherapy which not only recognizes man's spirit, but actually starts from it. Clinebell (1, p. 145) reports the case of a "seemingly hopeless alcoholic" who, just before committing suicide, was asked by a psychiatrist, "Who can help you?" He replied, "No person or institution. Only what I do not now possess—a belief, a faith in something outside myself, something stronger, even more overwhelming than my weakness—some form of spiritual substitute that yet evades me."

Logotherapy makes available that "spiritual substitute" for alcohol, or, better, the spiritual reality for which alcohol is a substitute. Logotherapy does not seek to replace religion, rather to provide a stance in dealing with persons whose needs extend beyond the physical and psychological. Viktor Frankl (2) speaks of "spiritually-concerned medicine"; and although he distinguishes between the "healing" function of medicine and the "saving" function of religion, he points to an area of overlapping concern to which he gives the name "medical ministry." This phrase is particularly suited for the alcoholic whose medical (physiological-psychological) ailment requires a pastoral, spiritual concern. With respect to the alcoholic, a therapist must deal with, indeed "minister to," areas of life which are as directly related to a minister's responsibility as to a physician's—namely suffering, guilt, and death—the three categories of existence which Frankl speaks of as the tragic triad.

To say the will to meaning is basic to the alcoholic and its frustration fundamental to his alcoholism is not to suggest that the psychophysical manifestations of alcoholism are unimportant. A careful understanding of both the physiological and psychological problems of alcoholism are most helpful in dealing with its victims. Logotherapy provides a frame of reference within which these dimensions of the problem take on proper perspective.

A Logotherapeutic Rationale for Alcoholism

Man's basic striving, the will to meaning, is found in the statement of an alcoholic, reported by Clinebell (1): "A fellow sleeps to get strong, so he can work to get money to eat and have a place to sleep, so that he can get strong and be able to work and get money, and so on." The anxiety expressed in such statements is the logical outcome of a natural quest; it is the alcoholic's response to the frustration arising from the existential vacuum. Emptying the bottle becomes either a frantic effort to fill the vacuum or an evasive action to avoid it. In either case the vacuum is dealt with inappropriately and self-destructively. This fundamental "sickness," when escaped by means of the bottle, becomes a "double sickness"; and the spiraling pattern of drinking becomes more convincing evidence of the meaninglessness of life. What begins as a question becomes a certainty. Treatment of the alcoholic requires handling the vacuum in a more appropriate and creative manner.

In my experience, the first point at which logotherapy helps the alcoholic is an affirmation that the questions plaguing him are legitimate, and his raising them is an essential human undertaking. An honest wrestling with such questions can be frustrating, painful and anxiety-producing. It is precisely as a sedative against anxiety that alcohol becomes increasingly appealing as an avenue to achieving "homeostasis," a state of tranquility or lack of tension.

Effective treatment of the alcoholic requires an examination of whatever stands in the way of an honest confrontation with his existence. Logotherapy identifies three principal obstacles. First is this very desire to achieve homeostasis, as if the ideal state for man is to be free of all tension and conflict. Although man must relieve certain levels of tension, an underlying tension is essential for his existence: the tension in a field where one pole is represented by a meaning to be fulfilled and the other by the person who has to fulfill it (MS, p. 167).

A second obstacle is reductionism through which man is seen in less than his fullness. Alcoholics who are likely to deny their noetic dimension need to acknowledge and appropriate that dimension of their being.

A third obstacle is "pan-determinism" whereby a person may be misled to assume that he is powerless to exercise his freedom—freedom that is never entirely extinguished no matter how limited it may become. Sociological, biological, and psychological factors may limit the development of the alcoholic's situation, but they do not abolish his attitudinal freedom.

The Meaning of Meaning

The search for meaning is central, but how does one come to terms with the question of the meaning *of* life or the discovery of meaning *in* life? To tell the alcoholic that his problem is rooted in his frustrated will to meaning may not, of itself, be very helpful. It may become more helpful, however, as the nature of this "will" and, in fact, "the meaning of meaning" is more clearly defined. This goes a bit beyond the thought of Frankl himself, but is an attempt to elaborate on his fundamental insight.

Meaning means many things. Ogden and Richards (5) list sixteen different definitions of the word "meaning." Four of these bear particularly upon the personal life quests of individuals, including alcoholics.

The first sense of meaning deals with coherence, the relatedness of everything. To ask, on this level, "What is the meaning of life?" is to ask, "How do all things fit together?" How, for example, do the complexities of life experiences hold together in any kind of discernible pattern? To ask "What is the meaning of *my* life?" is to ask "How do I fit in with all else that is in nature and in history?" Often alcoholism is brought on by an event which shakes a person's world or his understanding of it. He may sense that he "doesn't belong," that he is not related in any genuine way to others or to events. The sense of inferiority so often associated with the alcoholic personality is an expression of this unrelatedness. Feelings of failure or inadequacy, of being superfluous are all expressions of this sense of "loss of meaning." Alcohol takes the edge off that unpalatable sober existence until the addictive drinking itself adds to the inadequacy, further intensifying the sense of unrelatedness.

A second sense of meaning concerns definition. To ask what something means may be a request that it be defined. On this level the quest for "the meaning of life" is a desire to know what life really is or what "real living" is. The personal phrasing of this question is, "How am I defined? Who am I?" The alcoholic often suffers from an identity crisis, which increases as his drinking pattern seems to develop two different personalities—drunk and sober. He drinks to escape a self he finds unacceptable. With the support of alcohol he becomes a personality that is freer, more relaxed, apparently more pleasing to others and hence to himself. But again, the spiraling development of the drinking pattern becomes vicious. The drunken, illusional self is at first a welcome substitute for the sober, real self which gradually becomes more repellent. Yet in time the intoxicated self also becomes repellent, until the alcoholic loses any stable sense of selfhood.

A third sense of meaning is associated with the word purpose. To ask, "Does life have a meaning?" is to ask, "Is there an overall, encompassing purpose to life?" The personal question is, "What is the intention of my life? What is its goal, its direction?" A number of my alcoholic clients feel their existential frustration most keenly as an absence of direction or purpose. The pain of purposelessness may be dulled by the daily after-work martini or the suburban housewife's bourbon bottle, which may evolve into a more regular intoxication. One can endure limited purposes, or even purposelessness for a time; but ultimately the human spirit cries out for a goal. A case in point is the alcoholic quoted earlier who saw the endless cycle of sleep, strength, work, money, sleep as leading nowhere. The cry is for a sense of direction that links one's life with something beyond oneself.

The fourth aspect of meaning, and the one most crucial to the treatment of alcoholism, deals with what Ogden and Richards refer to as "the place of anything in a system." Here, meaning illuminates an event with reference to the past and the future. "What is the meaning of unemployment? How did it come about? Where will it lead? What is the meaning of my life? What are the influences of the past? Of my goals?" As the alcoholic experience develops, the consequences of his life become increasingly vague and the problem of meaninglessness is compounded. Life seems inconsequential, including the drinking itself, except in a negative way. It is on this level that such words as "obligation" and "responsibility" become relevant. This definition of meaning entails the nature of the alcoholic's response to all his past experiences and the future consequences of his decisions and actions. The question asked on this level is not so much "How do all things hang together?" or "Who am I?" or "Where am I going?" but "What should I do?" Life, to be meaningful, must not only attempt to answer the first three questions, but also it ultimately must be lived responsibly. The alcoholic's life is characterized by increasing irresponsibility. The more he drinks to satisfy the search for meaning, the further he gets from any genuine satisfaction of that search. Ultimately, the core of the alcoholic's treatment is the cultivation of a new kind of response to reality. Logotherapy is well equipped to kindle such response because its starting point is consciousness of responsibility.

Starts in Treatment

In outlining four distinct but related definitions of meaning, I have tried to refine the insight that the will to meaning is the underlying drive, and its frustration the underlying problem of the alcoholic. His successful treatment requires confrontation with all four definitions of the meaning quest. In terms of coherence, the alcoholic has to accept the fact of his alcoholism and include it within his total life spectrum rather than separate that reality from his consciousness, repress it, or pretend about it; treatment begins with the affirmation, "I am an alcoholic." In terms of identity, the alcoholic needs to regain a sense of personal worth—not an easy achievement in view of the degree of personal, professional, social, and family disintegration to which the alcoholic's drinking may have led. In terms of intention, treatment requires the discovery of a new purpose. Finally, treatment requires the development of a new response to reality. The starting point may vary with the individual. Logotherapy is, after all, an approach to therapy rather than a system. The techniques employed are not predetermined, but depend on the particular combination of therapist and patient.

One might begin, for example, at the point of the client's identity problem and his need to repair a badly damaged sense of personal worth. The logotherapist will stress the value of the patient's past contributions and of his potential for the future. The therapist's stress of "attitudinal values" will help the patient achieve or retrieve a sense of personal integrity and importance by seeing his opportunities. If the patient can not create anything, and thus possesses few "creative values"—and if his sphere of experience is limited, thus providing few "experiential values," he still has the limitless field of "attitudinal values" which arise from the manner in which he faces his particular situation.

Or the therapist might begin at the point of need for the discovery of a new purpose. Logotherapy maintains that no life is purposeless and every person can find purpose no matter what his history. The elderly citizen or the terminal patient, for example, can choose to look upon death as a fitting climax to a meaningful life, or his response to the inevitability of death can itself become an event of ultimate meaning—perhaps the highest meaning a mortal life can achieve. Alcoholism is sometimes like death in the sense that it is an inescapable fact. Some alcoholics cannot look hopefully to the day when they will not be alcoholics. They can only confront the fact, accept it, and decide how they are going to deal with it—respond to it.

What conceivable possibility is there that an alcoholic, often with besmirched reputation and a radical loss of self-respect, might ever regain a positive personal definition? What chance is there for him, having perhaps lost job and family, to discover a purpose that includes his alcoholism as part of the coherent pattern of his life rather than circumventing it? What is the hope that an alcoholic might respond to his own addiction and his own drinking history in such a way as to make it consequential to himself and others? On the surface the prospects look slim indeed, but the answer emerges from an understanding of the makeup of man and his needs. The founders of Alcoholics Anonymous came upon it in their own experience four decades ago; namely, that the alcoholic's own experience offers him the opportunity for personal spiritual and social growth and provides him with special credentials for making a positive contribution to the lives of others. Alcoholics Anonymous, in fact, without any conscious logotherapeutic orientation, provides striking evidence of the validity of Frankl's basic thesis: that a recovery of meaning is the ultimate avenue to the recovery of health. If man were really dominated by a will to pleasure, as Freud suggested, there would be little hope the alcoholic would suspend the pleasures of perpetual intoxication for the agony of sobriety. Of, if man were really dominated by the will to power, as Adler contended, there would be little expectation that the artificially empowered drunkard would yield to the weaker state of sobriety. It is in terms of a regained sense of meaning that the pain and frustration of sobriety are risked by the alcoholic as a viable option for life.

The Advantage of Group Therapy

This largely cerebral analysis of the meaning of meaning and its implications for treatment may lend precision to the meaning-quest of the alcoholic seeking help. But intellectualization is not the road to recovery from an ailment so complex. True therapy comes not through rational realignment alone, but through a new emotional understanding. A sense of meaning is both an intellectual perception and an emotional awareness. There is a severe limit to how successfully one can "talk someone into" adopting a more mature response to life and behavior patterns that make for sobriety. This is precisely what drives many family members and friends of alcoholics to distraction, to whom it seems so obvious that all the alcoholic needs to do is simply stop drinking.

Frankl warns that logotherapy "is as far removed from logical reasoning as it is from moral exhortation" (MS, p. 174), but reports that he frequently employs a good deal of argumentation. He speaks of the need to "correct" a patient, to "make him see," to "convince him" or to "change his attitude." No doubt there are situations in which this approach is appropriate, and flexibility of approach is one of the strengths of logotherapy. Alcoholics, however, are generally not among those upon whom such direct methods are successfully employed. For the alcoholic, genuine therapy results not so much from exhortation as from experience. To be sure, exposure to a dynamic and charismatic preacher or speaker or counselor may become considerably more than a lecture; it may become a total experience in which intellectual, emotional, and spiritual dimensions of the multidimensional man are touched. Frankl's counseling sessions undoubtedly are often so charged with his own personality that they become total human experiences; but few of us possess that kind of charisma.

A context broader than the one-to-one counseling situation has distinct advantages for eliciting a more complete experience. The group context offers such customary advantages as mutual support, the provision of a "laboratory" for working out and observing feelings and relationships, and a shift of responsibility from therapist to patient. For the alcoholic, these advantages are compounded, particularly when the group is comprised of alcoholics. The Alcoholics Anonymous group provides the most productive context for treatment through recovery of meaning (3).

This is true because the group provides acceptance, which is fundamental to therapy. The alcoholic believes he is unacceptable, especially to nonalcoholics. No matter how empathetic a therapist may try to be, he usually does not know the alcoholic experience from the inside. Alcoholics, knowing this, strongly suspect that no one can appreciate the agony of addiction or accept the degradation that often accompanies it. The Alcoholics Anonymous group, comprised of people who know what addiction to alcohol is like and whose personal histories leave no room for condemnation and judgment of others, provides a condition that cannot be successfully imitated.

Alcoholics Anonymous also offers an advantage in the discovery of a new purpose. It suggests that the most significant meaning an alcoholic may ever achieve can arise, not in spite of, but because of his alcoholism. When an alcoholic testifies to his own experience, he discovers that it is of value to others. The twelve-step program of spiritual growth outlined by Alcoholics Anonymous culminates with the alcoholic's willingness to be on call at virtually any hour and to travel any distance to be at the side of an alcoholic who has taken the initiative of calling for help. The realization that as an alcoholic he can perform some functions better than anyone else—even a psychiatrist or a minister—provides the ultimate satisfaction of his existential frustration. The knowledge that his alcoholic experience can become consequential enables him to make a fitting response to the undeniable fact of his alcoholism. It provides him with a viable and mature alternative to lifeless homeostasis and a creative content for his existential vacuum.

References

1. Clinebell, Howard Jr. (1956). *Understanding and Counseling the Alcoholic.* Nashville: Abingdon Press.
2. Frankl, V. E. (1975). *The Unconscious God.* New York: Simon and Schuster.
3. Holmes, Robert M. (1970). Alcoholics Anonymous as group logotherapy. *Pastoral Psychology.* March.
4. James, William (1910). *Varieties of Religious Experience.* Longmans, Green and Co.
5. Ogden C. K., and I. A. Richards (1960). *The Meaning of Meaning.* London: Routledge and Kegan Paul.
6. Wise, Carroll (1942). *Religion in Illness and Health.* New York: Harper.

Narcotics

Alvin R. Fraiser

The narcotics addict epitomizes the world of frustrated youths whose problems lie in the neglected dimension of the human spirit. Clashing values, spiritual suffering, degradation, fear, and lack of fulfillment move the addict to seek refuge in narcotics. He is not addicted when he takes the first fix. In many cases, the first use of a drug is an attempt to quell spiritual frustration and provide temporary solace from the storms of life. Even where group pressure seems to be the motivating force, the mere fact that such pressure can induce the drug experience is in itself an indication of spiritual malaise.

The addict's problems spring not only from his interpersonal, sexual, and work failures, but also from his struggles with the meaning of his life. He is no longer guided by the values that have assisted people in the past. Neither Marx's sociological theories nor Freud's theories of instinctual life provide him with solutions to his problems. In my work with addicts I have found them pushed to seek refuge in narcotics not by their motives, memories, or biological needs, but by inner conflicts over values, behavior, and conscience.

When a person first turns to narcotics to assuage his frustrations and feelings of inadequacy, he is saying to society, his family, and himself, "I am now disassociating myself from nature, my former self, and from anyone not in the drug culture." He is also saying,

"I am experiencing no mere social crisis but spiritual chaos." He is feeling intense guilt because he has compromised truth, has failed to combat injustice, has stolen from and exploited his friends and family, and, above all, has not realized his own potentials. The addict tends to possess high potential but is low in achievement. His very existence as an addict depends on his ability to hustle money to support his habit. Every day he may have to obtain and dispose of at least $1,000 worth of merchandise to support a $100-a-day habit. His spirit, his will, and his mind are ensnared in the bondage of addiction, and he becomes the prey of those who financially exploit his predicament.

The Personality of the Addict

Long-lasting societies have had creative value systems which allowed their members to actualize their unique potentials. Our technological society emphasizes organization and discipline, two conditions that blast the foundation from under the addict. He is unable to organize and to discipline himself. He resents the impositions of authority, yet, through his deviant behavior, gives up his rights to be self-determining and turns his life over to that hated authority.

Confident self-direction is impossible for the narcotics addict, because his self-doubts demean his own humanity. He cannot immerse himself in constructive, meaningful behavior, because he lacks self-esteem and confidence. He is filled with helplessness, anguish, and despair; he suffers acutely from a sickness of the spirit, a failure of nerve, a loss of hope.

To escape his predicament, he needs help in finding a content for his emptiness—a meaning to fulfill. The addict will resist the idea that, if he is to be a free human being, he must choose among the values that bind human beings together and yet preserve for each person his individuality. His past experiences do not permit him to trust such values. He prefers to create his own value system or to accept the values of the addict culture, because it is there that his loyalty lies as long as this group provides him with instant relief from his despair.

The addict views freedom as fantasy. He cannot see that freedom only exists in a framework of limits and cannot accept the responsibility of living within such a framework. He tends to think of life as moving merrily along on a monorail, unhindered, unchanging, static. He denies that a viable freedom can exist in dynamic living experiences in which basic human values are endlessly transformed.

The addict has enveloped himself in a host of assumptions that limit the need for serious thinking, acting, and experiencing human emotions. He assumes tomorrow will be a carbon copy of today, that he will be able to acquire the means of securing another "fix," and continue his static way of life. His intellect and cunning frequently permit him to accomplish these goals.

"Once an addict, always an addict," has long been found inappropriate. If we believe such clichés, we rule out the applications of some basic tenets of logotherapy: man is free to determine his actions and attitudes, to stand back, outside of himself, look at himself, and even confront himself about his attitudes and behavior. These human qualities enable him to resist the sociological and psychological forces that face him, to take a stand, and to change his attitudes. The addict, being human, can change his life style and shed his addiction; but, for the most part, society remains unwilling to make a major effort to help him, because it continues to view him as a dangerous criminal. Many therapists refuse to accept addicts because they consider them the most difficult patients. Working with addicts can result in many disappointments, shattered dreams, and heartbreaks; but I have found that the challenges and successes make the effort worthwhile.

Initially, the addict may have resorted to the use of narcotics because of some physical or psychic illness. But because his noös, according to logotherapeutic beliefs, cannot become ill, he can be assisted in his noëtic realm; with the help of a trained logotherapist, the addict can find a meaning to fulfill.

Hunger for meaning, far from being neurotic, makes life not only bearable, but enjoyable. Because of his noëtic urge to know, the addict can be guided to accept the idea that his use of drugs is only his futile attempt to satisfy one of his basic human needs—to know. As he works through this idea, he becomes capable of accepting another idea—that a person must feel free to use his most human attributes, and that no one can be free if he is continuously constrained to use and be numbed by the effects of narcotics.

Personal Experiences with Addicts

For the past ten years my life has been dedicated to working with hard-core narcotic addicts. It has been both rewarding and frustrating. When I began my work, I knew little about drugs, their effects upon human beings, the people who use them, and the culture which has grown around their use. I discovered that my academic background in sociology, psychology, and religion was insufficient as a basis from which to deal with the behavior of my clients. During the first three years, in the Illinois Correctional System, I worked with addicts who were under criminal commitment to an institution. The next four years I worked for the California Department of Corrections. My clients came to me, not because they wanted to, but because they were under court order. In the California System, addicts are under a seven-year civil commitment; they retain their civil rights but are committed by a court.

One of the most difficult tasks for the therapist working with clients who are forced to receive help, is to stimulate them to seek it. The average age of my clients was 26.5 years, which means their habits were well formulated and not easily changed. To benefit from therapy and academic or vocational training, they must experience growth toward adulthood. I have come to believe that such growth is accelerated or retarded by what a person decides about his life style and that some of these decisions may result in anxiety rather than homeostasis. I also believe that growth rarely comes without pain and anxiety and that a person's ability to make crucial decisions about his life provides him with an opportunity to experience fulfillment. These beliefs have enabled me to continue working with these challenging and difficult clients.

My experiences have led me to conclusions that contradict much of the literature about narcotics addiction and the addict as a person. Unable to accept the traditional approaches and premises of sociology, psychology, and religion, I moved toward developing my own. Then, while studying, under Frankl, at United States International University of San Diego, I realized I had been using the principles of logotherapy without the formalized framework.

A paper distributed by the Research Department of the California Rehabilitation Center entitled, "Personality Traits of Narcotic

Addicts," provided statistics about the age of the addicts committed to the institution, the number of years addicted, their ethnic backgrounds, their marital status, and the criminal offenses resulting in their commitment to the civil addict program. The paper failed to draw attention to any personality characteristics such as low self-esteem, high intelligence, low achievement, hypersensitivity, manipulation, nocturnalism, fear, guilt, and emotive responses.

The literature generally portrays addicts as mad, vicious fiends. On the contrary, I have found them to be high in a quality I call the "human perception." I prefer this term, which in my hierarchical order is at the top, to the more commonly used phrase, "extrasensory perception." Referring to this magnificent human quality as something extra or tacked on belittles it. I view the human perception as a quality innate in all persons. Its development is influenced by certain life experiences, especially traumatic ones. Human perception is highly developed in the addict because of the hyperaction of his other senses—touch, sight, taste, hearing, and smell. The keenness of his senses frequently makes the addict react on an emotive level, preventing him from bringing his superior intellect into play. His intellect and highly developed perceptive mechanisms are major stimuli to becoming an addict. He turns to drugs to allay his frustrations and feelings of inadequacy. The self-destructive use of drugs usually is an unconscious destructive impulse. The addict does not consciously know, nor will he admit, that drug use is self-destructive. At times, however, it becomes conscious and intentional, when the addict takes an overdose. Overdoses are common when the addict moves into the suicidal endogenous depressive state.

A Case in Point

Raul came to the California Rehabilitation Center three months after his third suicide attempt. Unable to overcome heroin addiction through his own efforts, and with no help available, Raul looked to suicide as the only way out. He was committed to the Center and assigned to the dormitory where I was a counselor. Raul was twenty-two, handsome, and the father of three small children. When he was sixteen, he had married his pregnant girl friend. She was several years his senior and was so motherly toward Raul that he felt like one of the children. He dropped out of high school and worked at menial jobs before he became addicted to heroin.

Because of his high-level intelligence—he had an I.Q. of 147—his treatment plan included high school graduation before he would be considered for release. He completed the required fifteen high school credits with highest honors.

Initially, Raul resisted being an active participant in the daily encounter group and made several attempts to be transferred to another dormitory which did not have such groups. Raul and I met several times in private therapy session before he became an active participant in group interactions, including small unstructured "rap sessions" in my office. He became open enough to discuss the reasons for his suicidal attempts and began to express some plans for his future. He found a meaning for his life in academic pursuits and expressed a realistic desire to make his contribution to society as an architectural engineer. He also decided not to return to his wife, whom he did not love, and agreed to pay child support. With these realistic goals established and aware of a meaning in life, Raul was released from the institution in the shortest time allowed by law, six months. After his release he worked full time for an art-supply house and attended college in the evenings. He also assisted in training seminars on drug abuse. After having remained drug-free for two years, he was discharged from the program.

Generalized Fear

Most addicts are filled with a "generalized fear," without apparent reason. They fear close interpersonal relationships, view themselves as being out of step with the general culture, and rarely talk about their feelings. This fear thwarts their ability to trust others, especially authority figures. Yet, their behavior consistently places them under police control and in the bondage of correctional institutions.

Lew, a Black man, came to the Center at the age of forty-four. He was born in Louisiana and was resentful toward Caucasians. In an effort to cope with his feelings of rejection, he began using heroin at the age of fourteen and was sentenced to state prison. For the next thirty years he lived in institutions, at times using heroin while incarcerated. After release, he remained in the community only two or three months before being returned for another crime.

In the treatment community, he tested my overtures of concern about him. After fourteen months in therapy, he was released to the outside community. He did not report to his supervising agent, but chose to return to his old pattern of living. Through a mutual friend, I got in touch with him and urged him to return to the Center for further treatment. When he returned, he expressed his gratitude to me. My counseling was one of the few times in his life that someone had cared. He began to make plans for the time after his new release. He wanted to work as an interior decorator and expressed his artistic talents, for personal satisfaction, through wood carving. The day before his second release I asked him what would be different this time. He said, "I now know what I want to do, and I cannot do it in an institution." Lew completed his two year drug-free program with few problems. He had discovered his will to meaning; at last, at the age of forty-seven, he was a free man.

The Search for Perfection

The salient personality trait of the addict is low self-esteem. He usually talks much about his self-sufficiency, but the self-destructive behavior of narcotic use gives the lie to his claim.

The addict operates at the ends of a continuum between total perfection and imperfection. When he is unable to fulfill his expectations to the point of perfection, he resorts to narcotics. He views failure to reach perfection as total defeat; he does not interpret it as a learning experience. He does not see any choice but to use narcotics, feeling himself pushed by his environment to the depths of despair. It is possible, however, for an individual with this distorted perception to acquire an understanding of himself, his motives, drives, and desires, and, through a will to live, to abstain from the use of narcotics.

When Bryant, twenty-six, came to the center, he had been a drug user for ten years. After experimenting with marijuana, LSD, methedrine, and barbiturates, he became addicted to heroin. At first, he insisted the reason why he used drugs, stole from his relatives, and exploited his friends was his father's rejection in divorcing his mother when Bryant was nine-years-old. Verbosity and keen intellect enabled him to avoid looking inward during the first few months in the dormitory community. His father, who had retired from the military and lived in a town close to the institution, accepted an invitation to attend a family group with Bryant once a week. After Bryant got to know his father and understand the reasons for his seeming rejection, he was faced with the fact that he could no longer use his old excuses. He began to make plans for his future. Since he had never acquired saleable skills, he took a business training course at the Center. He was released to the community after a twelve-month treatment, married, and had a daughter. He attended college while working full-time and remained drug-free for the required two years. He was discharged and has continued to be a good husband and father.

Manipulation is the Game

The addict is a master in manipulating others. He can instantaneously appraise other people. He reads body language and voice inflections to decide whether the person will be sympathetic toward him, so he can obtain money; he immediately spots an area of guilt or pity in the person and begins his manipulation; he is usually successful in establishing a relationship with someone who will excuse his failures.

Roy, nineteen, epitomizes these attributes. He had been a heroin addict for five years. At the age of nine months he had poliomyelitis, which left his legs severely damaged. All his life he had used his affliction as a manipulative tool. Although he was extremely bright, he had avoided academic training. He was unable to write more than his name. When he learned that his treatment process was to include academic instruction and physical therapy, he began manipulating to be transferred to another dormitory without such programs. When this failed, he sluggishly began to fulfill the requirements of his treatment plan. Special arrangements were made to enable him to study in spite of his physical handicap. He was allowed to take his school books out of the classroom. It took him almost five months to accept the idea that he was not primarily a cripple, but a bright young man who happened to have weak legs. He then became an ardent student and was able to complete all requirements to enter high school within six months. He was released from the institution with new motivations and goals. He completed his high-school requirements in two years and, at the last account, had entered college.

During my four years at the California Rehabilitation Center, approximately 260 narcotic addicts completed the treatment process in which I used logotherapy as the basis of treatment; 40 percent of these addicts remained drug-free in the community to which they were released. During the same four years, only 10 percent remained drug-free when released from dormitories in which traditional therapy was used.

A Supplementary Form of Therapy for Addicts

Elisabeth Lukas

People become addicts for two primary reasons: suffering and boredom. They want to forget a blow of fate that has become inescapable, or to fill an inner emptiness that has become unbearable. There are secondary reasons for taking drugs such as curiosity, peddlers, opposition to authority, peer pressure, or ignorance, but these come into play mostly when a primary reason is present.

In working with addicts of any kind—those taking hallucinatory drugs, alcohol, sleeping or other pills—logotherapy is a supplementary form of therapy. As a first step it is hopeless to try and help an alcoholic rediscover his life goals because his immediate goal is drinking. To remove his physical and psychological blocks to the resources of his spirit, other methods are necessary that remain on the physio-psychological level: chemical means, gradual detoxification, vitamins, behavior therapy, training in avoidance, conditioning, shock and relaxation therapy. These methods cannot be replaced by logotherapy.

But the therapy must not stop there. We know from experience what will happen when "cured" addicts leave the clinic detoxicated and with an indoctrinated aversion against drugs, but still full of fears, doubts, and frustrations, suffering from the traumas of the past and the uncertainties of the future. They will ask themselves if there was any sense of their being cured and what they will do with the life that was restored to them. We need a supplementary form of therapy that dares to enter the spiritual dimension of the addicts, to participate in their search for meaning, and to movitate them to find new outlooks and attitudes.

Although logotherapy is a supplementary form of therapy, it is essential. Drug addicts canot remain cured if the cure limits itself to their physical and psychological needs. Logotherapy is useful because it is flexible enough to be combined with any other form of therapy. It is not only supplementary therapy in overcoming addiction but also prophylactic in preventing a relapse.

In my work with addicts I first try to get the patients to go to a suitable clinic equipped with the medical and psychological means to help. But at the same time I promise to take them on as clients afterwards.

The treatment of the "cured" addicts consists of two phases. The first is still primarily psychological, but in the second I venture into the region of the human spirit with all its dormant resources. But even during the psychological phase I try to prepare the patients for the subsequent Socratic dialogue which is to explore their preferences for meanings, goals, and commitments.

In the first phase I open the way to logotherapy through relaxation and suggestion exercises, using tape cassettes. The technique may be autogenic training, progressive relaxation (Jacobson), or suggestive training of the will. In every case I let the patients take the cassette home. As long as they are in contact with the therapist and feel his support and patience, they will be able to remain calm and decide on starting afresh. But once they are home again, facing the demands of everyday life, their mood will change. They become restless, insecure, their intentions waver, and the new beginnings look doubtful. It would be expecting too much from them to lie down and do the relaxation exercises from memory.

Cassettes offer many advantages. They are easy to operate, one can relax, let the machine do the "thinking," and listen to the formulations. Although the cassette is a crutch, too, just as the drug was, it is less harmful, and the patients are used to relying on crutches. They also ordinarily respond well to suggestion, and their suggestibility is used in this phase of the therapy. A woman who was addicted to sleeping pills was able to gradually reduce and eventually eliminate her high intake of valium by replacing it with a cassette. She had been free of medication for nine weeks, and only occasionally requires a replaying of the cassette. This is not an ideal cure but it presents a "first aid," a change from a dangerous to a more harmless crutch.

Relaxation cassettes help patients calm their anxieties, gain distance from their tensions, and reduce their fears. After a while, the autogenic relaxation exercises can be followed by suggestive training of the will.

It is true that suggestions seem to violate the patients' freedom of free choice which is a basic tenet of logotherapy. But this first phase is still a transitional step from the drug dependency to the complete restitution of inner freedom, and in this phase the demands cannot be placed too high. I am using the suggestive training of the will as a detour to a genuine strengthening of the will, enabling the patients to gain the conviction that they can reach their conscious and unconscious goals—a conviction which, in turn, starts the real therapeutic process.

The second phase in the supplementary treatment consists of the self-discovery discourse. Here the therapist follows only one rule, all else is experience, improvisation, and intuition. The one rule demands that meaning is not given but found by the patients. The patients themselves must realize their unique possibilities, tasks, and goals, become aware of their value priorities, and learn to live for a task they feel worthwhile. The therapist challenges them, involves them in a Socratic dialogue, shows them meaning possibilities; but the final responsibility of the decisions rests with the patients.

After a successful first phase, the chances of a profitable self-discovery discourse are better than they would have been immediately after the withdrawal treatment. The patients had good intentions before but were not able to live up to them. This time it's different. The suggestive training improves their inner strength and gives them a better chance to resist a relapse. Even if anxiety should overwhelm them again, they can use their relaxation exercises—they are better equipped to face their weak ego strength.

In this second phase the patients' tendency to self-pity is counteracted. Self-pity is a whirlpool that drags them down to helplessness. They are inclined to deplore their fate, to ask why it happened to them, to blame parents, upbringing, and circumstances, to complain about their conditions, and to repeat that everything is senseless. The therapist must make every effort to change this paralyzing attitude to one that is constructive leading to the overcoming of the drawbacks. He must show his patients that their unhappy childhood, their failure in work and human relationships, and their instability offer opportunities for high human achievements, namely to build up a rich and meaningful life in spite of these impediments.

If all goes well in life, if one was born with talents, had a happy childhood, and was favored by breaks, it is easy to achieve happiness and success. The tougher the starting point, the more remarkable is even the smallest success accomplished by one's own efforts. The patients are led to see that, given their circumstances, they have reason to be proud of every accomplishment by which they have conquered their drawbacks. These small steps are proof of a far greater human achievement than the greatest possible success of others who were favored by natural gifts and upbringing. The patients must learn to defy their fate and be proud of their own strength—this pride is a great help to prevent a relapse.

The logotherapist educates his patients to take responsibility for their actions. They learn to free themselves from their feelings of dependency—on drugs and everything else. As long as they say, "I cannot love because my parents rejected me," they will be unable to love. But if they are courageous enough to say, "Just because I was rejected and know how it feels, I will make every effort not to spread rejection any further"—only when they change their attitude will they be able to love. Only then will they have conquered fate and proved that they accepted responsibility for their actions. The defiant power of the human spirit is an enormous reservoir of energy from which psychotherapy can draw.

The negative experiences of the ex-addict can be overcome if they are transformed into a positive aspect. It is always touching to see the enthusiasm and commitment of former addicts when they are asked to help others overcome their addiction. This task gives them the feeling of finally having found meaning in their unhappy experience. Their own suffering was not in vain: it now helps them understand the agony of other addicts and gain their confidence. Their own failure becomes retroactively filled with a meaning that had escaped their attention. In my work with addicts I always turn to patients who are on the mend and ask them to help me persuade others to take the first step and go to a clinic. Ex-addicts are doing an outstanding job, better than I could do myself, and that feeling of being useful, to have a task, is a further step in their rediscovery of meaningful life.

But all the training, experiences, and techniques of the therapist will not bring about a lasting cure without one ingredient that is central to logotherapy: a trust in the humanity of the patient. From everything the therapist does must emanate a deep conviction that behind all that chemistry that can be treated, and all those psychological forces that can be manipulated, stands a human spirit that can be appealed to. And a further conviction of the therapist that behind all that weakness and failure in the patient, there is a healthy core that can enable the patient to build a new, meaningful, and happy future from the ruins of the past. The patients must feel this basic trust by the therapist, and sometimes the trust of only *one* person is sufficient to prevent them from a relapse to addiction, sickness, and despair.

VIII

Community Concerns

This section opens a new world for logotherapy to become a guiding philosophy. The heading "Community Concerns" is at the same time too modest and too pretentious. It is too modest because the applications go beyond community to national, even global, concerns. Any school of thought that can make contributions to the problems of minorities, prisons, and administration of justice, labor-management relations, and community health has a claim to more than parochial influence. But it is easy to become too pretentious in such claims. As the essays in this section illustrate, logotherapy is beginning to have a demonstrable influence in all these fields. Critics may point out, however, that it is not so much logotherapy that provides new directions but the age-old truths on which its philosophy is based: that people care about each other, accept responsibility, and direct their attention to transcending goals is advice as old as human records go. But Frankl puts such advice not as a moral demand but as a prescription for mental health and, indeed, for human survival. If man continues to consider his will to pleasure and to power as his highest motivations, he exposes himself to frustration at best, and possibly to extinction. If man continues to seek mental health merely in stability and adjustment, he will not reach out for his potentials. If he emphasizes his drives rather than his goals, he will accept his reduction to the animal level. If he stresses his efficiency in a material world he will reduce himself to the level of a computer. If he sees his nature in terms of his animal past, it will be difficult for him to evolve to a stage of more complete humanity. Frankl puts his message in almost Darwinian terms: at this point of evolution, man, the meaning seeker, is the fittest in the struggle for survival.

Logotherapy's prescription for community health cannot be filled at the nearest drugstore but only by the conscious effort of every person to sharpen his or her ability to recognize the meanings of the moment. It is a prescription of the individual, by the individual, for the individual. Meshoulam discusses the promise of logotherapy for community health, and Lunceford, Briggs, Bodenheimer, Phillips, and Sargent write about specific aspects. It is not claimed that logotherapy is about to solve the problems discussed—merely that a first step has been taken. This, too, is the approach of logotherapy: meaning is not found once and for all, but step by step.

Many of those who carry the ideas of logotherapy to their various fields of endeavor are graduates of classes Frankl has conducted in the winter quarter at the United States International University in San Diego since 1970. They carry the ideas of logotherapy to many fields and many places in the Western and Eastern hemispheres. The essays in this section are samples of first steps taken in six distinct directions.

The Community Mental Health Movement

Uriel Meshoulam

The Community Mental Health Movement (CMHM) is a unique phenomenon in the history of psychology. No one dominant figure and no one theory can take credit for its emergence. It arose "out of an explosion of discontent" (7), as a result of numerous practical problems, such as disenchantment with the traditional psychotherapies, shortage of professional manpower, a growing need for help, and a general lack of satisfying answers to many contemporary problems of our society. The CMHM is a practical movement, aimed at solving concrete problems left unsolved by traditional psychology.

But discontent with the old paradigm and realization of its limitations are not sufficient for change; a new paradigm must emerge. Logotherapy's assumptions about human nature, and its phenomenological approach to the study of human behavior, justify its identification with a new paradigm. The logotherapeutic propositions have an implicit impact on the development of the CMHM, although no direct reference is made of this in its literature.

Logotherapy is an emergent theory which offers unconventional solutions to some of the community mental health problems. Thus, logotherapy can serve as a fruitful new frame of reference for the further development of the practice of community mental health, and the CMHM can offer its practical experience to be assimilated by logotherapy and thus stimulate refinement of the theory.

This essay presents four major logotherapeutic propositions: the noögenic nature of the "collective neurosis of our time"; the will to meaning as underlying human motivation; the concept of man as free and responsible; and logotherapy's development of short-term psychotherapeutic techniques.

The Noögenic Nature of the "Collective Neurosis of Our Time"

One of the CMHM's main concerns is the steadily growing gap between the need for psychotherapy and the supply of professional time. Frankl accounts for the "growth in psychotherapeutic need" by stating that "doctors today are approached by many patients who in the former days would have seen a pastor, priest, or rabbi; they are confronted with philosophical problems rather than emotional conflicts." These cases have become so common that they are justifiably called "the collective neurosis of our time" (PE, p. 17).

The increased psychotherapeutic need, therefore, is caused not by an increase in psychogenic neuroses and psychoses, but by a neurosis-like condition rooted in spiritual problems, moral conflicts, and existential crises. The collective neurosis is noögenic rather than psychogenic, and is characterized by a nihilistic attitude toward life, an alleged meaninglessness of life, conformism, a sense of boredom, and an inner emptiness.

These noëtic problems, presented by an existential vacuum, create a heavy burden on mental health clinics; and a large part of the professionals' time is spent on dealing with them. The problem is made acute by the limited resources of trained psychiatrists, clinical psychologists, social workers, and those in related professions. As early as 1959, Albee (1) cautioned that the shortage in professional manpower was ever-increasing. The Joint Commission on Mental Illness and Health (9) concluded that this shortage could be expected to worsen. The longer and more expensive the professional training is, the graver the want will be. "Physicians are in steadily decreasing supply in ratio to population. As psychiatry is a medical specialty, it does not seem logical to think that the supply of psychiatrists can increase" (2).

These two trends, the increase in psychotherapeutic need and the decrease of professional time, seem to be impossible to stop. Efforts to reverse the trend by training more professionals are doomed to failure, just as cleaning the environment can not be accomplished simply by training more sanitary workers. New approaches must be taken and unconventional programs initiated to find solutions to problems of this magnitude.

Logotherapy maintains that the collective neurosis of our time is spiritual, and thus should be dealt with on the noölogical dimension. There is an increased need for "noetic care" rather than psychological care. This implies that we are not restricted to traditional psychotherapists but can turn to other counseling professions, such as social workers and ministers, for assistance to people seeking meaning in life. Factual support is provided by a study (6) indicating that 42 percent of those in need of help consult their clergyman, 29 percent their physician, and 20 percent one of the helping professions.

Once personal problems are regarded as not necessarily medical or psychological, we are permitted to consider resources of care even beyond these counseling professions. The client's relatives and friends, the family lawyer or physician, may be well equipped to assist with spiritual and philosophical difficulties. Housewives, students, teachers, peers, parents and relatives can also be considered as possible providers of noëtic care. Actually, people often do seek assistance by turning to acquaintances for whom Caplan (3) coined the term "care-givers."

Besides supplying alternative manpower, nonprofessionals and care-givers as providers of noëtic care offer other advantages:

1. They are not biased by psychological theories and a medical approach. Their naiveté brings about new ideas and approaches based upon common sense rather than theoretical inclinations. This is not to say that theoretical orientation is identical with bias; rather, it is meant to emphasize that common sense and a sound life philosophy are in some situations more essential than professional expertise for helping a person in noëtic plight. Frankl cautions that traditionally the physician is not prepared to cope with the existential vacuum in any but medical terms and thus sees the problem as something pathological. Since noëtic problems are often nonpathological, the medical approach of the psychiatrist may be disadvantageous.

2. The mental-health professional tends to establish an expert-patient relationship with the client, which may impede the development of an amiable and egalitarian tie. The nonprofessional is more likely to develop a friendship-like relationship, because he is perceived, and is perceiving himself, as less of an authority figure. He is also more readily accepted by the client as equal in terms of social status and moral values; and friendship ensues more easily with one's equal. Schofield (13) agrees with logotherapy when he stresses the immense therapeutic value inherent in a friendship relationship for persons in noëtic plight. Cordial encounter on a truly human dimension, rather than psychological instruction and insight, encourages the client's endeavor to find and actualize meanings.

3. The person in need spontaneously selects that care-giver whom he expects to provide the best rapport. The teacher is often required to provide noëtic assistance to youths in philosophical conflict and is called upon to play the double role of teacher and care-giver. The physician is the natural source of support and consultation for the disabled and the incurable, concerned not only with the disease, but also with the patient's attitude toward it. This way the provided assistance fits the individual's needs.

The Will to Meaning

Since man is continuously in search of "something" or "someone" for whose sake it is worth living, the frustration of his will to meaning is a central factor in his unhappiness. The logotherapist's task is to fill the client's existential vacuum by helping him find meanings. How can the community assist persons suffering from an existential vacuum? What can be done to evoke man's will to meaning except supply him with "ready" assignments which might not be meaningful to him?

We encourage the development of the child's intellect by presenting him with stimuli to evoke his mental potential through his interplay with them. Similarly, we can call forth man's will to meaning by challenging him with potential meanings to be fulfilled; for instance, by introducing him to tasks which require personal commitment. Only in this way can a person freely choose tasks that are meaningful to him and accept responsibility for them.

Many people find meaning through helping others, and the world is in need of people who help fellow human beings; therefore, persons in the state of existential vacuum are a promising source of helping manpower. In addition to providing noëtic care to others, they may find in this experience the answer to their own questioning of the meaning of life, and thus be helped themselves. This phenomenon of being helped by helping others is realized by some authors engaged in community mental health issues. Riessman (12) termed this phenomenon the *"helper" therapy principle.* However, this principle is still awaiting elaboration and wider application.

The possibilities inherent in this principle for the solution of community mental health problems are recognized by Klein: "It is only a logical step, once having identified these [human services] needs, to place them in juxtaposition to the huge army of alienated and unemployed, who are desperately in need of meaningful, horizon-opening work such as can very easily come from giving service to a fellow human being" (11). Cowen, a leading spokesman of the CMHM, calls for the "need to plan for more systematic utilization of nonprofessionals who may need the opportunity to be genuinely helpful to others and can grow from such activity" (4).

Few existing projects use the helper principle and offer their participants an opportunity for actualizing meanings through acts of self-transcendence. Some of the large programs recognized by Riessman (12), such as Alcoholics Anonymous, Synanon (for drug addicts) and Recovery Incorporated (for former mental patients), were not consciously planned for this purpose. More planned programs are needed, to which people in need such as juvenile delinquents, bored housewives, school dropouts, and lonely old people could be directed to receive help through giving it. To demonstrate what can be done for people by letting them help others, two projects will be described: one for old people, the other for dropouts and delinquent youths.

Johnston (8) describes the Foster Grandparents Project, carried out in Summit County, Ohio. Each of the foster grandparents, needy people over sixty years of age, spent four hours a day with an emotionally-disturbed or physically-handicapped child of preschool age. Thus the children received personal attention which they could not get before. Foster grandparent and child developed a warm relationship which benefited both. The children became happier and more relaxed, and were reported to sleep better, play better, and eat better. The helpers seemed to find the experience most meaningful. One of the foster grandfathers is quoted as saying, "It gives me a reason for getting up in the morning." The participating old people devoted themselves most persistently, demonstrating how deeply concerned they were about the welfare of these children, and that they saw the project as an assignment well worth living and working for.

Klein (11) describes a series of projects initiated by the Institute for Youth Studies at Howard University, Washington, D.C. The program aimed at helping dropouts and delinquent youths by assigning them to help in various agencies in roles which demanded commitment and personal involvement. These young men and women were trained for a few months, and simultaneously started to work as aides in child-care centers, as youth leaders in a community mental-health center, as counseling aides with delinquent children, and as classroom aides in elementary schools. This project assisted the participating agencies in their work, and also helped the helpers. Although most participants brought with them fatalistic views of life, poor self-esteem, and strong senses of alienation, their styles of life changed, their educational aspiration levels rose, and some were reported preparing for and receiving high school equivalency certificates. The project succeeded in "finding *real* channels for moving these young people from their 'outsider' and 'spectator' roles . . . into *meaningful* 'participant' roles in society" (11).

Commitment is not necessarily limited to noëtic care tasks. Any task which makes man realize he is valuable and needed will prevent possible frustration of his will to meaning. Thus the community could develop programs in a wide variety of fields, such as the Peace Corps or Action projects. The individual, through actively participating in a program which is meaningful to him, would be defending himself against man's dangerous enemy—despair over the alleged meaninglessness of life.

The will to meaning as a fundamental concept in understanding human motivation has implications for the education of the young. The indoctrination of a hedonistic and materialistic philosophy of life is incompatible with the expectation to fulfill meanings. The community will do well to encourage the student's spontaneous concern with values and meanings, rather than explaining them away by a reductionist approach. Therefore, the aim of the community health revolution should be to fight, through education and appropriate projects, those approaches which reify man.

The Concept of Man as Free and Responsible

Disenchantment has been expressed about sending adults to institutions when they suffer from severe behavioral problems. Institutionalization is often dehumanizing. Basic human rights are taken from the inmates, along with their sense of responsibility and freedom. The patient is stripped of his everyday duties and becomes dependent upon the ward's staff. He trades in his freedom for the comfort of being released from the overwhelming burden created by the difficulties in his life. Hospitalization interferes with the patient's readjustment to his community, makes the process of resocialization difficult and often impossible, and in this sense is anti-therapeutic.

In the United States thousands of people are institutionalized in mental hospitals. The probability of their leading normal lives in the community is reduced by their being regarded, by the staff as well as by themselves, as chronic and lost cases. The situation has recently attracted public and professional attention. New ways of dealing with mental patients were explored which would be more potent, while preserving the patients' human dignity. To establish these new approaches, it was necessary to adopt an appropriate model of man, as a free and responsible being, and work within the appropriate theoretical framework. Logotherapy supplies the basis for such a model and framework.

Programs which place more responsibility on the individual and permit him more freedom have yielded encouraging results. The "therapeutic community" approach initiated by Jones (10) generated a pioneering project in which selected patients were encouraged in the democratic organization and management of their community life. Fairweather's (5) project at the Palo Alto Veterans Administration Hospital, California, was inspired by this "therapeutic community" approach. In accord with logotherapy's philosophy, the project aimed at restoring the patients to responsibility for their own affairs and those of their fellow patients. Rather than being excused from social duties, the patients were made collectively responsible for tasks previously taken care of by the staff. A patients' government was established; an employment service was independently run by the hospital patients; and responsibility and initiative rather than compliance was reinforced by the staff. Compared with a control group which was treated in a traditional way, Fairweather's patients improved their social functioning and were discharged sooner from the ward. Because conditions in the ward were similar to those in the outside world, the patients found it easier to adjust after their return to the outside community. Crises caused by sudden transitions from a "no responsibility" institute to the demanding community were prevented. Fairweather's patients stayed outside the walls of the institute longer and did better in their community and in their jobs.

Members of the therapeutic community within the ward are less dependent upon staff aid, and thus consume less of the professionals' time. The ratio between the number of members on the staff to the number of patients can be cut while the advantages of the therapeutic community remain intact.

Short-term Techniques

The traditional long-term talking therapies, stretching out over long periods, do not satisfy the community mental-health needs. The fact that they are not applicable to some psychiatric and social categories, such as diagnosed psychotics and members of lower social classes, also lessens their usefulness. Admittedly, long-term therapies are sometimes the best, and perhaps the only, available techniques for many patients. However, if we intend to solve mental-health problems from the community vantage point, we also need effective short-term techniques.

Logotherapy's contributions to therapeutic techniques—paradoxical intention and dereflection—are applicable only to a limited number of conditions, but these are conditions usually resistent to other kinds of treatment. Paradoxical intention and dereflection are useful in treatments of some behaviors regardless of their causes; they are not aimed directly at the elimination of symptoms but at changing the client's attitude toward them. The self-administration of the techniques has a number of advantages for community mental health: First, the client can practice them, after learning their application and rationale in a relatively short time, thus saving professional time. Second, the problem of transferring what is learned in the therapist's office to everyday life situations is avoided because the application of the techniques involves real-life behaviors. Third, because self-application of the techniques is encouraged, the client is reminded that he is always responsible for his own recovery by taking a healthy attitude toward himself and his symptoms. Identifying the application of the logotherapeutic techniques with attitude change toward one's own symptoms and toward one's concept of self as a responsible being explains the long-lasting effects of these therapies.

The encounter between the Community Mental Health Movement and logotherapy promises to be fruitful and points to further interaction between the two disciplines, for the benefit of both as well as for the benefit of community life.

References

1. Albee, G. W. (1959). *Mental Health Manpower Trends.* New York: Basic Books.
2. ______(1967). The relation of conceptual models to manpower need. In E. L. Cowen, E. A. Gardner and M. Zax, eds. *Emergent Approaches to Mental Health Problems.* New York: Appleton-Century-Crofts.
3. Caplan, G. (1964). *Principles of Preventive Psychology.* New York: Basic Books.
4. Cowen, E. L. (1967). Emergent approaches to mental health problems: an overview and directions for future work. In E. L. Cowen, E. A. Gardner, and M. Zax, eds. *Emergent Approaches to Mental Health Problems.* New York: Appleton-Century-Crofts.
5. Fairweather, G. W., ed. (1964). *Social Psychology in Treating Mental Illness.* New York: Wiley.
6. Gurin, G., Veroff, J., and Feld, S. (1960). *Americans View their Mental Health: A Nationwide Interview Survey.* New York: Basic Books.
7. Hersch, D. (1968). The discontent explosion in mental health. *American Psychologist* 23 (7): 497–506.

8. Johnston, R. (1967). Some casework aspects of using foster grandparents for emotionally disturbed children. *Children* 14 (2): 46–52.
9. Joint Commission on Mental Illness and Health (1961). *Action for Mental Health.* New York: Basic Books.
10. Jones, M. (1953). *The Therapeutic Community.* New York: Basic Books.
11. Klein, W. L. (1967). The training of human service aides. In E. L. Cowen, E. A. Gardner, and M. Zax, eds. *Emergent Approaches to Mental Health Problems.* New York: Appleton-Century-Crofts.
12. Riessman, F. (1965). The "helper" therapy principle. *Social Work* 10 (2): 27–32.
13. Schofield, W. (1964). *Psychotherapy: The Purchase of Friendship.* Englewood Cliffs, N.J.: Prentice-Hall.

Minorities

Ronald D. Lunceford

Logotherapy represents a school of thought with specific applications to blacks and other ethnic minorities. It speaks to the man in the street, helping him find meanings within the framework of his own individual system. The man in the street does not need to be convinced that life has meaning. He knows it intuitively, and this knowledge helps him survive in situations of pain, poverty, and suppression.

Part of the problem of mental health is economics. Until recently, psychotherapy was practiced by white, middle-class therapists for white, affluent persons with middle-class values. People receiving treatment were those who could afford it. Thus, psychiatrists and psychologists hardly faced blacks and minorities because, with few exceptions, minorities have been excluded from the affluent society. Therapists are now beginning to show concern with community health where money no longer is a major factor in obtaining help. Therapists are beginning to recognize the right of all people, regardless of race and economic background, to be mentally healthy, and to live in a society that allows them to grow up healthy within their own values.

As a community psychologist, I have found several tenets of logotherapy suitable for minorities. The central tenet is the emphasis on meaning. For blacks as a group, the pleasure principle in the form of sexuality is not a major issue because sexuality has not been suppressed in them by Puritan and Victorian mores; and power, until very recently, has not been an immediate concern for the blacks because it was beyond reach. But meaning is just as accessible to poor blacks as to rich whites. To be sure, meaning may not lie in the same direction for both groups, but logotherapy maintains that each individual can search for the meanings of his life in his own way, and that meaning does not depend on material success. In his capacity to find meaning, the poor black is equal to the rich white, and equality is the chief goal of today's minorities in the United States.

Meaning and Minorities

Logotherapy speaks of two kinds of meanings: the "absolute meaning" that is assumed to exist without proof, and the "meaning of the moment" that is available to each person in each situation. Both meanings have significance for minorities. Logotherapy stresses the spiritual dimension of man—not necessarily the religious, but the specifically human dimension in which religion may play a major part. Many psychiatrists have denied the importance of religion and called it a "crutch." But to many blacks, to deny religion is to deny a vital part of their existence—the part which holds their hope for salvation. The blacks have long found mental health in their religion. Because they could not afford psychologists and psychiatrists, they found strength in preachers and learned to mobilize their spiritual inner resources. To say it is unhealthy to be religious or spiritual is to be ignorant about the black religion or the strength and healing ability of the black church. The black church will remain a custodian of mental health until other legitimate ways are found to help blacks deal with realities, until other medicines replace the tranquilizers which most blacks feel are merely a device to adjust them to a society of white, middle-class values.

Logotherapy encourages a person to reach out for his own spiritual self, even if his values differ from those accepted by the majority. To effect healing, it reaches into the uniquely human dimension, the source of creativity, goal orientation, and faith. A probation officer once referred a fourteen-year-old girl to me as a "pathological" case. She had taken drugs, had been promiscuous, had been pregnant, had an abortion, refused to go to school, and now had run away from home. The clue to her case came in answer to my question about her fears. Was she afraid of something? She blurted out, "I am afraid the Lord does not like me; that Jesus is punishing me." She was relieved when I encouraged her to talk freely about her religious beliefs and hopes. What she had liked most in her life was to sing in her church choir, but she did not want to go to church because she was ashamed—because upon her father's insistence, she had agreed to an abortion, an act her church disapproved of. It became apparent that it was important for her to re-identify with her church. She realized that church was the place where she could transcend her shortcomings and be forgiven. She knew she could not undo the "sins" of her past, but there was a possibility to find a way out, and the church could help her find it. Instead of torturing herself with such questions as why she had been "punished," she focused on what was meaningful to her now; she rejoined her church choir, with the goal of making singing her career. She was able to sort out her guilt feelings and distinguish between those relating to the past, about which nothing could be done, and those from which she could learn by not repeating a behavior pattern she herself disapproved of. Her new behavior was not necessarily approved by American society, her parents, or even her church, but rather by her peers, with whom she could identify. She still hated school but went there for the sake of being able to continue in her choir and receive "free music lessons" for her career. She did not give up sex and drugs but conformed with the customs of her subculture, limiting sex to "steadies" and drugs to marijuana. With her life focused on a singing career, her self-esteem increased and she no longer felt the need to confirm herself by giving her body to any man who desired it. She turned out to be no "pathological case" at all but a human being struggling to find meaning in a framework that made sense to her.

The Meaning of Uniqueness

This case also illustrates the logotherapist's task to encourage each person to find the particular meanings of his life's particular situations. For the black, this message of uniqueness is twofold: it confirms his uniqueness as a black, and also his uniqueness as an individual.

In the past, blacks accepted their racial identity primarily in the negative terms of white society—they saw themselves as subservient, ugly, overemotional, childlike. Only slowly are they building up a self-image that stresses the positive aspects of these same qualities: their claim to "black power," their insistence that "black is beautiful," the emotional strength of their religiosity, and the positive qualities of the child—his creativity, his naturalness, his sense of wonder, his warmth, and his capacity to love. Here, logotherapy's message to the black is: do not try to be like the whites but teach them, by example, some of the human qualities with which the blacks are especially endowed.

Equally important is logotherapy's emphasis on the uniqueness of the individual. Most blacks at the People's Clinic in Santa Ana, California, cannot see themselves as individuals with unique characteristics and opportunities. The normal problems of childhood, marriage, and work are magnified for minorities in a white society. The value conflicts between accepted white values and those of an emergent black consciousness can become the source of noögenic neuroses against which traditional psychoanalytical treatments are largely ineffective.

Andrew, a ten-year-old black boy, was referred to me; three times he had attempted suicide. He suffered from traumas that have become widespread in our society: his mother had remarried, had a new baby, and was working, so Andrew did not get the attention to which he was accustomed. But in addition he also suffered from a personal conflict between the values of his neighborhood peer group and those of the private, predominantly white school to which his mother had sent him. His classmates rejected him because he was not interested in studying and in the "cultural" activities such as dancing classes about which they were excited; his pals in his community rejected him as a "snob" because he tried to emulate his white school mates. It was easy to see why he felt that nobody liked him, that he was "no good." He had to be shown that he was a unique individual with personal talents, hopes, and desires who had a specific place in his family, school, and neighborhood.

Part of Andrew's "therapy" was to provide for him the atmosphere of caring in the People's Clinic, which he felt he missed in his family and school, and make him understand the reality of what had happened: that, for instance, his mother's marrying and having another child was an extension of her love to a family of which he was an important part; or that her caring for him was expressed in her taking a job that enabled him to attend a private school, although her working made it difficult for her to spend much time with him.

This lack of communication and understanding is not restricted to children; it is a well-known cause of marital difficulties and is especially dangerous in racially mixed marriages. This misunderstanding emerges in many ways. I was asked for help by a couple whose marriage was in jeopardy. Harry, a black man, was studying to be a counselor, while his white wife, Betty, four years older, had already started on her counseling career. Betty felt that Harry was stifling her. He was unreasonably jealous and resentful of her friends and activities. Disputes about money were frequent. He wanted a child, while she preferred to wait until he was secure in a job, which he interpreted to mean that she planned to leave him. My talk with Harry convinced me that much of the marital trouble was caused by his insecurity, and that this insecurity had strong racial undertones. Deep inside, he doubted whether he was good enough for her and wondered whether he had married her because she was white, had a career, and had some money in the bank. He scorned her friends, and parties at which she felt at ease; he scorned her skiing trips. All these were foreign to him and his culture. He resented her buying liquor by the caseload for her parties, while he preferred to quietly sit home and "smoke a little grass" occasionally. He could not talk about his problems with his own friends because he felt they disliked him for having married a white woman and for going to school while they had manual jobs. I had to make Betty understand that it was natural for her husband, as a black man in a white society, to be jealous of her and fearful of her leaving him; that the world was wide open for her, that he needed her love and support, though she experienced this need as his attempt to smother her. Once they were able to talk to each other, not as a black and a white, not as a career woman and a struggling student, but as Harry and Betty, much misunderstanding was cleared away. He was surprised to find that she did not look down on him but admired his ambition to overcome his racial handicaps and appreciated his working for a degree in the helping professions. She had not been aware of his fear of her leaving him because she had always seen him as the strong partner in their marriage, the man she needed for physical and emotional support. She had no idea he resented her having her own bank account because she had been brought up in a family where the fear of an economic depression made it desirable for everyone to have his own nest egg. They listed the unique qualities they liked about each other, and also those which they disliked so they could work on changing them, and as a result they saw each other as the real persons they were, and helped each other to come closer to the ideal each of them had of the other.

The Significance of Free Choice

Closely connected with the stress logotherapy places on uniqueness is its insistence that every person, within unavoidable limitations, has a freedom of choice which enables him to find the meanings of his life.

The significance of this insight for blacks is obvious because they have, in addition to the "unavoidable limitations" they share with other people, the limitations of color. The black has to find meaning within the color of his skin, and in our society that means pain. In this respect they are in the same position as a person who is blind, or incurably ill, or in a concentration camp. The message of logotherapy is unmistakable: each person has to find meanings in the activities and experiences he selects, but where this is not possible, he still has the choice of finding meaning in the attitude he takes toward an unchangeable fact. This advice can easily be misunderstood as an inducement to meekly accept one's fate. This, however, is not what logotherapy advocates. It says to the minorities: The meaning of your lives is to improve your situation; but when you decide it is beyond your capacity to change your situation, you can rise above the unchangeable situation by accepting it and finding meanings within its limits.

My position as a logotherapist is to help minorities find personal worth and unique meanings in spite of the pain caused by the society in which they live. To change our situation in this society is our first task, but in the meantime, the freedom and mobility that is still denied to us in many areas is available to us by the stand we take—we either can fruitlessly ask ourselves why this pain was inflicted on us, or we can discover meaning potentials by asking ourselves what we still can do in our painful interim situation.

The lesson that meaning can be found even in situations of suffering is difficult to learn—and to teach. But pain has no color; it is universal. Here, perhaps, is the opportunity for blacks to find meaning in their suffering: to show others that if it is possible to change one's attitude about something as fundamental and unchangeable as the color of one's skin, it is possible to change one's attitude about any limitation. In individual counseling, I was able to show clients that they could find meaning by transcending their pain, by sharing themselves with others, by helping others feel good in their presence, by making use of their ability to give. Logotherapy's method of dereflection helps individuals to stop focusing on themselves, and to find meaning by reaching out to others or to causes in which they believe. It helps them find their uniqueness, a new self-image based on their personal potentials, and their capacity to grow toward them. These are not black goals—they are human goals, but they are harder to achieve for minority people.

In many ways, logotherapy is more important to blacks as a philosophy of life than as a therapy. Minorities are plagued not so much by phobias and psychoses as by the question of how to cope with life in a hostile environment—how to get over the pressure of finding a job, how to become mobile, how to live according to values society is not willing to grant, how to retain one's sense of humanity when a foot is on one's neck. In many ways, the primary problem of minorities remains a struggle for survival. Even affluent blacks do not feel safe yet. They still fear the power structure might take away what it has granted. Many still feel insecure and in doubt about their worth as human beings. To find their worth, they have to reach into their spiritual dimension and rely on their will to meaning. My life *has* to have meaning if I can take this continuous pain and still struggle to survive. This is an assumption for everybody but it is especially pertinent to blacks and the other minorities in America.

New Careers for Offenders

Dennie Briggs

Offenders constitute probably the greatest waste of human potential, especially if persons are included who are likely to *become* offenders, such as drug addicts, alcoholics, and juvenile delinquents. These persons are considered incorrigible, ineducable, or psychotic; not all of them are.

A new approach in the United States and Britain, "New Careers," identifies and mobilizes the neglected abilities of such persons and then encourages them to help others. New Careers was not directly inspired by Frankl's ideas but some New Career personnel, including myself, had heard him and read his books, and found his ideas valuable for young, violent offenders who had no purpose in life and tried to fill their inner emptiness with the temporary excitement and material advantages offered by crime. I have made the ideas of logotherapy available to prison inmates through books and discussion groups.

Many principles of logotherapy applied and appealed to the convicts: that a person has the power to change the direction of his life; that his main motivation is his will to meaning; that the drawbacks of the past can be at least partly overcome by the self-chosen goals of the future; that meaning potentials are available to everyone, even under the most restrictive circumstances; that to treat a person as a hopeless brute often makes him more so, and that to appeal to his human qualities may motivate him to develop his humanness; and that a person's life experiences give him unique knowledge that can help others in similar predicaments—former inmates can aid other prisoners, former addicts can assist drug takers.

New Careers in the United States

The New Careers movement was inspired by the study of Pearl and Riessman (3) and by some pilot projects carried out at Howard University in Washington, D.C.; the Mobilization for Youth project in New York; Lincoln Hospital, also in New York; and the psychiatric prison at Vacaville, California. I shall describe the Vacaville experiment with which I was connected as director of training.

In 1964, eighteen young offenders, some virtually illiterate and all with long histories of serious crime, were selected from among the 236 prisoners who had volunteered for the experiment. The program aimed at giving them a purpose and direction in life, and at helping them acquire the knowledge needed to pursue this new direction during and after their prison experience. They learned to see that their very experiences as criminals gave them a unique opportunity to help other criminals, thus turning their liabilities into assets society could use.

The Vacaville project tried to give the eighteen convict-trainees some understanding of the social problems from which they themselves suffered, and of the way in which the prison authorities dealt with these problems. The trainees studied the power structure of the prison system, interviewed the administrative staff to see how it functioned, listened to the views of the prison inmates, learned how psychiatrists chose their inmate clients, and how the educational system worked. The program set out to solve general problems rather than improve the situation of the participants directly. Each area of study was broken down in step-by-step tasks: to conduct an interview, write a report, collect material for study. The trainees were encouraged to make short-term commitments to complete their tasks by a fixed date. Failure to keep the commitment was discussed and analyzed in group meetings; likewise success (2, p. 26).

The trainees were motivated to seek a new life after release from prison by a vision of what could become different, and to acquire knowledge to make this vision a reality. J. Douglas Grant, the psychologist-director of the project, lists five conditions necessary for success: providing participatory roles, allowing autonomy of choice, building a group culture around a cause to which the trainee can commit himself, offering a meaningful future, and allowing natural leaders to emerge (1, p. 35).

In spite of the resistance of some prison authorities and the resentment of some inmates, and in spite of an initial mistrust of the trainees themselves that the project was a big "con game," the program had a promising start. There were no dropouts. Those who were paroled first knew they had an extra obligation: their progress would be watched; if they succeeded, others might have a chance. This chance, however, never developed. The newly elected administration in California, under Governor Ronald Reagan, abolished the program.

Yet, the experiment—limited as it was to eighteen participants—carried the seeds for other similar projects. Today, ten years after its start, twelve of the eighteen Vacaville trainees are still engaged in programs designed to bring about social change and also to have impact on individual participants. One Vacaville "graduate" today is chief of the New Career Branch of the National Institute of Mental Health of the Department of Health, Education and Welfare, in Washington, D.C. He has initiated eighteen projects in community mental health, many employing other offenders. Another trainee from the Vacaville experiment, a man who had been nearly illiterate, now has a Ph.D. and is professor at the University of Massachusetts. He is in charge of a pilot program in which students as part of their courses, spend three months in prison with selected confined adult offenders, forming a community of students, staff, and prisoners, all becoming students studying prisons, and it is hoped, agents of change. Early reports indicate some beneficial results of the project, including a significant increase in self-esteem of the convicts, in their preparation for a meaningful job and life, and a reduction in recidivism. Before that, he was one of the architects of a program which closed down all the institutions for youth confinement in that state.

Two former Vacaville trainees are in graduate school pursuing Ph.D.'s; and two more are working in New Career programs, one as project director, the other as training director. Only one out of the original eighteen is back in prison. Grant reports that none of the intelligence tests given to the eighteen had suggested they were capable of higher education. When the man who is now professor was in youth confinement, he was diagnosed as a schizoid personality. Another man, now in graduate school, was diagnosed as a person of dull intelligence. All were labeled at best psychopathic personalities. According to their clinical records, they were likely to be in and out of institutions most of their lives. Professionals had assumed that in these men, either prenatally or during early childhood, permanent structures were formed which made effective adult life extremely unlikely. Grant states that this assumption was without foundation.

The resistance against imaginative new approaches in the penal system is still deep-seated. Not all experiments are successful. Much depends on the selection of the offenders who have the potential of assuming responsibility, and on the patience and understanding of the program director in dealing with prison authorities, prospective employers, and the inmates themselves who are often suspicious, easily discouraged, and respond to negative peer pressure from fellow inmates.

Nevertheless, a widening circle of pilot projects is slowly spreading in several states and Washington, D.C. The projects permit selected offenders to work outside prison. In Massachusetts, some work with mentally retarded children, preparing themselves for careers in that field after their release from prison. In other parts of the country, convict-trainees work for city, state, and federal government, in hospitals, universities, and private corporations. They are employed as staff on special-education programs for inmates and potential offenders, and have been hired as researchers, trainers, community organizers, program developers and evaluators (1, p. 33). More than two hundred former convicts who have gone through the New Careers program work for the Los Angeles county probation service.

Experiments are under way with court diversion schemes as an "alternative to prison" project for persons charged with but not yet tried for a crime. If they are willing they are given, or trained for, a job, and report regularly to the judge who may drop charges and save court time if he decides the prospects are good for the accused to become a useful member of society (4).

Experiences in Britain

In Great Britain, a New Careers Development Office has been established by National Association for the Care and Resettlement of Offenders (NACRO) in London to help any agency or group start programs that will train offenders or other disadvantaged people to acquire steady jobs in fields where their experience can be useful. Again I shall limit myself to describe a pilot project in which I have cooperated. In Bristol, the local branch of NACRO selects young men aged 17 to 21, with extensive histories of delinquency and facing criminal charges. With the court's approval, they are put on one year probation to the New Careers Development Project instead of being given prison sentences. They are trained in teams of four with a leader who is a former offender, drug user, or mental patient. Their training program includes placement for half a day, five days a week, on jobs in a primary school, helping the teachers; the local probation office; an adventure playground; or a local social services department. The young men receive help in daily group discussions of their experiences and through learning techniques to improve their effectiveness as helpers. They are given the responsibility for managing the residence in which they live, and do their own budgeting, shopping, cooking, and caring for the property.

The experiment is in its early stages but it is hoped that steady jobs can be provided for those who want to remain in this kind of work. Job possibilities for ex-offenders are opening up, even if slowly. The Social Services department of the London Borough of Islington, for instance, chose not to increase the number of professional social workers, but instead to add one hundred salaried positions for people from the neighborhood, many of them offenders. Similarly, the Alcoholics Recovery Project in South London is hiring some of its former clients, including those convicted of offenses, to replace social workers.

The New Careers movement is a small beginning, and faces the obstacles of distrust by institutional officials, threat by the professionals, the reductionist tendencies in education and psychology and social work, and the fear and apathy of the general public. A better understanding of logotherapy can help overcome these obstacles and convince those who are, or should be, concerned, that the New Careers program is not out to produce second-rate social workers but to find new ways to offer new services to a wider range of disadvantaged persons.

When Frankl developed his principles of logotherapy, he could not foresee that a logical extension of his work would be illustrated some day by those who came to seek a cure and instead became providers of the cure; that those being taught responsibility would become the teachers. But logotherapy can at least claim a share in experiments that focus the attention of convicts away from their dehumanizing past and present toward new meanings; that stress the healing potential of tasks performed for others and promote a sense of the person's uniqueness by helping him overcome an unwanted pattern of crime or addiction, and then using this experience to help others to free themselves from the same unwanted pattern.

References

1. Grant, J. Douglas and Grant, Joan (1971). Contagion as a principle in behavioural change. In *Unique Programs in Behavior Readjustment*. Elmsford, N.Y.: Pergamon.
2. Hodgkin, Nancy (1972). The New Careers project at Vacaville: a Californian experiment. *Howard League for Penal Reform Journal.*
3. Pearl, Arthur and Riessman, Frank (1965). *New Careers for the Poor.* New York and London: Free Press.
4. Briggs, Dennie (1974). *In Place of Prison.* London: Morris Temple Smith.

Responsibility in Politics and Law

Edgar Bodenheimer

It is the main thesis of this essay that the overaccentuation of the power principle, which has characterized much of Western thinking in social science and political practice since the days of Machiavelli, Spinoza, and Hobbes, must give way to an increased emphasis on responsibility as the basis of political and social action, and that in the specific area of law, in which presence or absence of responsibility is of central importance, an increasing reliance on the findings of logotherapy might point the way to the solution of a perplexing impasse which presently exists in the administration of justice.

The Concept of Power

Beginning with the sixteenth century, a shift took place from the community-centered thinking of the Middle Ages to a political and social philosophy in which the concept of power assumed a prominent position. "Every individual has a sovereign right to do all that he can," said Spinoza. "In other words, the rights of an individual extend to the utmost limits of his power as it has been conditioned" (13, ch. xvi). Hobbes declared that "the Value, or Worth of a man is, as of all other things, his Price; that is to say, so much as would be given for the use of his Power" (6, Pt. 1, ch. 10). Machiavelli elevated the pursuit of power to the rank of a primary objective of statecraft, especially in the conduct of international relations; and he did not rule out the use of trickery and deception as a legitimate means for the attainment of governmental power goals.

It is true, on the other hand, that neither Spinoza, nor Hobbes, nor Machiavelli were willing to consider power an absolute and unrestricted principle of individual or collective action. Both Spinoza and Hobbes deemed it necessary for individuals to relinquish many freedoms and prerogatives to a government invested with authority to curb the anarchical use of power by laws designed to maintain social peace and security. Machiavelli declared in a seldom-quoted statement, "There are two ways of contesting: the one by law, the other by force; the first method is proper to men, the second to beasts" (8, ch. 18).

It was Nietzsche who elevated power to the rank of the highest goal and sought to relegate the institution of law to an inferior position. "There is nothing to life that has value, except the degree of power—assuming that life itself is the will to power" (10, p. 37). He considered law a biologically dangerous obstruction of "the real life-will, which strives after power" (10, p. 512).

Nietzsche's political disciples—although they may have misunderstood much of his teaching—were Mussolini and Hitler. But Nietzsche's ideas also influenced humanitarian thinkers like Bertrand Russell and Alfred Adler. Russell proclaimed that "the fundametal concept in social science is Power, in the same sense in which Energy is the fundamental concept in physics" (12, p. 12).

Adler declared, "The key to the entire social process is . . . that persons are always striving to find a situation in which they excel" (1, p. 74). Both Russell and Adler, however, rejected the consequences of Nietzsche's philosophy and advocated a taming of the power impulse through stimulation of social interest and promotion of cooperative attitudes.

The dynamics of the power principle, which to some extent were a necessary correlate of political and economic liberalism, produced many results beneficial to the development of civilization. In economics, power pursued as a search for profit was an important causal element in the expansion of industry and trade which brought about a sharp rise in the standard of living for the advanced countries. In the cultural sector, great thinkers and artists were able to obtain a powerful hold over the minds and sentiments of many men in a competitive struggle of ideas freed from a monolithic orthodoxy. In politics, the aspiration of nations to secure a position of prestige, recognition, and respect in the world community encouraged individual efforts on the part of many of their citizens to contribute achievements that would enhance national pride.

Every positive principle, however, carries the seeds of a negative complement. The pursuit of power by individuals, groups, and nations during the past few centuries, although greatly enriching civilization, at the same time placed its preservation and survival in jeopardy. The dangers inherent in a philosophy of power are particularly visible in the United States which has profited most conspicuously from the expansive, limit-rejecting ingredients of a radically self-assertive attitude toward life. American politics, in its internal as well as external dimensions, seem dominated today by a quest for power at any price. In the economic domain, capital as well as labor are often bent on an unrestrained pursuit of economic advantage, with insufficient regard for the interests of the public. In academic life, the play of power interests interferes with the building of a genuine community of scholars. Power warfare has also entered conspicuously into the relations between the sexes.

Power and Responsibility

The foregoing observations are not to imply that the concept of power be demoted to an inferior status in social theory or political practice. Power is an important instrument in the attainment of individual or group objectives. The willingness to fight for a worthy cause is meaningless without power to achieve the desired goal. The institution of law leans on a slender reed if the administration of justice lacks the power to enforce it. Nations threatening the peace of the world may succeed in their adventures if power to restrain them is absent in the world community.

On the other hand, the relentless striving for power as an end in itself is incompatible with present-day reality. The idea that politics is nothing but a struggle for power has become obsolete in an age in which social cohesion needs to be increased rather than decreased. Although some conflict appears to be healthy in the political life of a country, the ultimate aim of politics must be the promotion of the common welfare rather than the acquisition or maximization of power. The assertion that the aim of international politics is "either to keep power, to increase power, or to demonstrate power" (9, p. 36) is equally outdated. Although, in the absence of world government, some tenson between nations is unavoidable, the aim of averting atomic disaster necessitates a subordination of power considerations to the idea of a supranational common good. The precarious condition of mankind today lends credence to the words of Martin Buber, "Power withdrawn from responsibility, power which betrays the spirit, power in itself . . . corrupts the history of the world" (3, p. 153).

"Power withdrawn from responsibility," in Buber's opinion, can become the source of unmitigated evil. By "power" he understands, in accordance with common usage, the self-aggrandizement of men or nations. What does he mean by "responsibility"? The context of his remarks shows that a man or group imbued with the idea of responsibility is dedicated to a goal, a work, a calling which transcends the narcissistic search for individual or collective ego satisfaction. In addition, responsibility seems to imply concern for persons and things whose existence or condition may be affected by the acts of a decision maker. A responsible person considers the probable effects of his actions upon his environment (human and nonhuman), weighs their expected benefits against possible drawbacks, and endeavors to justify them in the light of motivations other than mere impulse-directed desire or instinctual urge.

Responsibility holds a central place in logotherapy. The will to power is relegated to a much less basic position in the analysis of the human psyche. Logotherapy thereby performs a historic mission which, one may hope, will have significant normative consequences. "Logotherapy is ultimately education toward responsibility" (DS, p. xiv), and man's responsibility is "always responsibility for the actualization of values" (DS, p. 84). Such responsibility is discharged by the artist concerned with furthering the aesthetic dimension of life, the scientist devoted to the discovery of truth, the statesman working for the promotion of the common good, the judge seeking to serve the cause of justice, and the individual who through love of another human being enhances the meaning of existence in an "I-

Thou'' relationship. Stressing the need for a responsible outlook on life thus carries with it a plea for dedication to the tradition-hallowed values of human existence. To seek power for the sake of power, on the other hand, is not an objective geared to the realization of values. Power is neutral toward value; it may be employed for constructive as well as destructive purposes. Irresponsible exercises of power have been a frequent phenomenon in the history of the human race.

Frankl distinguishes between ''responsibility'' and ''responsibleness.'' Responsibility is imposed by some authority, such as a government or organized church; responsibleness is taken by an individual upon himself through his own decision, which he seeks to justify in the forum of his conscience.

The distinction between responsibility and responsibleness is important and meaningful. On occasions the inner voice of an individual may tell him not to carry out a duty imposed upon him from the outside by law or governmental command which he feels to be repugnant to fundamental precepts of morality and justice. It is true that under normal conditions prevailing in a sane society, the dictates of individual conscience will ordinarily coincide with the guidelines of the social order dealing with the basic norms of human conduct. Responsible men will, as a general rule, refrain from harming the bodily and mental integrity of their fellow men, observe good faith in their contractual and personal relations, and attempt to render unto others that which is due them. These general obligations have become concretized in numerous rules of law. Ranyard West has observed that each man, consciously or unconsciously, desires that his social instinct—that is, the chief source of his responsible actions—be reinforced by the impersonal norms of the law (14, pp. 165–169). He needs this reinforcement of his autonomous responsibility because he cannot, in all circumstances, trust his rational faculties to prevail over his subconscious impulses of hostility and aggression. Law in this sense represents an extension of individual self-control, ''an external support for a man's social instinct against the anti-social activities of his self-assertive instinct'' (14, p. 168). Thus, wide areas exist in which self-directed ''responsibleness'' and other-directed ''responsibility'' go hand in hand and become fused for all practical purposes; however, inner-directed and outer-directed morality may on occasion part ways. In such cases, logotherapy maintains that nonconformist modes of behavior may sometimes be justified.

Freedom and Causality

There would be little merit in speaking about responsible conduct if human beings did not have a choice between acting properly and improperly according to personal or societal codes. If man's decisions are inexorably determined by genetic endowment and the social milieu, a charge of irresponsible action becomes futile. Logotherapy takes the position that man, within limits imposed by biological, psychological, and sociological factors, has freedom to accept or reject his impulses. This freedom is not a freedom from the hereditary or environmental conditions facing an individual, but "rather freedom to take a stand on whatever conditions might confront him" (WM, p. 16). Logotherapy, therefore, rejects the psychic determinism which has been characteristic of psychoanalytic doctrine and some versions of behaviorism. Although human decisions are causally induced, man has genuine choices.

In repudiating the view that human conduct is rigidly determined, logotherapy becomes the psychological counterpart of a new approach in the physical sciences. The modern theory of physics has moved away from the Newtonian supposition that every event in nature is controlled by an ineluctable, linear, mechanical causality. Many physicists assume there may be areas in which determinism exists, there may be others where we are confronted with a nondeterministic causality, and there may also be pure chance events. Even scientists who believe in the reign of universal causality—although they cannot at the present time prove it—would not necessarily conclude that this belief forces them to accept determinism. The physicist Max Born, a close collaborator of Werner Heisenberg, has shown that causality and determinism are not only different words but that they also have different referents. Causal research may mean no more than the discovery of a dependence of one physical situation upon another, a finding, in other words, that a certain state of events A was the precondition of a state of events B. Such a finding does not contain a necessary implication that state B was the inevitable consequence of state A. In the light of our present knowledge, the idea that all causes coerce their effects must be relegated to the status of an unproven metaphysical hypothesis. Stating a reason, for instance, why an atom hit a glass plate at a certain point is not tantamount to the assertion that the atom, under the same conditions, might not possibly have arrived at a different point.

This revision of thinking in the natural sciences is applicable to the science of human behavior. In this area, too, there is insufficient evidence that human actions must in all cases be attributed to the operation of mechanistic, uni-directional forms of causality which leave no room for self-determination and the exercise of an uncoerced will. Causal phenomena may appear on different levels, and one chain of causality may impinge upon another in a complex, interactional, and not always discernible manner.

In the case of a potential criminal offender, for example, we can no longer assume that a sequence of events which can be traced back to his early childhood experiences or character traits can under no circumstances be interrupted, offset, or nullified by another line of causation, or a new set of forces, that lead him to a reexamination and revision of his goals in life. This does not mean that an individual is always able to offer resistance to his irrational impulses, but neither can a determination be made that he is never in a position to oppose a set of conscious or unconscious inclinations and desires (2, p. 175). No convincing reasons prevent the conclusion that some human acts, although they are the end result of traceable causes, are nevertheless the product of free choice. This is the position of logotherapy, and it appears to be in harmony with the most advanced trends in scientific thinking.

Legal and Psychological Freedom

If the view of logotherapy with respect to human decisional freedom were to gain widespread acceptance, it would go a long way toward bridging a serious split which has developed in the United States between the legal and psychiatric professions. The breach exists in the area of criminal responsibility, and it relates to the question under what circumstances mental illness should absolve a criminal offender from liability. The law has traditionally insisted on formulating certain legal tests, as distinguished from psychiatric criteria, to determine whether an accused person is entitled to the defense of insanity. The tests that have been used in the courts are, singly or in some combination, whether the defendant was capable of distinguishing between right and wrong,[1]* whether he acted under an irresistible impulse[2] or was able to conform to the requirements of the law.[3] Whatever the nature of the psychiatric testimony offered in the court room might be, the judge or jury reached their ultimate conclusions in the light of the yardsticks provided by the law. Thus, even though the testimony of the psychiatrist might suggest that the accused was mentally ill in a medical sense, the administrators of justice could always come to an independent judgment that the legal requirements of insanity had not been met. The members of the psychiatric profession, on the other hand, most of whom were committed to a strictly deterministic psychology, felt that these legal criteria offered them little help in discharging the forensic part of their task.

In 1954, the Federal Court of Appeals for the District of Columbia attempted to lower the bars that had previously existed between law and psychiatry in the case of *Durham v. United States.*[4] In this decision, the Court announced a new test of responsibility, to be applied in all future criminal cases tried in the District, which was formulated as follows: "An accused is not criminally responsible if his unlawful act was the product of mental disease or defect" (p. 875). This new standard was to reconcile the legal rule of responsibility with modern developments in medical science and to heal the rupture between the professions by what in practical effect—though not in judicial intent—amounted to a self-renunciation of the law in favor of psychiatry.[5]

The effect of *Durham* was a substantial broadening of the class of criminal offenders eligible for exemption from criminal responsibility. One of the reasons for this development was a decision reached in 1957 by the staff of Washington's mental hospital, Saint Elizabeths, (in reversal of an earlier opinion) that psychopathic and sociopathic offenders were, from a medical standpoint, within the scope of the insanity defense. This ruling was apparently based on the premise that such offenders are so conditioned by their early childhood

*Numerals in this section refer to Notes on page 307.

experiences and subsequent environmental influences that their criminal conduct must be viewed as a necessary and inevitable consequence of their life history. Although under the *Durham* test, the ultimate decision on the existence or nonexistence of criminal responsibility was entrusted to the jury, the trial judge was not permitted to instruct a jury that a psychopath was not within the reach of the insanity defense.[6]

One of the early effects of *Durham* was the acquittal and release of a number of dangerous offenders. To remedy this situation, Congress enacted a statute in 1955 making hospitalization mandatory in every case tried in the District of Columbia where a defendant was adjudged not guilty by reason of insanity. This statute did not solve the problem created by *Durham* because some offenders acquitted under an extremely broad test of insanity were found, after their commitment to Saint Elizabeths, not to be in need of psychiatric treatment. These persons were released after a short period of confinement and resumed their criminal careers. It was discovered—in the district of Columbia as well as elsewhere in the country—that for genuinely psychopathic criminals commitment to a mental hospital was not necessarily a more humanitarian solution than a sentence served in prison, because there is generally no statutory limit on the length of time a person may be held in a mental institution.

In 1961, Judge Warren E. Burger, the present Chief Justice of the United States Supreme Court, charged that administration of the insanity defense under the *Durham* test had tended "to treat unsupported and dubious psychiatric theory as scientific knowledge."[7] He pointed out that "from ancient times the development of the law was always on the basic idea that man should be held criminally responsible for his voluntary acts resulting from an exercise of his will," but that the *Durham* test "ignores will or choice."

The difficulties encountered in administering the *Durham* rule prompted the District of Columbia Court, in a series of decisions beginning in 1962, to recede from an essentially medical test of insanity and return to the reinstatement of a legal criterion. Under *Durham,* it was not necessary, as a prerequisite for acquittal, to show that the defendant was unable to control his actions. Some psychiatrists pointed out that a person may suffer from a mental disease and yet be able to control most of his actions (4, pp. 13–15; 5, pp. 42–60). To the extent that a criminal offender was not forced into his crime by ineluctable necessity, there appeared to be no plausible reason to absolve him from responsibility for his conduct.

In the light of such considerations, the Court in 1962 framed a new instruction to the jury to the effect that "a mental disease or defect includes any abnormal condition of the mind which substantially affects mental or emotional processes and *substantially impairs behavior controls.*"[8] In 1972, the Court unanimously overruled *Durham*[9] and adopted the test of the Model Penal Code.[10] The significance of this step was the replacement of an essentially vague criterion of insanity, framed in terms of a causal relation between mental disease and criminal act, by a more concrete legal signpost for the guidance of the jury: its new task was to determine whether at the time of the unlawful conduct, in the light of all the evidence, the accused possessed substantial capacity to conform his actions to the requirement of the law. Even the judge who had written the *Durham* opinion acknowledged the need, in the wake of supervening experiences, of "distinguishing between the uniquely psychiatric elements of criminal responsibility and its legal and moral elements."[11] The fact that few American jurisdictions chose to adopt the *Durham* rule, while the Model Code test is gaining increasing favor with courts and legislatures (7, pp. 294–295), seems to indicate that these recent developments in the District of Columbia parallel national trends in this area of the law.

The new legal criterion of mental disease, which focuses on the presence or absence of behavior controls at the time of the unlawful act, implies a rejection of a radically deterministic philosophy. The adoption of this test holds no guarantees, however, that medical experts believing in psychic determinism will not, in many cases, testify in court that the accused person was lacking the capacity to conform his conduct to the requirements of the law to such an extent that he should not be held responsible for his acts. A growing acceptance of logotherapy's position by psychiatrists could contribute greatly to the solution of a problem which has created much ill-will between two disciplines whose cooperation is required at a time when the problem of crime has assumed unprecedented dimensions. The view taken by logotherapy would make it possible, in the administration of criminal justice, to start off from a presumption of responsibility. To overcome this presumption it would have to be proved by convincing evidence that the offender was deprived of rationality to such an extent that he had become the instrument of irrational forces; then responsibility should be denied and the insanity plea upheld.

An acceptance of this position would leave unsolved many acute and perplexing problems in the administration of criminal justice. It would, however, have the salutary effect of restoring the concept of responsibility to its proper place in the social and legal order. It would permit a renewed emphasis in the education and treatment of human beings on the fact that they are deemed responsible for their actions unless their decisional freedom has been destroyed or gravely impaired by a severe form of mental illness.

Notes

1. M'Naghten's Case, 8 Eng. Rep. 718 (1843).
2. *Commonwealth v. Rogers,* 7 Metcalf 502 (Mass., 1844).
3. See *Model Penal Code,* Proposed Official Draft (1962), Sec. 4.01, set forth *infra* n. 37.
4. 214 Fed. 2d 862 (1954).
5. The Court's opinion insisted that the new rule would leave the jury free to perform its traditional function of applying "our inherited ideas of moral responsibility." Since, however, the terms "mental disease" and "product" (in the sense of cause-effect relationship between mental disease and criminal act) remained undefined in the opinion, the rule provided the jury with no standard by which to judge the evidence and thus left it dependent upon the testimony of the experts.
6. *Taylor v. United States,* 222 Fed. 2d 398, 404 (1955).
7. *Blocker v. United States,* 288 Fed. 2d 853, 858 (1961).
8. *MacDonald v. United States,* 312 Fed. 2d 847, 850 (1962).
9. *United States v. Brawner,* 471 Fed. 2d 969 (1972).
10. *Model Penal Code,* Sec. 4.01 (0): "A person is not responsible for criminal conduct if at the time of such conduct as a result of mental disease or defect he lacks substantial capacity either to appreciate the criminality [wrongfulness] of his conduct or to conform his conduct to the requirements of law."
11. See Judge Bazelon's concurring opinion in *United States v. Eichberg,* 439, 2d 620, 621–628 (1971).

References

1. Adler, A. (1929). *The Science of Living.* New York: Greenberg.
2. Bodenheimer, E. (1967). *Treatise on Justice.* New York: Philosophical Library.

3. Buber, M. (1965). *Between Man and Man.* New York: Macmillan.
4. Davidson, H. A. (1962). The psychiatrist's role in the administration of criminal justice. In *Criminal Psychology.* New York: Philosophical Library.
5. Glasser, W. (1965). *Reality Therapy.* New York: Harper.
6. Hobbes, T. (1914). *Leviathan.* New York: Dutton.
7. LaFave, W. R. and Scott, A. W. (1972). *Handbook of Criminal Law.* St. Paul: West.
8. Machiavelli, N. (1908). *The Prince.* New York: Dutton.
9. Morgenthau, H. J. (1967). *Politics Among Nations,* 4th ed. New York: Knopf.
10. Nietzsche, F. (1968). *The Will to Power* (Kaufmann transl.). New York: Modern Library.
11. ______(1968). *Basic Writings* (Kaufmann transl.). New York: Modern Library.
12. Russell, B. (1938). *Power: A New Social Analysis.* New York: Norton.
13. Spinoza, B. (1895). *Tractatus Theologico-Politicus* (Elwes transl.). London: Routledge and Kegan Paul.
14. West, R. (1945). *Conscience and Society.* New York: Emerson Books.

New Course for Management

Oliver A. Phillips

Contemporary management theories which bring the human element into focus started in the early 1920s with the Harvard research at the Hawthorne works of the Western Electric Company. These studies mentioned noneconomic motivators, the concept of social equilibrium, the fact that man's actions cannot be determined by logical factors and that simple cause-and-effect analysis is insufficient in describing man (6). Other theorists such as McGregor (4) introduced the concept that man by nature is striving for goals other than those of a pure economic nature. Herzberg's research (5) further divided economic and noneconomic motivational goals into hygienic factors and motivators. Although these and other theories helped us understand human behavior within the context of the work environment, they remain isolated factors not integrated into a holistic understanding of man. Logotherapy offers the structure within which these various factors have relevance.

Existing management theories also fail to offer a satisfactory solution to the spreading problem of worker alienation. Companies have tried many remedies such as the use of psychological tests to weed out potentially dissatisfied workers; the increase of fringe benefits to "lock in" the employee; organizational changes to reduce worker alienation; and various procedures to control shoddy workmanship, often the result of such alienation. The purpose of this essay is to suggest the concepts of logotherapy that can be used to alleviate the problem.

Logotherapy Translated into a Management Theory

Logotherapy was developed in a clinical rather than a business environment. Its basic concept can be adjusted to application by management. As the accompanying chart shows, man's main motivation, his will to meaning, can be diverted in two directions, one leading to collective neurosis and the nihilistic view that life has no meaning, the other to existential frustration and reductionist view that man is a robot. Only when a person's will to meaning is allowed to develop freely and responsibly, will he find meaning—through his activities, experiences, and attitudes.

How far these psycho-philosophical concepts can be translated into the practical world of business is still an open question. This essay attempts to indicate how management can avoid the diversions of workers' will to meaning toward nihilism and reductionism. But to place the workers' will to meaning at the center of the production process would require fundamental changes in the value priorities of management, from efficiency toward human potential, from quantity of production toward quality of life, from power and money toward meaning. Few companies are willing to even explore such value shifts. However, economic and ecological necessity may force a new course in management. And it may turn out, as preliminary observations indicate, that in the long run efficiency and profits may increase if they no longer are the primary goals but emerge as byproducts of a management that aims at allowing workers to find fulfillment.

Collective Neurosis

One way for management to repress its workers' will to meaning is to create an environment that fosters the development of collective neurosis (left side of the chart). This can happen in companies run by authoritarian management that controls employees through fear. Such companies often succeed for long periods, reinforcing the belief that authoritarian management pays off. However, the consequences

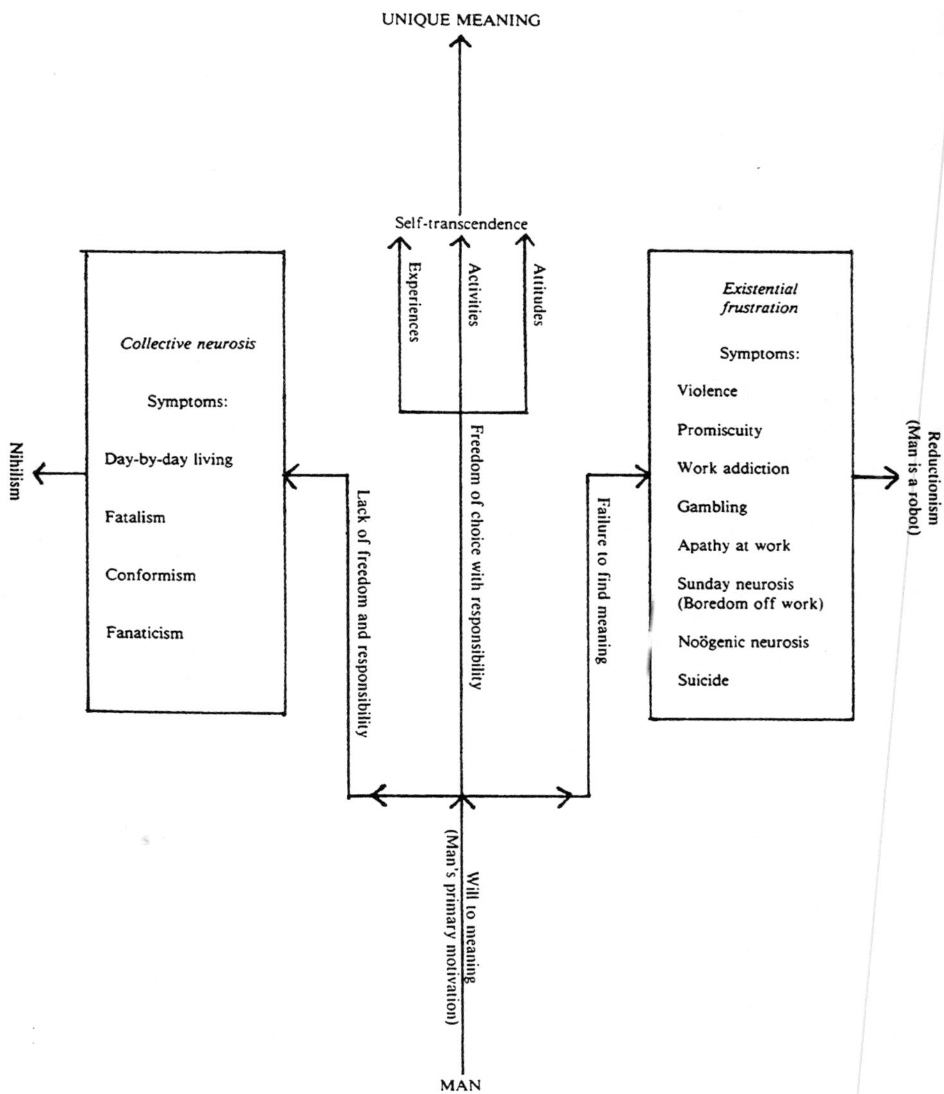
UNIQUE MEANING
Self-transcendence
Experiences
Activities
Attitudes
Collective neurosis
Symptoms:
Day-by-day living
Fatalism
Conformism
Fanaticism
Nihilism
Lack of freedom and responsibility
Freedom of choice with responsibility
Failure to find meaning
Existential frustration
Symptoms:
Violence
Promiscuity
Work addiction
Gambling
Apathy at work
Sunday neurosis (Boredom off work)
Noögenic neurosis
Suicide
Reductionism (Man is a robot)
Will to meaning (Man's primary motivation)
MAN

of the collective neurosis are eventually felt in the form of shoddy workmanship, increased rejection rates, careless mistakes, stagnated creativity, loss of efficiency, and a lowering of profits. Management is perplexed because everything seemed to be running smoothly. Everyone does exactly as he is told, dissenters are rare, company procedures are followed meticulously. To know what is happening, one must understand that the workers' will to meaning is repressed by the four symptoms of the collective neurosis: a day-by-day attitude, fatalism, collective thinking, and fanaticism (PE, p. 117 ff).

A day-by-day attitude among workers is induced by companies whose primary concern is profits. Workers are hired and fired to balance the accounting, with little consideration for their contributions to the organization, their accomplishments, or their loyalty. Under these circumstances, the employee is likely to develop a short-range attitude toward his job, waiting for his number to come up.

Fatalism results when the uniqueness of the employee is denied. He is not given a choice; he is "assigned" according to a management plan. Fifty draftsmen, seventy-five assembly workers, or ten engineers are needed; and what counts is getting a certain number of bodies on a certain job within a specified time.

Collective thinking is brought about by the company that does not tolerate dissent. The yes-man dominates. The supervisor is lulled into believing his directions are correct because everyone agrees. The employee is merely following directions and, rather than offering solutions himself, waits for management to solve the problems. The employee abandons himself as a free and responsible person.

Fanaticism is fostered by authoritarian companies among its supervisors and higher managers, occasionally also among its workers. It denies the individuality of others and does not tolerate differing opinions.

If a symptom of the collective neurosis is present, the worker's will to meaning is repressed. And because work and wages occupy a high position on the value scale of our society, most employees will feel that not only their work but their life lacks meaning. Managers of authoritarian companies will understand why their company starts losing money only if they can see that it is their very striving for profits that makes profits elusive. The will to power, in the form of profits, has become an end rather than a means to offer useful goods and services to the customer.

Existential Frustration

The second way in which a company can repress its workers' will to meaning (right side of the chart) is to create conditions that will frustrate the workers because they cannot see meaningful relationships to their work. Workers' frustration can have many causes, among them the categorizing and depersonalizing of jobs.

Categorizing jobs denies the worker his human qualities, making him a robot. This can be done on all levels, from the assembly-line worker to the engineer who designs nothing but airplane wing tips, or the supervisor who does nothing but fill out company forms. Depersonalizing undercuts the worker's uniqueness and can take many forms. A person is given a job with a fancy title but finds he is nothing more than an errand boy. Or a person is yanked from his job, his room, his desk, for no apparent reason but "efficiency." Or he is separated from his co-workers whose companionship has given him some meaning even if his work didn't. Many stages of inspection on the production line also have a depersonalizing effect: if the product turns out well, the inspector gets the credit; if it turns out badly, instead of asking the worker what the problem is, more inspection stations are installed.

These depersonalizing practices are often used by managers who feel they have a humanistic system. They have excellent personnel policies, retirement plans, liberal vacations. Missing is the understanding that each person is unique and wants to do something meaningful to him. If the employee is ignorant of his potentials, if management pays no attention to them, and if no opportunity exists to develop them, the employee will feel frustrated or empty without knowing why. The result of his frustration may be violence, promiscuity, excessive dedication to work (work addiction), alcoholism, gambling, apathy at work, boredom when off work (Sunday neurosis), and in extreme cases suicide. This is not to say that management has caused the lack of meaning in the employee's life but rather that a meaning in work can serve as a focal point toward fulfillment in all aspects of life.

Meaningful Work

A job does not necessarily become more meaningful if it offers better pay, guarantees more security, brings prestige, or is a challenge to intelligence. These conditions are important but do not provide a final solution. The American worker has been progressing toward affluence, job security, and employment that offers prestige and a challenge to intelligence. Yet worker dissatisfaction has been spreading.

No job is meaningful as such. What is interesting to one person is boring to another; self-esteem through status brings fulfillment for some but not every worker can take the extensive training needed for status jobs. And in the affluent society more people than ever downgrade money on their list of priorities, although for most it still ranks high. Organization theories that look for "things" to motivate the worker are bound to fail. Theories that offer physical advantages and psychological motivations will not succeed if they disregard the human spirit as a source of incentive: man's decision making, his uniqueness, his responsibility, his willingness to reach out beyond himself, his thirst to fulfill what he sees as his potentials.

Management cannot dictate what an employee's work meaning should be. It can only provide him with a freedom of choice with responsibility. This single concept of logotherapy probably has the most far-reaching effect in management theory. It means that an employee should be able to choose his work assignments and the type of work he wants to perform. Instead of fitting workers into job categories, a list of tasks to be accomplished could be set up, and the workers given the widest possible freedom to decide among themselves how and by whom these tasks are to be done. Freedom of choice is also improved by making the pay scale and fringe benefits more uniform among employees than they presently are. An employee who is offered a supervisor's position with higher salary, private office, and personal secretary is put under considerable pressure to accept that position even though it means leaving a job he enjoys doing, and leaving friends whose company he likes. This situation can hardly be said to allow free choice. Management would be hard pressed to justify giving a supervisor more money than those working under him. He is merely performing a different task under better working conditions. The implication is that those who advance in the hierarchy of management must be unhappy in their jobs or they would not be paid more. If someone enjoys his work he needn't be paid more to do it.

Two reasons usually are advanced to justify higher salaries to people in higher positions: their investment in the education needed to qualify for managerial work, and the responsibility they are taking on. Both reasons need reexamination. Education often has little relevance to the job being performed; on-the-job training may be more pertinent than a college degree. Important are not the initials or titles after a person's name, nor how fancy a resume he has, but what he can do and finds most meaningful. And responsibility need not be reserved for the supervisor but should be given to anyone doing a job. In fact, logotherapy demands that freedom of choice should be given only to the extent responsibility is accepted, or the result will not be meaning but chaos. To consider the work situation as an opportunity for education—to competence as well as responsibility—is a concept only few organizations in the United States are beginning to see.

The emphasis on job descriptions and employee qualifications reduces not only the worker's opportunity to make choices but also his uniqueness. The more a worker feels he is doing a job not because he is a special person but because he has certain general qualifications, the more he will feel replaceable. And the meaning potential of a job, regardless of its status and salary, increases with the worker's sense of being irreplaceable.

Just as management cannot give an employee meaning, it cannot directly motivate him. It only can, as McGregor (4) maintains, block his natural desire to work and do a good job. Logotherapy, however, goes one step further by identifying the direction in which man is pulled in his search for meaning: he reaches out beyond himself toward other people, and toward causes in which he believes.

The concept that dedication to something outside one's self-interest is a stronger motivation to work than money or power could not emerge in the pre-affluent society. Under conditions of poverty, a person found meaning in work because it helped him feed, house, and clothe himself and his family. But under conditions of affluence, the meaning of work takes on new levels. To some extent the affluent person still works for the sake of his family or for a higher standard of living, but if the assumption of logotherapy is correct, this will not satify him in the long run; it will leave him with a sense of emptiness. He will look for new meaning potentials in work that benefits his coworkers, minority groups he identifies with—women, the old, the blacks—and causes he considers worth supporting—the economic health of his country, ecology, the elimination of poverty and discrimination, peace.

Such concepts seem utopian and require an education to responsibility not offered widely in the home and the schools. Yet, without such an education to responsibility man will fill his inner emptiness with surrogates of meaning—violence, addiction, power, money. Work is still a major source of meaning but an increasing number of people realize that meaningful work and a paid job need not be identical. They switch careers, go back to school, or cut down their hours of meaningless employment while trying to find a lifestyle that allows them to live on less and to fill their increased leisure with creative and voluntary activities they find meaningful.

Management can offer meaning to workers by finding employees who believe in the causes the company is serving. Believers in organic food can work in plants manufacturing such foods, and believers in a strong America can work in munitions factories. Where such an approach is not practical, management can provide workers with satisfaction in other ways. A company may make products or furnish services that directly benefit the community; or it can indirectly help the community—for instance, through helping minorities or the underprivileged obtain training and jobs. Contributions to charities or scholarships for the underprivileged are other means of community service for companies too small to afford large-scale training programs. An organization has many ways to help the community, thereby giving its employees a sense of meaning.

Creative Values

Of the three roads to meaning—activity, experience, and attitude—the creative value of activity directly applies to work although the other two also have a place for the employee. In an industrialized, computerized society, meaningful work becomes more difficult to find; and we have indicated how choice, uniqueness, and responsibility need to be shifted to different levels, and how self-transcendence can be made to come into play. Even one of the most conservative management systems in the world, the military, has found new ways of giving its "employees" some limited choices by letting them volunteer their service, choose the school they wish to attend and the theater of operation in which they wish to serve.

But even in civilian employment it is impossible to let all workers choose their tasks. An alternative is to allow them to *rotate* the tasks no one likes to do. In this situation both attitudinal and experiential values are elicited. Undesirable tasks are unavoidable, but the employee still has the freedom of choice over his attitude toward the task and can therefore find meaning in braving it. In addition, because the undesirable task is now shared, he has an experiential value of knowing that by doing his share he is lightening the burden of his fellow workers. The unpleasant task, therefore, can actually allow an employee to experience meaning from its performance. This is true primarily when the undesirable task is freely shared among workers, and not when it is assigned to one or two workers as a permanent job.

Pleasure can be a by-product of performing a freely chosen or a shared, undesirable task. Attempts by management to provide pleasure for the employee by direct means—Christmas parties, company picnics, discount tickets to amusement parks and theaters, bowling leagues, company baseball teams, etc.—are likely to fail, except where they foster a closer human relationship among the employees. These activities are good adjuncts to the pleasure received at work, but they do not replace the happiness obtained indirectly through meaningful work involvement.

Examples

Some of the principles outlined in this essay have been tested by various companies. The examples offered here are taken from different parts of the world and from differing economic systems. They are not "based" on logotherapy but use many of its tenets, and thus indicate that these tenets can serve as a nucleus around which a new management philosophy can evolve.

In Kansas, the Topeka Gaines Pet Food plant employs semi-autonomous teams; each selects its own foreman, devises its own methods for doing the work, determines the production quota, and makes job assignments. Every team member is trained to learn all the jobs which are rotated so no one gets assigned to menial work all the time. The company has no time clocks, no special parking privileges, no separate dining rooms for managers. Each worker participates in the decision making, takes responsibility for it, and is actively interested in community affairs. As a result of this management system, absenteeism is only 1 percent compared with the "normal" 5 percent, and production is 20 to 30 percent higher than at comparable plants (3).

In Yugoslavia, workers participation in decision-making is assured by law. In the Energoinvest Company, Sarajevo, for instance, which owns 35 factories, six mines, and has 33 foreign-sales offices, the Workers Council participates in management decisions and has the power to hire and fire their management for poor performance. The Council defines the managerial prerogatives, and the chief executive's function is to implement the Council's decision. The worker's pay is directly proportional to the company's profits. The company also has worker teams, and direct community involvement is accomplished through the chief executive who is responsible for insuring that the company does nothing against the public interest (2).

In China, a management is emerging that uses meaning orientation as an incentive to work, although in a different manner. The Chinese worker finds meaning through his knowledge that a better standard of living for all will result from his toil. Here, too, a team of workers, the "revolutionary committee," nominally controls the factory. Each committee determines its production quota and targets for capital acquisition; status symbols such as titles are eliminated, and managers and workers wear the same clothes; the workers' efforts often directly benefit the community—in such forms as building a new bridge or constructing a new hydroelectric plant. The range of free choice is limited for the Chinese worker when compared with the American worker, but his dedication to a cause outside himself makes up the difference (7).

In Israel, the kibbutz offers an example of a socialist working community in a capitalist economy. Here, too, the workers rotate work, have no distinction in status and pay, wear no distinctive clothes, determine management decisions, and are motivated by a will to meaning expressed in the betterment of their society and in the service of their community.

These examples project the will to meaning as a pervading force pulling varying strands of mankind toward self-transcendence. The forms this force takes may vary; but when viewed through logotherapy, the variance disappears, and the unified will to meaning appears. A management realizing the consequences of the frustrated will to meaning in its work force will be able to unite with the workers in a common goal of dedication to a task beyond itself.

References

1. Aronowitz, Stanley (1973). *False Promises.* New York: McGraw-Hill.
2. Burck, Gilbert (1972). A socialist enterprise that acts like a fierce capitalist competitor. *Fortune,* Vol. LXXXV, No. 1.
3. Jenkins, David (1973). Democracy in the factory. *Atlantic,* Vol. 231, No. 4.
4. McGregor, Douglas (1960). *The Human Side of Enterprise.* New York: McGraw-Hill.
5. Herzberg, Frederick (1967). *Work and the Nature of Man.* Cleveland: World.
6. Roethlisberger, F. J., and Dickson, W. J. (1966). *Management and the Worker.* Cambridge: Harvard University Press.
7. Wheelwright, E. L., and McFarlane, B. (1971). *The Chinese Road to Socialism.* New York: Monthly Review Press.

The Work Situation

George A. Sargent

Work alienation has been recognized as a problem in the United States only recently. Before and during the depression, the question of meaningful work seldom arose. Just having a job was enough. Men worked because they had to survive. But in an affluent society, where survival no longer is a daily issue, rising expectations have allowed workers to stand aside from their work and look at it critically. And frequently they find their jobs unfulfilling.

Their attempts at individuality and creativity are often considered by management as blocks to efficient production. The split-and-simplify methods of the assembly line leave little room for the individual. Nor does the white-collar worker escape boredom; it comes from the preponderance of paperwork and administrative red tape that feeds the growing technological monster. Under these conditions, employee turnover and absenteeism have risen alarmingly.

Those studying the problem of work alienation—the meaninglessness on the job—usually base their analyses on implicit acceptance of psychoanalytic, stimulus-response, or need-deprivation models. Logotherapy provides a better alternative with its coherent motivational theory focusing on man's search for meaning. We shall, therefore, explore the untapped potentials offered by viewing work through logotherapy.

Work and Psychological Well-Being

A study by the Department of Health, Education, and Welfare (12) estimates that 17 percent of the labor force—11.9 million persons—can be considered unhappy in their jobs. As critics have pointed out, this also means that 83 percent are happy; and worker alienation, therefore, is no major problem. Indeed, job satisfaction research over the past twenty-five years has consistently found 80 to 85 percent of all workers generally satisfied with their work situation.

But Kornhauser (3) tends to qualify some of these studies. Most workers he studied were only "mildly satisfied." Their lack of strong dissatisfaction *or* satisfaction, he said, indicated an attitude more of apathy than approval.

Research by Lukas (4) supports Frankl's insistence that success and meaning do not necessarily go together, nor do failure and despair. "Successful" persons may be in despair; and "failure" in the material sense may be filled with a sense of meaning. Perhaps the amount of meaning workers find in their lives gives a better measure of work alienation than their self-reported job satisfaction. My own research in 1971 demonstrated that, though job satisfaction and purpose in life are correlated, they are different phenomena. It is a fallacy to assume that because 83 percent of workers report mild satisfaction with their jobs they do not suffer from a lack of meaning.

Freud and the psychoanalytic school saw work as a sublimation of the aggressive instincts but also as man's closest bond with reality and the human community. Ives Hendrick posited an actual work instinct; Erik Erikson recognized work as a crucial developmental stage; and Barbara Lantos saw work as a specifically human activity whose achievement contributed to ego satisfactions as opposed to id satisfactions—that is, satisfactions derived from work were less hedonistic and more rational. The real difference between work and play is in their purpose, not their content. Others have gone beyond the psychoanalytic school.

Maslow's hierarchy of needs, ranging from the need to survive all the way up to the need for self-actualization, translated into work terms, suggests that workers in the United States have substantially satisfied their lower-level needs: they are reasonably well assured of survival through jobs, social security, company pensions, and public-assistance plans. Machines have taken much toil out of many jobs. But now, as predicted in the hierarchy, with their lower-level needs satisfied, men look to self-actualization. Money is no longer enough to meet their needs; they want to feel they are growing and "becoming" all they can be, and too often their jobs seem to restrict their development. They want more control over their job situation, more responsibility, more interesting work.

This explanation of dissatisfaction is good as far as it goes. Unfortunately, many people, misinterpreting Maslow, attempt to pursue self-actualization directly, but this is not what is intended; "my experience agrees with Frankl's that people who seek self-actualization directly, selfishly, personally, dichotomized away from mission in life—i.e., as a form of private and subjective salvation—don't, in fact, achieve it" (6, p. 108). Man achieves some level of self-actualization not by aiming directly at it but through a devotion to a cause or accomplishment of a task.

Meaning and Work

The major lesson of this exploration of the work situation in logotherapy's terms is that work may fulfill a person's needs for comfort, recognition, money, and companionship, and still leave him miserable. Above all, employees must see some sense in their work before they will find true satisfaction in performing it. A mass of literature points to this conclusion, without producing convincing theoretical explanations of why it is true. Explanations are based on self-esteem, the need hierarchy, mastery instincts, and philosophical hedonism; but none explains the phenomenon as well as logotherapy: man seeks meaning in his work because meaning is what he seeks in his life.

Meaning may be found in devotion to a cause, performance of a task, or in true encounter with another person. The ability to work is neither a necessary nor a sufficient condition for living meaningfully, but during a person's life much of his meaning can be found within his occupational activity (DS, pp. 94 ff).

Men and women relate to their work in three broad stages: prevocational (preparation and selection), vocational, and postvocational (separation from work through unemployment or retirement).

The Prevocational Stage

The search for meaningful work starts in the prevocational stage. But the search is made difficult because the prospective job seeker faces situations for which tradition has not prepared him. Today, people are entering the work force at a later age than ever before because a technological society requires more education, and rising affluence makes it less necessary to begin work at an early age. In fact, many young people postpone entrance indefinitely. They opt for lives with relatively low levels of income; many drop out, set up communes, work only part time, or choose not to join the labor force at all. But most people still plan a lifetime of work; and their value priorities, too, are changing. Several large-scale studies of college youth, sponsored by the National Institute of Mental Health, have found that career interest is now secondary to "finding a purpose and meaning in life" (5).

Not only young persons are in this prevocational stage but also veterans, housewives, the disadvantaged and disabled, rehabilitated criminals, and mental patients of all ages. The entire group is faced with the staggering problem of having to select work from the 20,000 different types of jobs officially listed (1). Never before has the potential employee faced so many highly specialized job possibilities. Today's career choice also represents a choice of life style. Whatever the decision of the job seeker, it will limit future choices. Since educational requirements are specialized for many vocations, he must make the right choice early or exclude himself from many careers. A young person who is unaware of the range of opportunities may eliminate many meaningful career possibilities before knowing they exist. And when he decides on a career it may become obsolete. New discoveries may wipe out a lifetime of training and experience, bringing frustration and insecurity to the area of career preparation and choice.

With the work ethic weakening, the family's influence on the wane, and without tradition as a guide, the young person is likely to focus his attention on the material benefits of a job rather than on a task that needs to be done—a needed product or service. Sadder still, he may grab the first thing that comes along, simply to ward off nothingness. Work selected under such circumstances may provide temporary meaning if it is done to achieve a purpose; for instance, the young person may derive meaning from any job because it gives him the desired independence from his parents, or a woman may find meaning in her gaining a sense of equality with her husband. But unless such persons can find long-lasting meaning in work, they may drop out or bury themselves in work—responses which are often motivated by an intense desire to find meaning, coupled with frustration of not being able to do so.

The logotherapist can be helpful to prevocational career seekers in several ways. First, dereflection can assist in refocusing toward the life tasks and away from themselves. To be sure, proper vocational counseling procedures must be used. Current talents, assets, and liabilities should be objectively appraised in the light of the requirements of the various occupations. The therapist can help the job seeker make an inventory of his assets and goals. But beyond a certain point the career seeker must start his job before he can assess it. In the absence of a final objective, which few young people see clearly, a step-by-step approach may gradually illuminate the path to an emerging goal. The therapist can also function as a "logo-educator" who starts the career seeker on an educative effort that should become a lifelong process. He needs to learn cognitively and emotionally that a person really can have a choice and probably can accomplish what he thinks needs to be done. He can also learn why it is important that the job needs to be done. Commitment must have reasons. A therapist who helps job seekers see those reasons may kindle their enthusiasm.

Such a message is conveyed through action as well as words. Because this educational effort must start early, parents are the primary sources conveying these messages. During the crucial life stages, between the ages of five and ten, identification with a responsible, meaning-seeking worker will teach logotherapy's lesson far better than mere words or a combination of actions and words later.

The Vocational Stage

In the vocational stage, workers may be overcome by meaninglessness because our society prompts them to see their own worth in terms of their economic value to others. They suppress their own needs in order to be what others want them to be, or what they *think* others want them to be. They forget who they are, what satisfies them, or for what or for whom they would be willing to live, work, or die. Here, logotherapy helps by its reorientation of the person toward his personal uniqueness, the human core, and self-transcendence.

Logotherapy also can help the worker by showing him that happiness in work, as any other happiness, cannot be pursued directly but results from a meaningful job motivation. Job satisfaction, in the long run, will not come from direct approaches, such as providing recreational facilities, improved lighting, or piped-in music. Primary motivation comes from the meaning the task has for the individual. For this reason, logotherapy places primary responsibility for job satisfaction on the worker, not the job. This is consistent with the research of Kornhauser (3, p. 266) and Weiss and Riesman (11, p. 504): those who find most satisfaction in their work are also those who find the most satisfaction in their off-the-job activities. Maslow put it this way, "The only happy people I know are the ones who are working well at something they consider important" (7, p. 6).

The evidence, however, is not clear-cut whether all workers have needs for self-actualization. Morse and Weiss, for instance, showed that a white-collar worker most often sees his job as a purpose in life, while the blue-collar worker finds in work a way to keep active (10, p. 198). Research has also indicated that many blue-collar workers are less concerned with job content than with security, good pay, short hours, and long vacations. Nonetheless, recent indications of deep unhappiness in the blue- and white-collar ranks suggests a shift of the central concerns of employees toward the higher-level needs Maslow mentioned. Workers feel they are missing something in their lives. As long as that something was beyond reach, it did not make them too unhappy. But now that realization appears possible—as has happened in this era of media-stimulated rising expectations—the innocence is shattered. This is as true for intangibles like "peace of mind" and "personal fulfillment" as it is for material goods.

Alienation seems to be more pronounced in routine, repetitive jobs, the kind found in large, impersonal organizations. Here one also finds loss of identity, apathy, and job dissatisfaction, especially toward the bottom of the organization hierarchy. A vast potential for violence accumulates as a result of the unused talents and frustrated goals of today's workers at all levels. These energies must be redirected into areas of creative, meaningful productiveness.

One alternative chosen by some young people in the vocational stage has been to recombine their work, play, and family activities in work communes. Whether this solution is good or even possible for a large segment of the population remains to be seen. The potential for solving deadly work problems seems to lie in making work itself more meaningful. This may be done by eliminating jobs that are dehumanizing; reconstructing jobs that have been excessively fragmented; and offering the public products and services which the workers feel are needed. If no redeeming social contribution is found in the production of plastic war toys, then perhaps their production should be stopped, even though people buy them. With modern advertising methods influencing demand, it becomes increasingly difficult for entrepreneurs to justify their supply solely on the basis of that demand. Too often top value is placed on what is profitable or technically feasible rather than on what is humanly or ecologically desirable.

Employers in recent years have used "job enrichment" programs focused on improving the work itself to make jobs more significant to workers. But as long as these programs remain primarily techniques to improve work quality or to lower absenteeism and turnover, and are dropped or "tightened up" if profits do not increase, they will accomplish little. Techniques *as* techniques are counterproductive. They treat the worker not as a unique human being but as a piece of equipment that can be manipulated, thus reinforcing the worker's bias that he cannot be himself but needs only to learn the right technique of manipulation in order to live a fulfilling life.

Enlightened managers in the sixties and early seventies have taken their cue from McGregor's Theory X and Theory Y (9). Theory X managers have negative expectations of their workers; they feel people have to be forced to work and to be watched carefully. Theory Y managers believe people want to work and expect the best from them—a self-fulfilling prophecy. Today's managers need more than this oversimplified philosophy to guide them into the eighties. McGregor's formulations are helpful, but as managers have become increasingly aware of industry's role and responsibility in the world, a more sophisticated approach is needed. Logotherapy translates the self-understanding of the man in the street into scientific terms (2a, p. 131) and Fabry (2, p. viii) has tried to retranslate that scientific theory for that same man in the street. Logotherapy does the same with the man on the job: It takes his understanding of work and translates it into scientific and philosophical terms, and it now needs to be retranslated for the man on the job.

Men at work, suffering from meaninglessness, tend to blame themselves, thus adding guilt to their suffering. The logotherapist can help them distinguish between the collective neurosis which is not their fault and which they can learn to recognize, and personal feelings of emptiness which they have the capacity and responsibility to fill.

Therapists, counselors, management, family, and clergy can help a person cope with work alienation that makes him feel his job is without meaning. These "helpers" cannot give the employee meaning in his work but they may lead him toward seeing the meaning already present in what he is doing; making him aware of the choices available to him within his job or through a change in jobs; and assisting him to realize that there is more to life than work and that he may find meaning and purpose outside his job. It would be just as fatal to suggest he find all his meaning on the job as it would be to suggest he find none.

The Postvocational Stage

Morse and Weiss (10, p. 192) found that 80 percent of blue- and white-collar workers would continue to work even if they no longer needed the money. "It does not mean that people cannot readjust to not working," they said, "rather it means that not working requires considerable readjustment." Most workers have nonfinancial reasons for working—they need to keep busy or it gives them purpose. Some persons are lost without a job. Those who manage without working, usually enjoyed their work but can live meaningfully without it. This view confirms Frankl's findings, in the depression days of the thirties, that the despair of the unemployed lifted if they found some worthwhile activity, even if it was unpaid. The healthiest people keep busy with something or someone. "They have grasped the fact that the meaning of human life is not completely contained within paid work, that unemployment need not compel one to live meaninglessly'' (DS, p. 99).

This is true for the retired as well as for the unemployed. The problems of the retired include not only the loss of work but also the lack of some life-organizing activity to structure their time, and the threat of senility and death. Impending death prompts them to evaluate their lives, asking themselves, ''What have I done with my work life?'' The logotherapist will make the retired person see his past as a storehouse of experience that can be used during the newly gained leisure. The therapist will dereflect the retired away from an overconcern with the loss of work and toward new life tasks now available. Old persons have the opportunity to do what they had always wanted to do, to experience beauty in nature, adventure in art, and the pursuit of knowledge which they had to neglect during their working years. And they can use their wisdom, time, and experience to help others—children in school, patients in hospitals, oldsters in retirement homes. Friends and family need counsel, help, and caring. Unemployment or retirement, forced or voluntary, is no excuse for not contributing to the world.

References

1. *Dictionary of Occupational Tables* (1965). 3rd ed. Washington, D.C.: U.S. Dept. of Labor.
2. Fabry, Joseph B. (1968). *The Pursuit of Meaning*. Boston: Beacon Press.
2a. Frankl, V. E. (1975). *The Unconscious God.* New York: Simon and Schuster.
3. Kornhauser, Arthur (1965). *Mental Health of the Industrial Worker: A Detroit Study.* New York: Wiley.
4. Lukas, Elisabeth S. (1972). Logotherapie als Persönlichkeitstheorie. In Frankl, *Der Wille sum Sinn,* Bern-Stuttgart-Wien: Hans Huber.
5. Marks, John B., and Glaser, Edward M. (1972). *The Meaning of Work . . . to Five Different Categories of Young Men.* Los Angeles: Human Interaction Research Inst.
6. Maslow, Abraham H. (1966). Comments on Dr. Frankl's paper. *Journal of Humanistic Psychology,* VI (1): 7–12.

7. ______(1965). *Eupsychian Management.* Homewood, Ill.: Richard D. Irwin.
8. ______(1951). Higher needs and personality. *Dialectica,* 5: 257–265.
9. McGregor, Douglas (1960). *The Human Side of Enterprise.* New York: McGraw-Hill.
10. Morse, Nancy C., and Weiss, Robert S. (1955). The function and meaning of work and the job. *American Sociological* Review, 20:191–198.
11. Weiss, Robert S. and Riesman, David (1961). Social problems and disorganization in the world of work. *Contemporary Social Problems,* Robert K. Merton and Robert A. Nisbet, eds. New York: Harcourt Brace Jovanovich.
12. *Work in America* (1972). Report of a Special Task Force to the Secretary of Health, Education, and Welfare.

Epilogue

Reuven P. Bulka

The wide range of areas where logotherapy has had its impact is evidence that it has come into its own. From its theoretical beginnings, through its further development in face of its founder's harrowing experiences, logotherapy has spread its horizons beyond the reaches of one man's charisma. It now speaks effectively to many ills of modern society. This book has been compiled to illustrate the applications of logotherapy and to consolidate its position as a major school of psychological-philosophical thought.

Logotherapists, however, have now to make a crucial decision. Should logotherapy remain an autonomous system or strive to become an ecumenical force complementing other schools of thought and therapy?

This question is not easily answered, because the trend, as the contributions to this book indicate, is in both directions at once. In medical applications, logotherapy is often effective as a complement to standard medical procedures, in psychotherapy as well as for physical illness. In psychotherapy, the technique of paradoxical intention, founded on man's ability to defy and overcome, can be used in conjunction with behavior techniques such as reconditioning and desensitization. The second technique, dereflection, can be easily adapted to most methods of therapy. These two techniques can be used as complements to traditional therapeutic approaches whenever an unwanted pattern needs to be broken, as may be the case in alcoholism, drug addiction, juvenile delinquency, emotional disturbances in children, and for minority groups. In addition, Takashima shows how the internist can use logotherapy, Jepsen illustrates its use for dentists, and Travelbee its applicability to the field of nursing. Also, as is evident from the introduction to the section on "Medical Uses," logotherapy can be used in a supplementary role in other related fields such as neurosurgery.

However, in one field logotherapy functions autonomously. When a person suffers from the existential vacuum, as a consequence of his repressed or inactive will to meaning, the philosophy and methods of logotherapy are indicated. Hogan explains this specific use of logotherapy for patients suffering from a noögenic neurosis, Lukas presents a step-by-step approach for such neuroses, Crumbaugh develops his logoanalysis for existentially frustrated clients, and Fabry describes the use of logotherapy for people who are not mentally ill but mentally searching. Meshoulam discusses the implications of logotherapy for the Community Mental Health Movement, Brandon for the counselor facing clients suffering mental anguish, Tweedie for religious counselors, and Leslie for counselors of the aged. In all these situations mental health is improved by a redirection of goals and a refocusing on meaning. In the past, this was the almost exclusive task of organized religion. The logotherapist is oriented toward helping all people, religious and nonreligious, to find and respond to the meanings of the moment. Logotherapy itself maintains a neutral stance on religion; it neither prescribes nor denies it as as possible therapeutic vehicle. Logotherapy is a secular discipline open to the religious dimension, ecumenical in theory and practice.[1]

Logotherapy's central emphasis on finding the meanings of the moment is helpful beyond the medical and counseling areas. Wirth sees logotherapy as a potent force in education, Bodenheimer points to the part logotherapy can play in the attainment of justice, Briggs indicates how logotherapeutic principles can improve our prison system, and Sargent and Phillips suggest how logotherapy may serve

1. The full implications of this ecumenical ingredient in logotherapy are discussed in Reuven P. Bulka, The ecumenical ingredient in logotherapy, in *Journal of Ecumenical Studies,* Vol. 11, no. 1, pp. 13–23.

as the philosophical foundation of a new, more humanely responsive labor ethic. As indicated in the introduction to the section on youth, the far-reaching implications of logotherapy extend even to the area of sports.

In all, logotherapy appears, from the totality of these contributions, to be well endowed as an autonomous system, founded as it is on the human dimension, and well equipped to treat the human condition. At the same time, its role in the world of psychotherapy appears to be that of a rehumanizing force. Arnold and Gasson show how logotherapy is more inclusive than other clinical schools, going beyond even the world view of humanistic psychology.

In 1968, Abraham Maslow, in the preface to the second edition of *Toward a Psychology of Being,* expressed a feeling that humanistic psychology, the so-called third force, is a transitional phase, a prelude to a higher, "fourth psychology," which would be transhuman, centered in the cosmos instead of in human needs. Logotherapy, it can be argued, is this fourth psychology, emphasizing the existence of objective values, the ultimate, unconditional meaningfulness of existence, and man's orientation to self-transcendence rather than self-actualization. Higher dimensions, however, are higher only to the extent that they incorporate the lower dimensions in their scope, and are more inclusive or even all-inclusive.

It is ironic that at the same time as we contemplate logotherapy as a "higher," fourth psychology, it goes "down" to the very core of man's essence. Paradoxically, yet understandably, the fourth dimension of psychology is the natural dimension of man. Meshoulam's suggestion that logotherapy can be used by the man in the street in his role as care-giver is perhaps founded implicitly on logotherapy's affinity with natural, uncomplicated man, indicating that indeed every human being, in his core, expresses the verities contained in logotherapy. The reader may at times be struck by the simplicity of logotherapy, yet logotherapy is aware and proud of this. In the words of Emerson, "Nothing is more simple than greatness; indeed, to be simple is to be great." This statement concerning man applies equally to theories of man. The human being is not complicated—he becomes complicated when his true humanness is not expressed but repressed. Logotherapy humanizes, and thus uncomplicates. The basic tenets of logotherapy, while they are validated clinically, were born in the common sense of the experiential world.

The role, therefore, of logotherapy, is to effect a monanthropism, a oneness of mankind, and a wholeness of man, through its philosophy and psychology. The question is how this is best accomplished.

The desire to remain autonomous, to have control of one's direction, can be overwhelming. The politics of psychology are such that many schools are separate entities for this reason. These schools might use overlapping terminologies, work generally within the same framework, be directed toward the same purpose, and yet, because of distinct differences, refuse to amalgamate their common ground. In the desire to remain distinct, to have a separate identity, the dangers of polarization are accentuated, as is the case with the Freudian school of psychoanalysis and its relation to Jungian and Adlerian psychology. The lack of unity toward a common purpose is most keenly felt by those who can least afford it, the burdened souls seeking help.

Logotherapy is now in an enviable position. It has firmly established itself as a vital voice in human affairs but is open-ended about its future. Logotherapists can break the grip of politics in psychology. They can do this by developing the concepts of logotherapy toward autonomy, making logotherapy an independent school, or becoming an ecumenical, unifying force, transcending itself toward the other schools of psychology; in effect, initiating a psychological synthesis as prelude to a human synthesis. This is not to imply that logotherapy must go one way or the other. Rather it indicates the possibilities open to it. This confrontation by logotherapy with its own meaning of the moment is not so vital for logotherapy as it is for the world of the clinic, and for the wider, pervading clinic we call the world.

A Bibliography of Logotherapy

1. Books

Crumbaugh, James C., *Everything to Gain: A Guide to Self-fulfillment Through Logoanalysis.* Chicago, Nelson-Hall, 1973.

———, and John Russell, *Logotherapy: New Help for Problem Drinkers.* Chicago, Nelson-Hall, in press.

Fabry, Joseph B., *The Pursuit of Meaning: Logotherapy Applied to Life.* Preface by Viktor E. Frankl. Boston, Beacon Press, 1968; revised paperback edition, New York, Harper and Row, 1979.

Frankl, Viktor E., *Man's Search for Meaning: An Introduction to Logotherapy.* Preface by Gordon W. Allport. Boston, Beacon Press, 1959; paperback edition, New York, Pocket Books, 1977.

———, *The Doctor and the Soul: From Psychotherapy to Logotherapy.* New York, Alfred A. Knopf, Inc.; second, expanded edition, 1965; paperback edition, New York, Vintage Books, 1977.

———, *Psychotherapy and Existentialism: Selected Papers on Logotherapy.* New York, Washington Square Press, 1967; Touchstone paperback, 1978.

———, *The Will to Meaning: Foundations and Applications of Logotherapy.* New York and Cleveland, The World Publishing

Company, 1969; paperback edition, New York, New American Library, 1976.

______, *The Unconscious God: Psychotherapy and Theology.* New York, Simon and Schuster, 1977.

______, *The Unheard Cry for Meaning: Psychotherapy and Humanism.* New York, Simon and Schuster, 1978.

Leslie, Robert C., *Jesus and Logotherapy: The Ministry of Jesus as Interpreted Through the Psychotherapy of Viktor Frankl.* New York and Nashville, Abingdon Press, 1965; paperback edition, 1968.

Tweedie, Donald F., *Logotherapy and the Christian Faith: An Evaluation of Frankl's Existential Approach to Psychotherapy.* Preface by Viktor E. Frankl. Grand Rapids, Baker Book House, 1961; paperback edition, 1972.

______, *The Christian and the Couch: An Introduction to Christian Logotherapy.* Grand Rapids, Baker Book House, 1963.

Takashima, Hiroshi, *Psychosomatic Medicine and Logotherapy.* Foreword by Viktor E. Frankl. Oceanside, New York, Dabor Science Publications, 1977.

Ungersma, Aaron J., *The Search for Meaning: A New Approach to Psychotherapy and Pastoral Psychology.* Philadelphia, Westminster Press, 1961; paperback edition, Foreword by Viktor E. Frankl, 1968.

2. Chapters in Books

Arnold, Magda B., and John A. Gasson, "Logotherapy and Existential Analysis," in *The Human Person.* New York, Ronald Press, 1954.

Ascher, L. Michael, "Paradoxical Intention," in *Handbook of Behavioral Interventions,* A. Goldstein and E. B. Foa, eds. New York, John Wiley, in press.

Barnitz, Harry W., "Frankl's Logotherapy," in *Existentialism and The New Christianity.* New York, Philosophical Library, 1969.

Bruno, Frank J., "The Will to Meaning," in *Human Adjustment and Personal Growth: Seven Pathways.* New York, John Wiley, 1977.

Downing, Lester N., "Logotherapy," in *Counseling Theories and Techniques.* Chicago, Nelson-Hall, 1975.

Elmore, Thomas M., and Eugene D. Chambres, "Anomie, Existential Neurosis and Personality: Relevance for Counseling," in *Proceedings,* 75th Annual Convention, American Psychological Association, 1967, 341–342.

Frankl, Viktor E., contributions to *Critical Incidents in Psychotherapy,* S. W. Standal and R. J. Corsini, eds. Englewood Cliffs, Prentice-Hall, 1959.

———, "Logotherapy and the Collective Neuroses," in *Progress in Psychotherapy,* J. H. Masserman and J. L. Moreno, eds. New York, Grune & Stratton, 1959.

———, "The Philosophical Foundations of Logotherapy" (paper read before the first Lexington Conference on Phenomenology on April 4, 1963), in *Phenomenology: Pure and Applied.* Erwin Straus, ed. Pittsburgh, Duquesne University Press, 1964.

———, "Fragments from the Logotherapeutic Treatment of Four Cases. With an Introduction and Epilogue by G. Kaczanowski." in *Modern Psychotherapeutic Practice: Innovations in Technique,* Arthur Burton, ed. Palo Alto, Science and Behavior Books, 1965.

———, "The Will to Meaning," in *Are You Nobody?* Richmond, Virginia, John Knox Press, 1966.

———, "Accepting Responsibility" and "Overcoming Circumstances," in *Man's Search for a Meaningful Faith: Selected Readings,* Judith Weidmann, ed. Nashville, Graded Press, 1967.

———, "Comment on Vatican II's Pastoral Constitution on the Church in the Modern World," in *World.* Chicago, Catholic Action Federations, 1967.

———, "Paradoxical Intention: A Logotherapeutic Technique," in *Active Psychotherapy,* Harold Greenwald, ed. New York, Atherton Press, 1967.

———, "The Significance of Meaning for Health," in *Religion and Medicine: Essays on Meaning, Values and Health,* David Belgum, ed. Ames, Iowa, The Iowa State University Press, 1967.

———, "The Task of Education in an Age of Meaninglessness," in *New Prospects for the Small Liberal Arts College,* Sidney S. Letter, ed. New York, Teachers College Press, 1968.

———, "Self-Transcendence as a Human Phenomenon," in *Readings in Humanistic Psychology,* Anthony J. Sutich and Miles A. Vich, eds. New York, The Free Press, 1969.

______, "Beyond Self-Actualization and Self-Expression," in *Perspectives on the Group Process: A Foundation for Counseling with Groups,* C. Gratton Kemp, ed. Boston, Houghton Mifflin Company, 1970.

______, "Logotherapy," in *Psychopathology Today: Experimentation, Theory and Research,* William S. Sahakian, ed. second edition. Itasca, Illinois, F. E. Peacock Publishers, 1979.

______, "Reductionism and Nihilism," in *Beyond Reductionism: New Perspectives in the Life Sciences* (The Alpbach Symposium, 1968), Arthur Koestler and J. R. Smythies, eds. New York, Macmillan, 1970.

______, "Universities and the Quest for Peace," in *Report of the First World Conference on the Role of the University in the Quest for Peace.* Binghamton, New York, State University of New York, 1970.

______, "What is Meant by Meaning?" in *Values in an Age of Confrontation,* Jeremiah W. Canning, ed. Columbus, Ohio, Charles E. Merrill Publishing Company, 1970.

______, "Dynamics, Existence, and Values" and "The Concept of Man in Logotherapy," in *Personality Theory: A Source Book,* Harold J. Vetter and Barry D. Smith, eds. New York, Appleton-Century-Crofts, 1971.

______, "Youth in Search of Meaning," in *Students Search for Meaning,* James Edward Doty, ed. Kansas City, Missouri, The Lowell Press, 1971.

______, "Address before the Third Annual Meeting of the Academy of Religion and Mental Health," in *Discovering Man in Psychology: A Humanistic Approach,* Frank T. Severin, ed. New York, McGraw-Hill, Inc., 1973.

______, "Beyond Pluralism and Determinism," in *Unity Through Diversity: A Festschrift for Ludwig von Bertalanffy,* William Ray and Nicholas D. Rizzo, eds. New York, Gordon and Breach, 1973.

______, "Meaninglessness: A Challenge to Psychologists," in *Theories of Psychopathology and Personality,* Theodore Millon, ed. Philadelphia, W. B. Saunders Company, 1973.

______, "Encounter: The Concept and Its Vulgarization," in *Psychotherapy and Behavior Change 1973,* Hans H. Strupp *et al.,* eds. Chicago, Aldine Publishing Company, 1974.

———, "Paradoxical Intention and Dereflection: Two Logotherapeutic Techniques," in *New Dimensions in Psychiatry: A World View,* Silvano Arieti, ed. New York, John Wiley & Sons, Inc., 1975.

———, "Logotherapy," in *Encyclopaedic Handbook of Medical Psychology,* Stephen Krauss, ed. London and Boston, Butterworth, 1976.

———, "Man's Search for Ultimate Meaning," in *On the Way to Self-Knowledge,* Jacob Needleman, ed. New York, Alfred A. Knopf, Inc., 1976.

———, "The Depersonalization of Sex," in *Humanistic Psychology: A Source Book,* I. David Welch, George A. Tate, and Fred Richards, eds. Buffalo, New York, Prometheus Books, 1978.

Freilicher, M., "Applied Existential Psychology: Victor Frankl and Logotherapy," in *PsychoSources,* Evelyn Shapiro, ed. New York, Bantam Books, 1973.

Frey, David H., and Frederick E. Heslet, "Viktor Frankl," in *Existential Theory for Counselors.* Boston, Houghton Mifflin Company, 1975.

Friedman, Maurice, "Viktor Frankl," in *The Worlds of Existentialism.* New York, Random House, 1964.

Gale, Raymond F., "Logotherapy," in *Who Are You? The Psychology of Being Yourself.* Englewood Cliffs, Prentice-Hall, 1974.

Howland, Elihu S., "Viktor Frankl," in *Speak Through the Earthquake; Religious Faith and Emotional Health.* Philadelphia, United Church Press, 1972.

Kiernan, Thomas, "Logotherapy," in *Shrinks, etc.: A Consumer's Guide to Psychotherapies.* New York, The Dial Press, 1974.

Lande, Nathaniel, "Logotherapy (Viktor Frankl)," in *Mindstyles, Lifestyles: A Comprehensive Overview of Today's Life-Changing Philosophies.* Los Angeles, Price, Stern, Sloan, 1976.

Ledermann, E. K. "Viktor E. Frankl's Ontological Value Ethics," in *Existential Neurosis.* London, Butterworths, 1972.

Leslie, Robert, "Frankl's New Concept of Man," in *Contemporary Religious Issues,* Donald E. Hartsock, ed. Belmont, California, Wadsworth Publishing Company, 1968.

Liston, Robert A., "Viktor Frankl," in *Healing the Mind: Eight Views of Human Nature.* New York, Praeger, 1974.

McCarthy, Colman, "Viktor Frankl," in *Inner Companions.* Washington, D.C., Acropolis Books Ltd., 1975.

McKinney, Fred, "Man's Search for Meaning," in *Psychology in Action.* New York, Macmillan, 1967.

Marks, Isaac M., "Paradoxical Intention ('Logotherapy')," in *Fears and Phobias.* New York, Academic Press, 1969.

______, "Paradoxical Intention," in *Behavior Modification,* W. Stewart Agras, ed. Boston, Little, Brown and Company, 1972.

______, "Paradoxical Intention (Logotherapy)," in *Encyclopaedic Handbook of Medical Psychology,* Stephen Krauss, ed. London and Boston, Butterworth, 1976.

Maslow, Abraham H., "Comments on Dr. Frankl's Paper," in *Readings in Humanistic Psychology,* Anthony J. Sutich and Miles A. Vich, eds. New York, The Free Press, 1969.

Misiak, Henry, and Virginia Staudt Sexton. "Logotherapy," in *Phenomenological, Existential, and Humanistic Psychologies: A Historical Survey.* New York. Grune & Stratton, 1973.

Page, James D., "Frankl," in *Psychopathology.* Chicago, Aldine Publishing Company, second edition, 1975.

Patterson, C. H., "Frankl's Logotherapy," in *Theories of Counseling and Psychotherapy.* New York, Harper & Row, 1966.

Price, Johanna, "Existential Theories: Viktor Frankl," in *Abnormal Psychology: Current Perspectives.* Del Mar, California, Communication Research Machines, 1972.

Reynolds, David K., "Logotherapy," in *Morita Psychotherapy.* Berkeley, University of California Press, 1976.

Sahakian, William S., "Viktor Frankl," in *History of Psychology.* Itasca, Illinois, F. E. Peacock Publishers, Inc., 1968.

______, "Logotherapy," in *Psychotherapy and Counseling: Studies in Technique.* 2nd edition. Chicago, Rand McNally, 1976.

______, "Logotherapy Approach to Personality," in *Psychology of Personality.* 3rd edition. Chicago, Rand McNally, 1977.

______, "Logotherapy: The Will to Meaning," in *History and Systems of Psychology.* New York, John Wiley & Sons, Inc., 1975.

______, and Mabel Lewis Sahakian, "Viktor E. Frankl: Will to Meaning," in *Realms of Philosophy.* 2nd edition. Cambridge, Massachusetts, Schenkman Publishing Company, Inc., 1974.

Salit, Norman, "Existential Analysis; Logotherapy—the Gulf Narrows," in *The Worlds of Norman Salit,* Abraham Burstein, ed. New York, Bloch, 1966.

Schilling, S. Paul, "'The Unconscious God': Viktor Frankl," in *God Incognito.* Nashville and New York, Abingdon Press, 1974.

Schneider, Marius G., "The Existentialistic Concept of the Human Person in Viktor E. Frankl's Logotherapy," in *Studies in Philosophy and the History of Philospohy,* John K. Ryan, ed. Washington D.C., Catholic University of America Press, 1974.

Spiegelberg, Herbert, "Viktor Frankl: Phenomenology in Logotherapy and *Existenzanalyse,*" in *Phenomenology in Psychology and Psychiatry.* Evanston, Illinois, Northwestern University Press, 1972.

Strunk, Orlo, "Religious Maturity and Viktor E. Frankl," in *Mature Religion.* New York and Nashville, Abingdon Press, 1965.

Tyrell, Bernard J., "Logotherapy and Christotherapy," in *Christotherapy: Healing through Enlightenment.* New York, The Seabury Press, 1975.

Vanderveldt, James H., and Robert P. Odenwald, "Existential Analysis," in *Psychiatry and Catholicism.* New York, McGraw-Hill, 1952.

Zavalloni, Roberto, "Human Freedom and Logotherapy," in *Self-Determination.* Chicago, Forum Books, 1962.

3. Articles and Miscellaneous

Alter, Maragaret G., "The 'Ally' Approach in Teaching and Counseling." *The International Forum for Logotherapy,* Vol. 1, No. 19 (Winter 1978-Spring 1979), 26–28.

Ansbacher, Rowena R., "The Third Viennese School of Psychotherapy." *Journal of Individual Psychology,* XV (1959), 236–237.

Ascher, L. Michael, "Employing Paradoxical Intention in the Behavioral Treatment of Urinary Retention." *Scandinavian Journal of Behavioral Therapy,* Vol. 6, Suppl. 4, 1977, 28.

———, "Paradoxical Intention: A Review of Preliminary Research." *The International Forum for Logotherapy,* Vol. 1, No. 1 (Winter 1978-Spring 1979), 18–21.

______, and Jay S. Efran, "Use of Paradoxical Intention in a Behavior Program for Sleep Onset Insomnia. *Journal of Consulting and Clinical Psychology,* 1978, 547–549.

______, and Ralph M. Turner, "A Controlled Comparison of Progressive Relaxation, Stimulus Control, and Paradoxical Intention Therapies for Insomnia." *Journal of Consulting and Clinical Psychology,* in press.

Ballard, R. E., "An Empirical Investigation of Viktor Frankl's Concept of the Search for Meaning: A Pilot Study with a Sample of Tuberculosis Patients." Doctoral dissertation, Michigan State University, 1965.

Birnbaum, Ferdinand, "Frankl's Existential Psychology from the Viewpoint of Individual Psychology." *Journal of Individual Psychology,* XVIII (1961), 162–166.

Bordeleau, Louis-Gabriel, *"La Relation entre les valeurs de choix vocationnel et les valeurs creatrices chez V. E. Frankl."* Doctoral dissertation, University of Ottawa, 1971.

Bulka, Reuven P., "An Analysis of the Viability of Frankl's Logotherapeutic System as a Secular Theory." Thesis presented to the Department of Religious Studies of the University of Ottawa as partial fulfillment of the requirements for the degree of Master of Arts, 1969.

______, "Denominational Implications of the Religious Nature of Logotherapy." Thesis presented to the Department of Religious Studies of the University of Ottawa as partial fulfillment of the requirements for the degree of Doctor of Philosophy, 1971.

______, "Logotherapy and Judaism." *Jewish Spectator,* XXXVII, No. 7 (Sept. 1972), 17–19.

______, "Logotherapy and Judaism—Some Philosophical Comparisons." *Tradition,* XII (1972), 72–89.

______, "Death in Life—Talmudic and Logotherapeutic Affirmations." *Humanitas* (Journal of the Institute of Man), X, No. 1 (Feb. 1974), 33–42.

______, "The Ecumenical Ingredient in Logotherapy." *Journal of Ecumenical Studies,* XI, No. 1 (Winter 1974), 13–24.

______, "Logotherapy as a Response to the Holocaust." *Tradition,* XV (1975), 89–96.

______, "Logotherapy and Talmudic Judaism." *Journal of Religion and Health,* XIV (1975), No. 4, 277–283.

———, "Logotherapy—A Step Beyond Freud: Its Relevance for Jewish Thought." *Jewish Life* (Fall, Winter 1977–78), 46–53.

———, "Is Logotherapy a Spiritual Therapy?" *Association of Mental Health Clergy Forum,* Vol. 30, No. 2 (January, 1978).

———, "The Work Situation: Logotherapeutic and Talmudic Perspectives." *Journal of Psychology and Judaism,* Vol. 2, No. 2 (Spring, 1978), 52–61.

Burck, James Lester, "The Relevance of Viktor Frankl's 'Will to Meaning' for Preaching to Juvenile Delinquents." A Master of Theology thesis submitted to the Southern Baptist Theological Seminary, Louisville, Kentucky, 1966.

Calabrese, Edward James, "The Evolutionary Basis of Logotherapy." Dissertation, University of Massachusetts, 1974.

Carrigan, Thomas Edward, "The Meaning of Meaning in Logotherapy of Dr. Viktor E. Frankl." Thesis presented to the School of Graduate Studies as partial fulfillment of the requirements for the degree of Master of Arts in Philosophy, University of Ottawa, Canada, 1973.

Cavanagh, Michael E., "The Relationship between Frankl's 'Will to Meaning' and the Discrepancy Between the Actual Self and the Ideal Self." Doctoral dissertation, University of Ottawa, 1966.

Cohen, David. "The Frankl Meaning." *Human Behavior,* (July, 1977) 56–62.

Crumbaugh, James C., "The Application of Logotherapy." *Journal of Existentialism,* V (1965), 403–412.

———, "Cross Validation of Purpose-in-Life Test Based on Frankl's Concepts." *Journal of Individual Psychology,* XXIV (1968), 74–81.

———, "Frankl's Logotherapy: A New Orientation in Counseling." *Journal of Religion and Health,* X (1971), 373–386.

———, "Aging and Adjustment: The Applicability of Logotherapy and the Purpose-in-Life Test." *The Gerontologist,* XII (1972), 418–420.

———, "Changes in Frankl's existential vacuum as a measure of therapeutic outcome." *Newsletter for Research in Psychology* (Veterans Administration Center, Bay Pines, Florida), Vol. 14, No. 2 (May 1972), 35–37.

———, "Frankl's Logotherapy: An Answer to the Crisis in Identity." *Newsletter of the Mississippi Personnel & Guidance Association,* IV, No. 2 (Oct 1972), 3.

______, "Patty's Purpose: Perversion of Frankl's Search for Meaning." *J. Graphoanalysis.* July 1976, 12–13.

______, "Logoanalysis," *Uniquest* (The First Unitarian Church of Berkeley), No. 7, 1977, 24–25.

______, and Leonard T. Maholick, "The Case for Frankl's 'Will to Meaning.'" *Journal of Existential Psychiatry,* IV (1963), 43–48.

______, "An Experimental Study in Existentialism: The Psychometric Approach to Frankl's Concept of *Noögenic Neurosis.*" *Journal of Clinical Psychology,* XX (1964), 200–207.

______, Sister Mary Raphael and Raymond R. Shrader, "Frankl's Will to Meaning in a Religious Order" (delivered before Division 24, American Psychological Association, at the annual convention in San Francisco, August 30, 1968). *Journal of Clinical Psychology,* XXVI (1970), 206–207.

______, and G. L. Carr, "Treatment of Alcoholics with Logotherapy." *International Journal of Addiction,* XIV (1979), No. 4

Dansart, Bernard, "Development of a Scale to Measure Attitudinal Values as Defined by Viktor Frankl." Dissertation, Northern Illinois University, De Kalb, 1974.

Dickson, Charles W., "Logotherapy and the Redemptive Encounter." *Dialogue,* Spring 1974, 110–114.

______, Logotherapy as a Pastoral Tool." *Journal of Religion and Health,* XIV, No. 4, 207–213.

"The Doctor and the Soul: Dr. Viktor Frankl." *Harvard Medical Alumni Bulletin,* XXXVI, No. 1 (Fall 1961), 8.

Duncan, Franklin D., "Logotherapy and the Pastoral Care of Physically Disabled Persons." A thesis in the Department of Psychology of Religion submitted to the faculty of the Graduate School of Theology in partial fulfillment of the requirements for the degree of Master of Theology at Southern Baptist Theological Seminary, Louisville, Kentucky, 1968.

Eger, Edith Eva, "Viktor Frankl & Me." *Association for Humanistic Psychology Newsletter,* February 1976, 15–16.

Fabry, Joseph, "A Most Ingenious Paradox." *The Register-Leader of the Unitarian Universalist Association,* Vol. 149 (June 1967), 7–8.

______, "The Quest for Meaning." *Uniquest,* Vol. 1 (1), (Fall 1974), 8–11.

———, "Positive Forces in Your Past." *PHP,* (October 1974), 45–49.

———, "Application of Logotherapy in Small Sharing Groups." *Journal of Religion and Health,* Vol. 13 (2) (April 1974), 128–136.

———, "The Health Tension." *PHP,* (September 1975), 24–28.

———, "Logotherapy and Eastern Religions." *Journal of Religion and Health,* Vol. 14 (4) (October 1975).

———, "Meaning as Therapy." *Dharma World,* Vol. 4 (2), (1977), 14–17.

———, "The Crises of Mid-Life." *PHP,* (September 1977), 78–83.

———, ed. "Viktor Frankl Festival of Meaning." *Uniquest,* 7, (1977) 1–44.

———, and Lukas, Elisabeth, "Therapy through Meaning May Help Many Addicts," *Drug Survival News,* Vol 5. (1977), 9.

———, and Max Knight (pseud. Peter Fabrizius), "Viktor Frankl's Logotherapy." *Delphian Quarterly,* XLVII, No. 3 (1964), 27–30.

———, "The Use of Humor in Therapy." *Delphian Quarterly,* XLVIII, No. 3 (1965), 22–36.

———, "The Father of Logotherapy." *Existential Psychiatry,* Vol. I (1967), 439.

Farr, Alan P., "Logotherapy and Senior Adults." *The International Forum for Logotherapy,* Vol. 1, No. 1 (Winter 1978-Spring 1979), 14–17.

Forstmeyer, Annemarie von, "The Will to Meaning as a Prerequisite for Self-Actualization." Thesis presented to the faculty of California Western University, San Diego, in partial fulfillment of the requirements for the degree of Master of Arts, 1968.

Fox, Douglas A., "Logotherapy and Religion." *Religion in Life,* XXXI (1965), 235–244.

Frankl, Viktor E., "Logos and Existence in Psychotherapy." *American Journal of Psychotherapy,* VII (1953), 8–15.

———, "Group Psychotherapeutic Experiences in a Concentration Camp" (paper read before the Second International Congress of Psychotherapy, Leiden, Netherlands, Sept. 8, 1951). *Group Psychotherapy,* VII (1954), 81–90.

———, "The Concept of Man in Psychotherapy" (paper read before the Royal Society of Medicine, Section of Psychiatry,

London, England, June 15, 1944). *Pastoral Psychology,* VI (1955), 16–26.

______, "From Psychotherapy to Logotherapy." *Pastoral Psychology,* VII (1956), 56–60.

______, "Guest Editorial." *Academy Reporter,* III, No. 5 (May 1958), 1–4.

______, "On Logotherapy and Existential Analysis" (paper read before the Association for the Advancement of Psychoanalysis, New York, April 17, 1957). *American Journal of Psychoanalysis,* XVIII (1958), 28–37.

______, "The Search for Meaning." *Saturday Review,* (Sept. 13, 1958.)

______, "The Will to Meaning." *Journal of Pastoral Care,* XII (1958), 82–88.

______, "The Spiritual Dimension in Existential Analysis and Logotherapy" (paper read before the Fourth International Congress of Psychotherapy, Barcelona, Sept. 5, 1958). *Journal of Individual Psychology,* XV (1959), 157–165.

______, "Beyond Self-Actualization and Self-Expression" (paper read before the Conference on Existential Psychotherapy, Chicago, Dec. 13, 1959). *Journal of Existential Psychiatry,* I (1960), 5–20.

______, "Paradoxical Intention: A Logotherapeutic Technique" (paper read before the American Association for the Advancement of Psychotherapy, New York, Feb. 26, 1960). *American Journal of Psychotherapy,* XIV (1960), 520–535.

______, "Dynamics, Existence and Values." *Journal of Existential Psychiatry,* II (1961), 5–16.

______, "Logotherapy and the Challenge of Suffering" (paper read before the American Conference on Existential Psychotherapy, New York, Feb. 27, 1960). *Review of Existential Psychology and Psychiatry,* I (1961), 3–7.

______, "Psychotherapy and Philosophy." *Philosophy Today,* V (1961), 59–64.

______, "Religion and Existential Psychotherapy." *Gordon Review,* VI (1961), 2–10.

______, "Basic Concepts of Logotherapy," *Journal of Existential Psychiatry,* III (1962), 111–118.

———, "Logotherapy and the Challenge of Suffering." *Pastoral Psychology,* XIII (1962), 25–28.

———, "Psychiatry and Man's Quest for Meaning." *Journal of Religion and Health,* I (1962), 93–103.

———, "The Will to Meaning." *Living Church,* CXLIV (June 24, 1962), 8–14.

———, "Angel as Much as Beast: Man Transcends Himself." *Unitarian Universalist Register-Leader,* CXLIV (Feb. 1963), 8–9.

———, "Existential Dynamics and Neurotic Escapism" (paper read before the Conference on Existential Psychiatry, Toronto, May 6, 1962). *Journal of Existential Psychiatry,* IV (1963), 27–42.

———, "Existential Escapism." *Motive,* XXIV (Jan.-Feb. 1964), 11–14.

———, "In Steady Search for Meaning." *Liberal Dimension,* II, No. 2 (1964), 3–8.

———, "The Will to Meaning" (paper read before the Conference on Phenomenology, Lexington, April 4, 1963). *Christian Century,* LXXI (April 22, 1964), 515–517.

———, "The Concept of Man in Logotherapy" (175th Anniversary Lecture. Georgetown University, Washington, D.C., February 27, 1964). *Journal of Existentialism,* VI (1965), 53–58.

———, "Logotherapy and Existential Analysis: A Review" (paper read before the Symposium on Logotherapy, 6th International Congress of Psychotherapy, London, August 26, 1964). *American Journal of Psychotherapy,* XX (1966), 252-260.

———, "Self-Transcendence As a Human Phenomenon." *Journal of Humanistic Psychology,* VI, No. 2 (Fall 1966), 97–106.

———, "Time and Responsibility." *Existential Psychiatry,* I (1966), 361–366.

———, "What is Meant by Meaning?" *Journal of Existentialism,* VII, No. 25 (Fall 1966), 21–28.

———, "Logotherapy." *The Israel Annals of Psychiatry and Related Disciplines,* VII (1967), 142–155.

———, "Logotherapy and Existentialism." *Psychotherapy: Theory, Research and Practice,* IV, No. 3 (Aug. 1967), 138–142.

———, "What is a Man?" *Life Association News,* LXII, No. 9 (Sept. 1967), 151–157.

———, "Experiences in a Concentration Camp." *Jewish Heritage,* XI (1968), 5–7.

______, "The Search for Meaning" (abstract from a series of lectures given at the Brandeis Institute in California). *Jewish Heritage,* XI (1968), 8–11.

______, "The Cosmos and the Mind. (How Far Can We Go?) A Dialogue with Geoffrey Frost." *Pace,* V, No. 8 (Aug. 1969), 34–39.

______, "Eternity Is the Here and Now." *Pace,* V, No. 4 (April 1969), 2.

______, "Youth in Search for Meaning" (Third Paul Dana Bartlett Memorial Lecture). *The Baker World (The Baker University Newsletter),* I, No. 4 (Jan. 1969), 2–5.

______, "Entering the Human Dimension." *Attitude,* I (1970), 2–6.

______, "Fore-Runner of Existential Psychiatry." *Journal of Individual Psychology,* XXVI (1970), 12.

______, "Determinism and Humanism." *Humanitas (Journal of the Institute of Man),* VII (1971), 23–36.

______, "The Feeling of Meaninglessness: A Challenge to Psychotherapy." *The American Journal of Psychoanalysis,* XXXII, No. 1 (1972), 85–89.

______, "Man in Search of Meaning." *Widening Horizons* (Rockford College), Vol. 8, No. 5 (Aug. 1972).

______, "Encounter: The Concept and Its Vulgarization." *The Journal of the American Academy of Psychoanalysis,* I, No. 1 (1973), 73–83.

______, "The Depersonalization of Sex." *Synthesis (The Realization of the Self),* I (Spring 1974), 7–11.

______, "Paradoxical Intention and Dereflection." *Psychotherapy: Theory, Research and Practice,* XII, No. 3 (Fall 1975), 226–237.

______, "A Psychiatrist Looks at Love." *Uniquest* (The First Unitarian Church of Berkeley), 5, 1976, 6–9.

______, "Some Thoughts on the Painful Wisdom." *Uniquest* (The First Unitarian Church of Berkeley), 6, 1976, 3.

______, "Survival—for What?" *Uniquest* (The First Unitarian Church of Berkeley), 6, 1976, 38.

______, "Logotherapy." *The International Forum for Logotherapy,* Vol. 1, No. 1 (Winter 1978-Spring 1979), 22–23.

______ and Joseph Fabry, "Aspects and Prospects of Logotherapy." *The International Forum for Logotherapy,* Vol. 1, No. 1 (Winter 1978-Spring 1979), 3–6.

Funke, Gunther. "'Rebirth' of a Marriage." *The International Forum for Logotherapy,* Vol. 1, No. 1 (Winter 1978-Spring 1979), 29–30.

Garfield, Charles A., "A Psychometric and Clinical Investigation of Frankl's Concept of Existential Vacuum and of Anomie." *Psychiatry,* XXXVI (1973), 396–408.

Gerz, Hans O., "The Treatment of the Phobic and the Obsessive-Compulsive Patient Using Paradoxical Intention sec. Viktor E. Frankl." *Journal of Neuropsychiatry,* III, No. 6 (July-Aug. 1962), 375–387.

———, "Experience with the Logotherapeutic Technique of Paradoxical Intention in the Treatment of Phobic and Obsessive-Compulsive Patients" (paper read at the Symposium of Logotherapy at the 6th International Congress of Psychotherapy, London, England, August 1964). *American Journal of Psychiatry,* CXXIII, No. 5 (Nov. 1966), 548–553.

———, "Reply." *American Journal of Psychiatry,* CXXIII, No. 10 (April 1967), 1306.

Gill, Ajaipal S., "An Appraisal of Viktor E. Frankl's Theory of Logotherapy as a Philosophical Base for Education." Dissertation, American University, 1970.

Gleason, John J., "Lucy and Logotherapy: A Context, a Concept, and a Case." *Voices: The Art and Science of Psychotherapy,* 7(1971), 57-71.

Green, Herman H., "The 'Existential Vacuum' and the Pastoral Care of Elderly Widows in a Nursing Home." Master's thesis, Southern Baptist Theological Seminary, Louisville, Kentucky, 1970.

Grollman, Earl A., "Viktor E. Frankl: A Bridge Between Psychiatry and Religion." *Conservative Judaism,* XIX, No. 1 (Fall 1964), 19–23.

———, "The Logotherapy of Viktor E. Frankl." *Judaism,* XIV (1965), 22–38.

Grossman, Nathan, "The Rabbi and the Doctor of the Soul." *Jewish Spectator,* XXXIV, No. 1 (Jan. 1969), 8–12.

Guldbrandsen, Francis Aloysius. "Some of the Pedagogical Implications in the Theoretical Work of Viktor Frankl in Existential Psychology: A Study in the Philosophic Foundations of Education." Doctoral dissertation, Michigan State University, 1972.

Hall, Mary Harrington, "A Conversation with Viktor Frankl of Vienna." *Psychology Today,* I, No. 9 (Feb. 1968), 56–63.

Harrington, Donald Szantho, "The View from the Existential Vacuum." *Academy Reporter,* IX, No. 9 (Dec. 1964), 1-4.

Havens, Leston L., "Paradoxical Intention." *Psychiatry & Social Science Review,* II (1968), 16–19.

Haworth, D. Swan, "Viktor Frankl." *Judaism,* XIV (1965), 351–352.

Henderson, J. T., "The Will to Meaning of Viktor Frankl As a Meaningful Factor of Personality." Master's thesis, The University of Maryland, 1970.

Hirsch, Bianca Z., "The Boy Who was Afraid to Come to School." *The International Forum for Logotherapy,* Vol. 1, No. 1 (Winter 1978-Spring 1979), 31–32.

Holmes, R. M., "Meaning and Responsibility: A Comparative Analysis of the Concept of the Responsible Self in Search of Meaning in the Thought of Viktor Frankl and H. Richard Niebuhr with Certain Implications for the Church's Ministry to the University." Doctoral dissertation, Pacific School of Religion, Berkeley, California, 1965.

______, "Alcoholics Anonymous as Group Logotherapy." *Pastoral Psychology,* XXI (1970), 30–36.

Humberger, Frank E., "Practical Logotherapeutic Technique." *Uniquest* (The First Unitarian Church of Berkeley), No. 7, 1977, 24–25.

Hyman, William, "Practical Aspects of Logotherapy in Neurosurgery." *Existential Psychiatry,* VII (1969), 99–101.

Johnson, Paul E., "Logotherapy: A Corrective for Determinism." *Christian Advocate,* V (Nov. 23, 1961), 12–13.

______, "Meet Doctor Frankl." *Adult Student,* XXIV (Oct. 1964), 8–10.

______, "The Meaning of Logotherapy." *Adult Student,* XXVI, No. 8 (April 1967), 4–5.

______, "The Challenge of Logotherapy." *Journal of Religion and Health,* VII (1968), 122–130.

Jones, Elbert Whaley, "Nietzsche and Existential Analysis." Dissertation in the Department of Philosophy submitted to the faculty of the Graduate School of Arts and Sciences in partial fulfillment of the requirements for the degree of Master of Arts, New York University, 1967.

Kaczanowski, Godfryd, "Frankl's Logotherapy." *American Journal of Psychiatry,* CXVII (1960), 563.

———, "Logotherapy—A New Psychotherapeutic Tool." *Psychosomatics,* Vol. 8 (May-June 1967), 158–161.

Klapper, Naomi, "On Being Human: A Comparative Study of Abraham J. Heschel and Viktor Frankl." Doctoral dissertation, Jewish Theological Seminary of America, New York, 1973.

Klitzke, Louis L., "Students in Emerging Africa: Humanistic Psychology and Logotherapy in Tanzania." *Journal of Humanistic Psychology,* IX (1969), 105–126.

Kosukegawa, Tsugio, "A Comparative Study of the Differences Between Christian Existence and Secular Existence, and of Their Existential Frustration." *Japanese Journal of Educational and Social Psychology,* VII, No. 2 (1968), 195–208.

Lamontagne, Ives, "Treatment of Erythrophobia by Paradoxical Intention." *Journal of Nervous and Mental Disease,* Vol. 166, No. 4 (1978), 304–306.

Lapinsohn, Leonard I., "Relationship of the Logotherapeutic Concepts of Anticipatory Anxiety and Paradoxical Intention to the Neurophysiological Theory of Induction." *Behavioral Neuropsychiatry,* III, No. 304 (1971), 12–14 and 24.

Leslie, Robert C., "Viktor E. Frankl's New Concept of Man." *Motive,* XXII (1962), 16–19.

Lukas, Elisabeth S., "The Four Steps of Logotherapy." *Uniquest* (The First Unitarian Church of Berkeley), No. 7, 1977, 24–25.

———, "Logotherapy's Message to Parents and Children." *The International Forum for Logotherapy,* Vol. 1, No. 1 (Winter 1978-Spring 1979), 10–13.

Marrer, Robert F., "Existential-Phenomenological Foundations in Logotherapy Applicable to Counseling." Dissertation, Ohio University, 1972.

Maslow, A. H., "Comments on Dr. Frankl's Paper." *Journal of Humanistic Psychology,* VI (1966), 107–112.

———, "Meaning in Life." *Time* (Feb. 2, 1968), 38-40.

Meier, Augustine, "Frankl's 'Will to Meaning' as Measured by the Purpose-in-Life Test in Relation to Age and Sex Differences." Dissertation presented to The University of Ottawa, 1973.

______, "Frankl's 'Will to Meaning' as Measured by the Purpose-in-Life Test in Relation to Age and Sex Differences." *Journal of Clinical Psychology,* XXX (1974), 384–386.

Meshoulam, Uriel, "Some Implications of Logotherapy on Community Health." *The International Forum for Logotherapy,* Vol. 1, No. 1 (Winter 1978-Spring 1979), 7–9.

Muilenberg, Don T., "Meaning in Life: Its Significance in Psychotherapy." A dissertation presented to the faculty of the Graduate School, University of Missouri, 1968.

Muller-Hegemann, D., "Methodological Approaches in Psychotherapy: Current Concepts in East Germany." *American Journal of Psychotherapy,* XVII (1963), 554–568.

Murphy, Leonard, "Extent of Purpose-in-Life and Four Frankl-Proposed Life Objectives." Doctoral dissertation in Department of Psychology, The University of Ottawa, 1967.

Murphy, Maribeth L., "Viktor Frankl: The New Phenomenology of Meaning." *The U.S.I.U. Doctoral Society Journal,* III, No. 2 (June 1970), 1–10, and IV, No. 1 (Winter 1970–1971), 45–46.

Newton, Joseph R., "Therapeutic Paradoxes, Paradoxical Intentions, and Negative Practice." *American Journal of Psychotherapy,* XXII (1968), 68–81.

Noonan, J. Robert, "A Note on an Eastern Counterpart of Frankl's Paradoxical Intention." *Psychologia,* XII, (1969), 147-149.

Norman, Robert, "A Note on an Eastern Counterpart of Frankl's Paradoxical Intention." *Psychologia,* XII (1969), 147–149.

O'Connell, Walter E. "Viktor Frankl, the Adlerian?" *Psychiatric Spectator,* Vol. VI, No. 11 (1970), 13–14.

______, "Frankl, Adler, and Spirituality." *Journal of Religion and Health,* XI (1972), 134–138.

______, "Originator of Logotherapy Discusses Its Basic Premises" (interview). *Roche Report: Frontiers of Clinical Psychiatry,* Vol. 5, No. 1 (Jan. 1, 1968), 5-6.

Offutt, Berch R., "Logotherapy, Actualization Therapy or Contextual Self-Realization?" Dissertation, United States International University, 1975.

Palma, Robert J., "Viktor E. Frankl: Multilevel Analyses and Complementarity." *Journal of Religion and Health,* XV (1976), 12–25.

Pervin, Lawrence A., "Existentialism, Psychology, and Psychotherapy." *American Psychologist,* XV (1960), 305–309.

Petraroja, Sergio D., "The Concept of Freedom in Viktor Frankl." *Catholic Psychological Record,* Vol. 4, Fall, 1966.

Polak, Paul, "Frankl's Existential Analysis." *American Journal of Psychotherapy,* III (1949), 517–522.

Raskin, David E., and Zanvel E. Klein, "Losing a Symptom Through Keeping It: A Review of Paradoxical Treatment Techniques and Rationale." *Archives of General Psychiatry,* Vol. 33, No. 5 (May 1976), 548–555.

Richmond, Bert O., Robert L. Mason and Virginia Smith, "Existential Frustration and Anomie." *Journal of Women's Deans and Counselors* (Spring 1969).

Rose, Herbert H., "Viktor Frankl on Conscience and God." *The Jewish Spectator* (Fall 1976), 49–50.

Rowland, Stanley J., Jr., "Viktor Frankl and the Will to Meaning." *Christian Century,* LXXIX (June 6, 1962), 722–724.

Ruggiero, Vincent R., "Concentration Camps Were His Laboratory." *The Sign,* XLVII (Dec. 1967), 13–15.

Sahakian, William S., and Barbara Jacquelyn Sahakian, "Logotherapy As a Personality Theory." *The Israel Annals of Psychiatry and Related Disciplines,* X (1972), 230–244.

Sargent, George Andrew, "Job Satisfaction, Job Involvement, and Purpose in Life: A Study of Work and Frankl's Will to Meaning." Thesis presented to the faculty of the United States International University in partial fulfillment of the requirements for the degree of Master of Arts, 1971.

———, "Motivation and Meaning: Frankl's Logotherapy in the Work Situation." Dissertation, United States International University. San Diego, 1973.

Schachter, Stanley J., "Bettelheim and Frankl: Contradicting Views of the Holocaust." *Reconstructionist,* XXVI, No. 20 (Feb. 10, 1961), 6–11.

Shea, John J., "On the Place of Religion in the Thought of Viktor Frankl." *Journal of Psychology and Theology,* III, No. 3 (Summer 1975), 179–186.

Shilup, Margaret, "A Quadruplegic Finds Meaning." *The International Forum for Logotherapy,* Vol. 1, No. 1 (Winter 1978-Spring 1979), 33–34.

Solyom, L., J. Garza-Perez, B. L. Ledwidge and C. Solvom, "Paradoxical Intention in the Treatment of Obsessive Thoughts: A Pilot Study." *Comprehensive Psychiatry,* Vol. 13, No. 3 (May 1972), 291–297.

Stropko, Andrew John, "Logoanalysis and Guided Imagery as Group Treatments for Existential Vacuum." Dissertation, Texas Tech University, 1975.

Turner, R. H., "Comment on Dr. Frankl's Paper." *Journal of Existential Psychiatry,* I (1960), 21–23.

Victor, Ralph G., and Carolyn M. Krug, "Paradoxical Intention in the Treatment of Compulsive Gambling." *American Journal of Psychotherapy.* XXI, No. 4 (Oct. 1967), 808-814.

———, "Victor Frankl." *The Colby Alumnus.* LI (Spring 1962), 5.

Waugh, Robert J. L., "Paradoxical Intention." *American Journal of Psychiatry,* Vol. 123, No. 10 (April 1967), 1305–1306.

Weiss, M. David, "Frankl's Approach to the Mentally Ill." *Association of Mental Hospital Chaplains' Newsletter,* (Fall 1962), 39–42.

Weisskopf-Joelson, Edith, "Some Comments on a Viennese School of Psychiatry." *Journal of Abnormal and Social Psychology,* LI (1955), 701–703.

———, "Logotherapy and Existential Analysis." *Acta Psychotherapeutica,* VI (1958), 193–204.

———, "Paranoia and the Will-to-Meaning." *Existential Psychiatry,* I (1966), 316–320.

———, "Some Suggestions Concerning the Concept of Awareness." *Psychotherapy: Theory, Research and Practice,* VIII (1971), 2–7.

———, "Logotherapy: Science or Faith?" *Psychotherapy: Theory, Research and Practice,* XII (1975), 238–240.

Yeates, J. W. "The Educational Implications of the Logotherapy of Viktor E. Frankl." Doctoral dissertation, University of Mississippi, 1968.

4. Films, Records, and Tapes

Frankl, Viktor E., "Frankl and the Search for Meaning," a film produced by Psychological Films, 110 N. Wheeler Street, Orange, CA 92669.

———, "Logotherapy," a film produced by the Department of Psychiatry, Neurology, and Behavioral Sciences, University of Oklahoma Medical School.

———, "Some Clinical Aspects of Logotherapy. Paper read before the Anderson County Medical Society in South Carolina," "Man in Search of Meaning. Address given to the Annual Meeting of the Anderson County Mental Health Association in South Carolina," and "Man's Search for Ultimate Meaning. Lecture given at the Peachtree Road Methodist Church in Atlanta, Georgia," videotapes cleared for television upon request from WGTV, the University of Georgia, Athens, GA 30601.

———, "Meaning and Purpose in Human Experience," a videotape produced by Rockland Community College. Rental or purchase through the Director of Library Services, 145 College Road, Suffern, NY 10901.

———, "Education and the Search for Meaning. An Interview by Professor Willaim Blair Gould of Bradley University," a videotape produced by Bradley University television. Available by request from Bradley University, Peoria, IL 61606 ($25 handling charges for usage).

———, "Youth in Search for Meaning. The Third Paul Dana Bartlett Memorial Lecture," a videotape produced by KNBU and cleared for television upon request from President James Edward Doty, Baker University, Baldwin City, KA 66006.

———, "Clinical Aspects of Logotherapy," a videotaped lecture. Replay available by arrangement with Medical Illustration Services, Veterans Administration Hospital, 3801 Miranda Avenue, Palo Alto, CA 94304.

———, "Logotherapy," a videotaped lecture. Available for rental or purchase from Educational Television, University of California School of Medicine, Department of Psychiatry, Langley Porter Neuropsychiatric Institute, 3rd Avenue and Parnassus Avenue, San Francisco, CA 94112.

———, "Logotherapy Workshop," a videotaped lecture. Available for rental or purchase from Middle Tennessee State University, Learning Resource Center, Murfreesboro, TN 37130.

———, "The Rehumanization of Psychotherapy. A Workshop Sponsored by the Division of Psychotherapy of the American

Psychological Association," a videotape. Address inquiries to Division of Psychotherapy, American Psychological Association, 1200 Seventeenth Street, N.W., Washington, DC 20036.

______, "Youth in Search of Meaning," a videotape produced by the Youth Corps and Metro Cable Television. Contact: Youth Corps, 56 Bond Street, Toronto, Ontario M5B 1X2, Canada.

______, "Man in Search of Meaning," a film interview with Jim Corey of CFTO Television in Toronto. Contact: Youth Corps. 56 Bond Street, Toronto, Ontario M5B 1X2, Canada.

______, "Human Freedom and Meaning in Life" and "Self-Transcendence—Therapeutic Agent in Sexual Neurosis," videotapes. Copies of the tapes can be ordered for a service fee. Address inquiries to the Manager, Learning Resource Distribution Center, United States International University, San Diego, CA 92131.

______, Two 5-hour lectures, part of the course *Human Behavior 616,* "Man in Search of Meaning," during the winter quarter, 1976. Copies of the videotapes can be ordered for a service fee. Address inquiries to the Manager, Learning Resource Distribution Center, United States International University, San Diego, CA 92131.

______, A videotaped convocation. Address inquiries to President Stephen Walsh, St. Edward's University, Austin, TX 78704.

______, A videotaped lecture given at Monash University, Melbourne, Australia, on March 6, 1976. Inquiries should be addressed to Royal Australian College of General Practitioners, Family Medicine Programme, Audio Visual Department, 70 Jolimont Street, Jolimont, 3002, Melbourne, Australia.

______, Lecture given at Monash University, Melbourne, Australia on March 6, 1976. An audiocassette available from Catholic Family Welfare Bureau, 491 Nicholson Street, Carlton North, 3054, Melbourne, Australia.

______, Interview with Dr. Viktor E. Frankl by Dr. Paul W. Ngui, President, Singapore Association for Mental Health; 16 mm. film. Inquiries should be addressed to Controller, Central Production Unit, Television Singapore, Singapore, 10.

______, "Three Lectures on Logotherapy," given at the Brandeis Institute, Brandeis, CA 93064. Long-playing records.

———, "Man in Search of Meaning: Two Dialogues," "Self-Transcendence: The Motivational Theory of Logotherapy," "What is Meant by Meaning?" and "Logotherapy and Existentialism," audiotapes produced by Jeffrey Norton Publishers, Inc., 145 East 49th Street, New York, NY 10017.

———, "The Student's Search for Meaning," an audiotape produced by WGTV, the University of Georgia, Athens, GA 30601.

———, "The Existential Vacuum" ("Existential Frustration As a Challenge to Psychiatry," "Logotherapy as a Concept of Man," "Logotherapy as a Philosophy of Life"), tapes produced by Argus Communications, 3505 North Ashland Avenue, Chicago, 7400 Natchez Avenue, Niles, IL 60648. $18.00.

———, "The Existential Vacuum: A Challenge to Psychiatry: Address given at The Unitarian Church, San Francisco, California, October 13, 1969," a tape produced by Big Sur Recordings, 2015 Bridgeway, Sausalito, CA 94965.

———, "Meaninglessness: Today's Dilemma," an audiotape produced by Creative Resources, 4800 West Waco Drive, Waco, TX 76703.

———, "Logotherapy Workshop," an audiotape produced by Middle Tennessee State University, Learning Resource Center, Murfreesboro, Tennessee 37130.

———, "Man's Search for Meaning. An Introduction to Logotherapy." Recording for the Blind, Inc., 215 East 58th Street, New York, NY 10022.

———, "Youth in Search of Meaning." Word Cassette Library, 4800 West Waco Drive, Waco, TX 76703 ($4.98).

———, "Theory and Therapy of Neurosis: A Series of Lectures Delivered at the United States International University in San Diego, California." Eight 90-minute cassettes produced by Creative Resources, 4800 West Waco Drive, Waco, TX 76703 ($79.95).

———, "Man in Search of Meaning: A Series of Lectures Delivered at the United States International University in San Diego, California." Fourteen 90-minute cassettes produced by Creative Resources, 4800 West Waco Drive, Waco, TX 76703 ($139.95).

———, "The Neurotization of Humanity and the Re-Humanization of Psychotherapy," two cassettes. Argus Communications, 7440 Natchez Avenue, Niles, IL 60648 ($14.00).

______, Robin W. Goodenough, Iver Hand, Oliver A. Phillips and Edith Weisskopf-Joelson, "Logotherapy: Theory and Practice. A Symposium Sponsored by the Division of Psychotherapy of the American Psychological Association," an audiotape. Address inquiries to Division of Psychotherapy, American Psychological Association, 1200 Seventeenth Street, N.W., Washington, DC 20036.

______, "Therapy Through Meaning." Psychotherapy and Social Science Review Tape Library, 111 Eighth Avenue, New York, N.Y. 10011, T656, One-Hour cassette, $15.

______, and Huston Smith, "Value Dimensions in Teaching," a color television film produced by Hollywood Animators, Inc., for the California Junior College Association. Rental or purchase through Dr. Rex Wignall, Director, Chaffey College, Alta Loma, CA 91701.

Gale, Raymond F., Joseph Fabry, Mary Ann Finch and Robert C. Leslie, "A Conversation with Viktor E. Frankl on Occasion of the Inauguration of the 'Frankl Library and Memorabilia' at the Graduate Theological Union on February 12, 1977," a videotape. Copies may be obtained from Professor Robert C. Leslie, 1798 Scenic Avenue, Berkeley CA 94709.

Hale, Dr. William H., "An Interview with Viktor E. Frankl. With an Introduction by Dr. Edith Weisskopf-Joelson, Professor of Psychology at the University of Georgia," a videotape cleared for television upon request from WGTV, the University of Georgia, Athens, GA 30601.

"The Humanistic Revolution: Pioneers in Perspective," interviews with leading humanistic psychologists: Abraham Maslow, Gardner Murphy, Carl Rogers, Rollo May, Paul Tillich, Frederick Perls, Viktor Frankl and Alan Watts. Psychological Films, 1215 East Chapman Ave., Orange, CA 92666. Sale $250; rental $20.

Murray, Dr. Edward L., and Dr. Rolf von Eckartsberg, A discussion with Dr. Viktor E. Frankl on "Logotherapy: Theory and Applied" conducted by two members of the Duquesne University Graduate School of Psychology, filmed July 25, 1972. Available for rental, fee $15. Mail request to Chairman, Department of Psychology, Duquesne University, Pittsburgh, PA 15219.

5. Braille Editions

The following Braille editions are available on loan at no cost from Woodside Terrace Kiwanis Braille Project, 850 Longview Road, Hillsborough, California 94010:

Fabry, Joseph B., *The Pursuit of Meaning: Logotherapy Applied to Life.*

Frankl, Viktor E., *Man's Search for Meaning: An Introduction to Logotherapy.*

———, *The Unheard Cry for Meaning: Psychotherapy and Humanism.*

Authors

MAGDA B. ARNOLD is professor emeritus of psychology and chairman of the Social Science Division at Spring Hill College, Mobile, Alabama. She received her Ph.D. from the University of Toronto, Canada, in 1942, and has taught at the University of Toronto, Wellesley College, Bryn Mawr College, Barat College, and the Loyola University of Chicago. She also taught summer sessions at Harvard University, the University of British Columbia, and the University of Prince Edward Island. She has published several books and many articles on her main interests—personality, emotion and motivation, and brain function. Her first critical evaluation of logotherapy in the United States, in cooperation with Gasson, appeared in *The Human Person* (edited by Arnold and Gasson) in 1954. It was based on Frankl's *Aerztliche Seelsorge.*

LOUIS S. BARBER is Assistant Superintendent of Special Schools and Services for the Riverside County Schools Office. He received his Ph.D. at the United States International University, San Diego, in 1972, where he took special training from Dr. Frankl. Previous positions include those of director of Extension Education, College of the Desert, Palm Desert, California; and principal of Twin Pines High School, Banning, California.

EDGAR BODENHEIMER is professor of law (emeritus) at the University of California, Davis. He received his doctoral degree from the University of Heidelberg, Germany, and was a member of Justice Jackson's legal staff at the war criminals trials in Nuremberg. He is the author of numerous journal articles and of the book, *Treatise on Justice.*

OWEN BRANDON retired in 1973, after 39 years in the ordained ministry of the Church of England. He was Rector of Fordwich and Fellow of St. Augustine's College, Canterbury. His field of research and specialization has been psychology of religious belief and experience. He has used logotherapy in his counseling work since 1964 and introduced Frankl's philosophy to clergy and ordinands in theology, psychology and pastoral care. He is the author of *The Battle for the Soul, Christianity from Within,* and *The Pastor and his Ministry.*

DENNIE BRIGGS is training officer, New Careers Development Office, National Association for the Care and Resettlement of Offenders, London, and a lecturer at the University of London. He received his B.S. in education from the Western Illinois University, 1949; his M.A. in sociology from the University of Southern California, 1952; and is a Ph.D. candidate in social psychology at Groningen University, Holland. Previous positions include clinical psychologist, U.S. Navy; administrator, Intensive Treatment Project, California Dept. of Corrections; Director of Training, New Careers Development Project, Sacramento, California. He has published more than 60 journal articles in the United States and Britain, is the co-author of *Dealing with Deviants,* and author of *In Place of Prison.*

REUVEN P. BULKA is editor of the *Journal of Psychology and Judaism* and is rabbi of Congregation Machzikei Hadas in Ottawa, Canada. He received his Ph.D. from the University of Ottawa in 1971; his thesis dealt with the implications of logotherapy's religious nature for specific religious systems. He is the author of many articles on logotherapy and of the book, *The Wit and Wisdom of the Talmud.*

JAMES C. CRUMBAUGH is clincial psychologist at the Veterans Administration Hospital, Gulfport, Mississippi. He received his Ph.D. from the University of Texas in 1953 and his postdoctoral training in clinical psychology at the University of Tennessee. Previous positions include those of clinical psychologist at the VA Hospital at Augusta, Georgia; clinical psychologist and research director at the Bradley Center, Inc., at Columbus, Georgia; and chairman of the Department of Psychology at MacMurray College, Jacksonville, Illinois. He is the co-author of the "Purpose in Life Test," an attitude scale constructed from the orientation of logotherapy, and the author of many publications, including the books, *Everything to Gain: A Guide to Self-Fulfillment through Logoanalysis,* and *Logotherapy: New Help for Problem Drinkers.*

JOSEPH B. FABRY is director of the Institute of Logotherapy, Berkeley, California, and editor of *The International Forum of Logotherapy.* He received his doctor of law degree from the University of Vienna in 1933 but spent most of his life as an editor, including 24 years with the University of California, Berkeley. Since 1963 he has been a student of Dr. Frankl and has become his spokesman to the American public. He is the author of *The Pursuit of Meaning,* a summary of Frankl's ideas, and a lecturer, seminar and group leader in logotherapy.

ALVIN R. FRAISER teaches sociology and criminal justice at San Diego City College, and the United States International University, San Diego. He received his Ph.D. under Dr. Frankl. Fraiser worked with drug addicts in the Illinois Correctional System, and as correctional counselor at the California Rehabilitation Center. Since 1970 he is a parole agent for the California Department of Corrections, San Diego.

J. A. GASSON is professor of psychology at Spring Hill College, Mobile, Alabama. He received his Ph.D. from the Gregorian University in Rome in 1931 and did some postdoctoral work there in 1935–1937. He has taught at the Jesuit School of Philosophy and in the department of psychology at Spring Hill College. From 1963 to 1971, he was director of the program in psychology at Spring Hill

College. He has published journal articles on the philosophical foundations of psychology.

HANS O. GERZ is a practicing psychiatrist in Middletown, Connecticut. He received his M.D. from the University of Düsseldorf, Germany, in 1953, came to the United States for training in psychiatry, and served as senior psychiatrist at Rockland State Hospital, Orangeburg, N.Y., and as clinical director of the Connecticut Valley (State) Hospital, Middletown. During a postdoctoral study in Europe he became familiar with the practice of paradoxical intention which he introduced to his work at the Connecticut Valley Hospital. He is a leading practitioner of this technique and has published numerous papers on his experiences. During a four-year stay in Europe he received personal advice and instruction from Dr. Frankl. Dr. Gerz organized and directed the 1964 Symposium on Logotherapy at the Sixth International Congress on Psychotherapy in London.

JOSEPH P. GHOUGASSIAN is professor of philosophy at the University of San Diego, presently researching psychopathology and its relation to the philosophy of man. He received his B.A. and M.A. in philosophy in Rome and his Ph.D. from Louvain University, Belgium, at the *Institut Supérieur de Philosophie.* He is the author of *Gordon Allport's Ontopsychology of the Person* and *Kahlil Gibran: Wings of Thought.*

DEREK L. T. GILL is an international journalist, author, and lecturer. He was born in Uganda, educated in England (London and Cambridge Universities), edited two daily newspapers, and traveled as a journalist on four continents. His book *Dove,* co-authored with Robin Lee Graham, is a Book of the Month Club selection. The interview with Dr. Frankl was taped by Gill when he was the editor of *Pace Magazine.*

TIMOTHY V. HOGAN is a clinical psychologist, assistant professor in the School of Psychology and the School of Medicine at the University of Ottawa, Canada, and consultant psychologist at the Royal Ottawa Hospital. He received his Ph.D. from the University of Ottawa in 1966. He is a "logotherapist" only to the extent that he has read Frankl's work and incorporated logotherapeutic principles in his practice. He has not studied under Frankl, nor met him. In his essay, Hogan describes his "improvisations" that were inspired by Frankl's philosophy and methods, and states his personal experiences as a therapist with patients in whom he noticed the presence of what Frankl had described as noögenic neuroses.

ROBERT M. HOLMES is chaplain/counselor and associate professor of Christian Thought at the Rocky Mountain College, Billings, Montana. He received his degree of Doctor of Theology at the Pacific School of Religion, Berkeley, California, where he met Dr. Frankl and became interested in logotherapy. As campus pastor, Holmes counsels with many young people as well as persons throughout the surrounding community, many of whom are struggling with the problems of alcoholic addiction. He is the author of the book, *The Academic Mysteryhouse* and of numerous articles in journals and magazines.

CARL H. JEPSEN is on the dental staff of the Coronado Hospital, and maintains a practice of family dentistry in Coronado, California. He received his D.D.S. from the University of Washington, Seattle, School of Dentistry, in 1965 and is presently studying for his Ph.D. at the United States International University Graduate School of Leadership and Human Behavior, San Diego, California, where he took classes from Dr. Frankl. Jepsen has published essays linking dentistry with the practices and theories of psychotherapies.

KURT KOCOUREK is the head of the Neurological and Psychiatric Outpatient Clinic of the Poliklinik Hospital, Vienna, Austria. He received his M.D. from the University of Vienna in 1950, and became assistant to Dr. Frankl at the neurological department of the Poliklinik Hospital.

ROBERT C. LESLIE is dean of the Pacific School of Religion, Berkeley. He received his S.T.B. at Boston University School of Theology and his Ph.D. at Boston University. He has served as a pastor, chaplain in the U.S. Army, hospital chaplain, and instructor of psychology of religion at Boston University School of Theology. For the past

25 years, he has been with the Pacific School of Religion where he taught pastoral psychology and counseling. He studied with Dr. Frankl in Vienna during the academic year 1960–1961. He is the author of *Jesus and Logotherapy* and *Sharing Groups in the Church.*

ELISABETH LUKAS is director of an educational counseling center in Munich, Germany. She received her Ph.D. in psychology from the University of Vienna where she studied under Dr. Frankl and wrote her Ph.D. thesis on the empirical validation of logotherapy, reporting original research which is extracted in Frankl's *Der Wille zum Sinn* (Hans Huber Verlag, Bern-Stuttgart-Vienna). In doing her research she worked closely with Frankl from 1969 to 1972. From 1973 to 1977 she worked as a therapist in counseling centers in Kaiserslautern and Wiesbaden, Germany.

RONALD D. LUNCEFORD is associate professor of sociology, California State University, Long Beach, a staff member of the University of California, Irvine, College of Medicine, Department of Psychiatry and Human Behavior, and consultant for the hospice program at the Hospital Home/Health Care Agency, Torrance. Previous positions include that of community psychologist and director of The People's Clinic, Santa Ana. Together with his wife Judith Lunceford, he authored the book *Attitudes on Death and Dying.* He received his Ph.D. from the United States International University, San Diego, where he studied under Dr. Frankl.

MARIO C. MACARUSO is chief psychiatric social worker for the Windsor System, Windsor, Connecticut. He received his Master of Science in Social Service from Boston University in 1949 and has been a certified social worker since 1957. While working in the Norwich Hospital outpatient clinic he made the acquaintance of Dr. Gerz who introduced Macaruso to the technique of paradoxical intention.

URIEL MESHOULAM is assistant professor of psychology, Merrimack College, N. Andover, Massachusetts. Born in Israel, he graduated from the Hebrew University of Jerusalem. In 1970 he came to the

United States to do graduate work in clinical psychology at the State University of New York, Albany. He studied with Dr. Frankl during a graduate seminar at Duquesne University, Pittsburgh, Pennsylvania, in 1972 and received his Ph.D. in clinical psychology from the State University of New York. He worked as instructor of psychology in Berklee College, Boston, and in Lesley College, Cambridge, and as assistant professor of psychology at Wellesley College, Wellesley, Massachusetts.

OLIVER A. PHILLIPS since 1957 has held positions of project engineer, chief engineer, and department manager in various aerospace companies in California. He received his Ph.D. in psychology at the United States International University, San Diego, where he studied under Dr. Frankl. He had previously been introduced to logotherapy at Pepperdine University in 1971 while still a department manager at TRW Systems Groups.

GEORGE C. PURVIS is the minister of the Asbury United Methodist Church, Denver, Colorado. He received his B.D. degree in 1967 from the Perkins School of Theology, S.M.U., Dallas, Texas, where he studied under Dr. Frankl during a summer program. He did postgraduate work at the University of London and served as minister of the Palmers Green Congregational Church. Since 1968 he served as minister in churches in Colorado, including Minister of Youth at the First Methodist Church at Fort Collins. He also worked with "Parents without Partners" and on the Committee on Drug Education.

WILLIAM S. SAHAKIAN is professor of psychology and philosophy, Suffolk University, Boston. He completed graduate studies at Harvard and Boston universities, receiving his Ph.D. from the latter institution. Among the 20 books in his over 50 publications are *Psychopathology Today, Psychotherapy and Counseling,* and *History of Psychology.* As a licensed psychologist, Sahakian practices logotherapy in Boston.

GEORGE A. SARGENT is clinical psychologist at The Family Center, Vista, California. He received his Ph.D. in Leadership and Human

Behavior from the United States International University, San Diego, where he studied under Dr. Frankl. Previous work included that of a therapist at the Western Institute of Human Resources, vocational group facilitator at the San Diego Community Mental Health Clinic, personnel development supervisor at the American Telephone and Telegraph Company, and clinic director at Western Institute North Coastal.

HIROSHI TAKASHIMA is director of Noöpsychosomatic Medicine at Central Hospital of Social Health Insurance; guest professor in existential psychology at the Tokyo Rissho Junior College for Women; consulting physician at Maruzen Clinic; and consulting cardiologist at Kaneko Clinic, all in Tokyo. He received his Ph.D. in pharmacology from the Keio University in 1948. In the past he was assistant of internal medicine, St. Luke's Hospital, Tokyo; assistant of pharmacology at Keio University School of Medicine, and lecturer of internal medicine at Nihon University School of Medicine. He became interested in logotherapy while studying with Dr. Frankl in Vienna in 1964, and has translated the Japanese edition of Frankl's book, *Psychotherapy and Existentialism.* Dr. Takashima is the author of several books, including *Medicine and Existence, Purpose in Life and Health, Psychogenic Disease and Psychogenic Health,* and *Psychosomatic Medicine and Logotherapy.*

JOYCE E. TRAVELBEE was, at the time of her death, director of graduate education at Louisiana State University School of Nursing, New Orleans. She received her M.S.N. from Yale University in 1959 and was a member of the Kappa Delta Phi Honorary Education society. Her past positions included professor of psychology of nursing at the University of Mississippi, Jackson, Mississippi, and project director of the curriculum of nursing at Hotel Dieu School of Nursing, New Orleans, Louisiana. She was the author of numerous papers. Her major books were *Interpersonal Aspects of Nursing* and *Intervention in Psychiatric Nursing.* She became interested in logotherapy through Dr. Frankl's lectures in New Orleans and his writings.

DONALD F. TWEEDIE, JR. is professor emeritus of psychology in the Fuller Theological Seminary Graduate School of Psychology,

Pasadena, California, and director of Hacienda Psychological Services, Hacienda Heights. He received his Ph.D. from Boston University in 1954, and did postdoctoral studies at Harvard Divinity School and the University of Vienna where he worked with Dr. Frankl. Before his present position, Professor Tweedie was chairman of the department of psychology at Gordon College and director of the Pasadena Community Counseling Center. His major publications include the books, *Logotherapy and the Christian Faith, The Christian and the Couch,* and *The Christian and Sex.*

ARTHUR G. WIRTH is professor of history and philosophy of education at Washington University, St. Louis, Missouri. He received his Ph.D. in philosophy of education from the Ohio State University in 1949. His major previous academic appointments included Ohio State University (1946–1949) and Brooklyn College (1949–1961). He is the author of *John Dewey as Educator* and *Education in the Technological Society: The Vocational Liberal Controversy in the Twentieth Century.* He was editor of the John Dewey Society Lecture Series, and of the Society's monographs in educational theory.

Index